NEOLIBERALISM AND POLITICAL THEOLOGY

To my entire family

Sunny, Erik, Jikke, Kes, Casjen and Falk

NEOLIBERALISM AND POLITICAL THEOLOGY

From Kant to Identity Politics

Carl Raschke

EDINBURGH
University Press

Edinburgh University Press is one of the leading university presses in the UK. We publish academic books and journals in our selected subject areas across the humanities and social sciences, combining cutting-edge scholarship with high editorial and production values to produce academic works of lasting importance. For more information visit our website: edinburghuniversitypress.com

Edinburgh University Press Ltd
The Tun – Holyrood Road, 12(2f) Jackson's Entry, Edinburgh EH8 8PJ

First published in hardback by Edinburgh University Press 2019

Typeset in Warnock Pro by Biblichor Ltd, Edinburgh

A CIP record for this book is available from the British Library

ISBN 978 1 4744 5455 1 (hardback)
ISBN 978 1 4744 5456 8 (paperback)
ISBN 978 1 4744 5457 5 (webready PDF)
ISBN 978 1 4744 5458 2 (epub)

Contents

Acknowledgements

IN PREPARING THIS work I would like to acknowledge the work of a number of my graduate assistants at the University of Denver – Kara Roberts, Stefanie Fajardo, Rebekah Gordon, Jeff Appel and Rachel Thomas – who helped me in different ways in conducting research and developing the manuscript. I would also like to recognise Joshua Hanan, my colleague in Communication Studies, who has the same passion for, and facility with the literature on, the topic of neoliberalism in its variegated aspects as I do. As co-instructor for a class on 'The Critique of Neoliberalism' in the spring of 2018, Joshua's insight and research instructions were invaluable. I should also like to thank Joshua Ramey of Grinnell College for offering through a number of interviews and conversations many productive insights. In addition, I would like to thank with extreme gratitude Professor Kurt Appel, Jakob Deibl and Lisa Achathaler at the University of Vienna for inviting me to offer through their interdisciplinary research platform a series of workshops and lectures in 2015, 2016 and 2017, out of which this book evolved. I would also like to thank Daniel Macintyre, Dean of the Division of Arts, Humanities, and Social Sciences at the University of Denver for the opportunity to deliver a special all-university faculty lecture in the fall of 2016 on which the first chapter is based.

Finally, I would like to thank David True and Vincent Lloyd, editors of the journal *Political Theology* and its online counterpart *Political Theology Network* (formerly *Political Theology Today*), for their support and encouragement in the development of this project, chiefly for providing a forum for some initial blog pieces out of which the book crystallised. Portions of Chapters 4 and 5 originally appeared in *Political Theology Today*. Much of Chapter 1 was first published in *The Journal for Cultural and Religious Theory*, and

Chapter 6 originally appeared in the online magazine *The New Polis*. Portions of Chapter 3 have been published with the proceedings of an invited international conference entitled 'The Crisis of Representation', held at the Melk Conference Centre at the University of Vienna in June 2017, and published in an open source format in early 2019 with University of Vienna Press.

Introduction

IN RECENT YEARS there has been a slowly rising tide of academic books and articles on the topic of neoliberalism. In the previous decade much of the discussion had centred on the fundamentally economic question of the consolidation of the new global capitalism and the changes wrought on erstwhile socialist countries following the demise of the Soviet Union in the early 1990s. The term 'neoliberalism', first applied as far back as the late 1930s as a term of leverage to argue against fascist and other species of totalitarian political system, throughout that earlier period became a kind of master signifier for the ascendant dogma of libertarian, monetarist, or 'free market', economic theories, especially those of the brand favoured by the so-called Chicago School of Milton Friedman, and counted among itself such other intellectual luminaries as Gary Becker, Ronald Coase, Richard Posner, Lars Peter Hansen and Eugene Fama. Variants of the Chicago School, the immediate heirs of the Mont Pelerin Society who gave original currency to the term 'neoliberal', had a powerful ear throughout the Ronald Reagan and George H. W. Bush administrations.[1] After the United States seemingly came out the victor in the Cold War following the events of 1989–91, the phrase gradually stuck among economists and political theorists as a serviceable descriptor for the new order that was emerging.

Both criticism and caution regarding the heady triumphalism among neoliberalism, however, began to percolate towards the end of the 1990s, especially when it became obvious following various debacles in the economies of Russia, Latin America and East Asia (excluding China), that such triumphalism should be taken with a grain of salt. The puncture of the so-called 'dot.com bubble' and the brief recession it caused right around the end of the Clinton presidency also gave pause to the prevailing, uncritical enthusiasm for unregulated global markets. But belief in the inherent superiority of the neoliberal paradigm would largely remain unchallenged until the global economic catastrophe of 2008. With the discrediting of the new worldwide 'financial capitalism' by the deep and sustained Great Recession that did not begin to significantly abate for nearly a decade, scholars and researchers during the years that followed began to seek increasingly for broader trends and factors that could be cited to elucidate the new global malaise.

The landmark book that exposed the need for a deeper critique of the neoliberal paradigm turned out to be political philosopher Wendy Brown's *Undoing the Demos: Neoliberalism's Stealth Revolution*, published in 2015.[2] Brown both mined and expanded on what had been the alternative socio-political – in contrast with the economistic – account of neoliberalism that had been sketched out by French philosopher Michel Foucault in the 1970s, but had at the same time been generally given short shrift except by compilers and chroniclers of the latter's work. Brown's argument, which was both penetrating in its insight and passionate in its polemics, brought to the fore a fundamental claim that neoliberalism constitutes, using Foucault's earlier nomenclature, the dominant *episteme* of the early twenty-first century, one that in fact embraces not just economics and politics, but the whole of culture itself.

Then came the summer of 2016, which brought with it like a violent Midwestern storm cell, a sudden global groundswell of seemingly angry populist and nationalist uprisings at the ballot box. The weather line was not confined to the presidential election of that year, as signalled in the surprising defeat of Hilary Clinton by financial tycoon and media celebrity Donald Trump. It also spread across Europe and certain regions of the developing world. The press and the Western intelligentsia were aghast and sought to explain this roiling tide as some atavistic upsurge of darker political proclivities and anxieties, routinely comparing trends to the 1930s and at times ineptly mimicking the Frankfurt School's favoured distinction between 'myth' and 'enlightenment'. But the comparison was more superficial than genuine. Something else was afoot, and certain other political theorists such as New School political theorist Nancy Fraser, who had already established herself as a leading exponent of gender theory and identity politics, immediately saw hidden causal connections between the regime of neoliberalism and the antagonism towards it on the part of the new populists, which so many her counterparts, including perhaps Wendy Brown herself, seemed to have missed. Fraser in a sequence of key articles in prominent publications, starting as early as the fall of 2016, coined the seemingly oxymoronic expression 'progressive neoliberalism' to set in relief the planetary hobgoblin to which populist politics appeared to be reacting.

Fraser's insights, however, which ironically seem counterintuitive while consistently offensive to the sensibilities of so much of the Western academic establishment, serve as the point of departure for this project. The thesis of this book, pursuant to the socio-political model of Foucault and Brown (and of course other prominent international figures such as Bernard Stiegler, Axel Honneth and Wolfgang Streeck who are not so well known in American academic circles), is that Fraser is definitely onto something, and it is our aim to tease as much of it out as we can so that we truly understand what is happening politically at so many levels. But what even these writers tend to skip over is the *genealogical* question of how neoliberalism came to be the *hegemonic* thought template that is increasingly grinding with 'seismic' repercussions against the material interests of those among the new 'populists', and is reflected in the ever more toxic political conflicts that are upending democratic government after democratic government. It is our position that these conflicts are ultimately the output of deeper *moral and religious* forces that are dividing both the West, and the Westernised 'rest' of the world that has been bewitched by neoliberalism.

We shall hypothesise at the outset, therefore, that neoliberalism is not so much an economic or a political formation as it is a *value configuration* against which much of the world is now in open revolt. A genealogy of neoliberal morals, or moral valuations, therefore demands a kind of Nietzschean intervention that grapples with, and unmasks, the pretences under which it so effectively perpetuated. The pretence has been one of 'democratic capitalism' in tandem with a certain social ethics of *cosmopolitan humanitarianism* that conceals its underlying agenda of economic exploitation and predation. It is history's most recent version of Europe's 'civilising mission' to the 'backward' nations of the world throughout the nineteenth century. Neoliberalism, however, is not simply a new 'colonialism' in a strictly economic sense. It turns out to be what Foucault called alternately an *appareil* or a *dispositif* (often translated as 'apparatus', but perhaps better rendered as an 'operation of power relations') that employs *as a full ensemble* various strategies of discourse, valuations, social pressure, economic mechanisms and political instrumentalities both to colonise effectively those outside its realm and to maintain control over those whom it has already subjugated.[3] It is hence a kind of scarcely perceptible *mega-apparatus* that is everywhere 'killing us softly with [its] song' (to borrow from the lyrics of a popular song from the early 1970s). Its silent toxicity has less to do with any application of overt coercion, or visible force, than with its capacity for an excessive burdening of private conscience, a promiscuous attention to blaming and shaming, derived from what it passes off as *a priori* moral authority with a complex, sophisticated and *transcendental* justification for its overreach.

As I sketch out in later chapters, that transcendental justification is decidedly religious in character. It tallies unquestionably with what figures such as Carl Schmitt, Mark Lilla, Giorgio Agamben and like-minded thinkers have consistently reminded us; namely, that much – if not all – normative political thought is grounded in some set of transcendental system of convictions that are ultimately *theological* in origin. Hence, we find Schmitt's phrase 'political theology' to be a highly useful general signifier for these convictions, one that can be introduced as a vital *appareil* in its own right for comprehending the meaning of the expression 'neoliberalism'. In that respect, our own 'genealogical' project then undertakes the venture of mapping *the deep political theology of neoliberalism.* Once we have performed the necessary surgery, we will begin to explore how the patient might consider the road to recovery and arise from the desperation of 'bare life' (to invoke Agamben's term) that neoliberalism has afforded to billions of people, not just the Western working class, but all peoples.

Chapter 1 ('Towards a Genealogy of Neoliberalism') roughs out a more capacious project of decoding neoliberalism as a system of signifiers in the fashion Foucault himself undertook in his greater *oeuvre* (not merely his lectures in the 1970s and 1980s), laying the foundation for what we now call 'cultural studies' along with the newest iterations of critical theory. Following up on my earlier book *Force of God: Political Theology and the Crisis of Liberal Democracy,*[4] the chapter frames the question of neoliberalism as a wider cultural and political one, as what Foucault himself hinted was the source of our new world disorder – a 'crisis of representation'. In *Force of God* I sought to administer Foucault's genealogical principles in exploring the 'valuational' substructure of the emerging political economy of the twenty-first century. I also offered a provisional (though admittedly not wholly sufficient) outline of how a new 'political theology' might 'save us'. Such an approach would have to be adequate to what French theorists Jean-Joseph Goux and Jean Baudrillard identified as the new epoch of 'symbolic' capitalism associated with electronic currency, planetary media and what language philosophers at the time implied was a *death of the referent.* In this book I contextualise the problem far more tangibly by naming the 'rough beast' responsible for the rapacity of the new symbolic economy – i.e. *neoliberalism*. I launch the lengthy anatomy of this covert leviathan, which this book constitutes, in sketching the multidimensional makeup of neoliberalism while relying on the work of French-Italian social philosopher Maurizio Lazzarato. Lazzarato has pinpointed the crucial interplay of signifying processes within the larger operating system of neoliberalism that keeps it going – in other words, the reinforcing mechanisms of financial debt and moral obligation and guilt, a relationship which Nietzsche first portrayed in *A Genealogy of Morals* more than a century ago.[5]

Chapter 2 ('Progressive Neoliberalism and its Discontents') characterises the American Presidential election of 2016 as a pivotal moment that threw into relief for the first time the contest between neoliberalism and the new global populism. It focuses on the usage of the current political term 'cosmopolitan' and its genesis in both ancient philosophy and twentieth-century Marxist rhetoric. It also clarifies and elaborates significantly as one of my book's central theses an argument by New School political scientist Nancy Fraser that neoliberalism is not, as commonly understood, a conservative ideology, but a 'progressive one' – hence her notion of 'progressive neoliberalism'. In addition, this chapter analyses how the word 'neoliberal' functions as a vague, yet suitable, descriptor for what Antonio Gramsci termed the distinctive ideological 'hegemony' of our day. More importantly, it links this sort of perspective with Nietzsche's diagnosis in his unpublished works with 'modern nihilism' whereby the 'highest values devalue themselves'. As a valuational structure that Nietzsche saw as a permanent condition of 'mass society', neoliberalism has fulfilled much of his prophetic vision. These observations segue into a summary of Brown's analysis and conclude with some comparative musings from Lilie Chouliaraki's notion of the 'ironic spectator'.

Chapter 3 ('Mediatic Hegemony: The Kingdom, the Power, the Glory and the Tawdry') explores Giorgio Agamben's celebrated 'double paradigm of sovereignty', which introduces the Christian idea of *oikonomia* ('economy') as a foundational political concept in Western thinking. In this section I argue that Agamben's far-ranging discussion improves our understanding of how Foucault's notion of biopower actually develops historically from the matrix of early Christian theology and how it becomes its own kind of 'political theology' to undergird the contemporary categoreal scheme of neoliberalism. Following Agamben, my argument also builds on his thesis that 'economic sovereignty' today is cemented through the power of modern forms of media in much the same way that the critical theorists of the interwar period identified the 'culture industry' as the genuine hegemon of capitalism. Throughout this chapter I also devote extensive attention to the work of the French social philosopher and media theorist Bernard Stiegler and his notion of 'cognitive capitalism'.

In Chapter 4 ('Killing Us Softly: On Neoliberal "Truth" Protocols') I return to Foucault briefly concerning what he calls the problem of 'veridiction', or truth-telling. I make the case that neoliberal 'truth' claims as its heritage the quest for a *mathesis universalis* of knowledge inaugurated by Descartes. The combining of modernist epistemology with 'pastoral power' from the eighteenth century onwards has built the scaffolding for the neoliberal regimen. Here I bank heavily on the insights of the German sociologist Wolfgang Streeck and the French social theorist Pierre Bourdieu to elaborate on what is entailed in neoliberal truth protocols. It is these kinds of protocols along with the politics inherent in them that have kept 'capitalism alive' all these centuries, as Streeck puts it. In addition, I explain through historical observations how so-called 'progressivist' politics from its inception in the nineteenth century has always earmarked neoliberal prototypes of governance, and how such a politics is inextricably bound up with such truth procedures. Finally, I take up again the matter of moral cosmopolitanism and its intimate relation with colonialism and the market-driven expansion of global capitalism. And I single out the eighteenth-century German philosopher Immanuel Kant – somewhat strangely in the minds of readers perhaps – to be in many regards the authentic 'grey eminence' of neoliberalism.

In Chapter 5 ('The Epistemic Crisis') I connect the trend towards the *mediatisation of the political* à la Agamben as a type of 'economic sovereignty' with what I call the 'epistemic crisis' of 'high modernism', a more exacting and formal philosophical analysis of the current 'crisis of representation'. 'High modernism' is a locution coined by political scientist and anthropologist James C. Scott. I enquire into the relationship between the high modernist epistemology and what I call the 'new political theology' lurking behind the innovations of Thomas Hobbes, Adam Smith, Kant and the arch-theorist himself of present-day neoliberalism – Friedrich Hayek.

In Chapter 6 ('Globalism, Multiculturalism and the "Politics of Recognition"') I come back to Fraser's idea of 'progressive neoliberalism' and show how its signature motif – 'identity politics' – has *devolved* from the speculative philosophy of Hegel through the New Left Marxism of the 1960s and 1970s, ultimately having been absorbed and 'captured' by the neoliberal agenda. Chapter 7 ('The Deep Political Theology of Neoliberalism') provides a tableau of diverse, but clearly 'theological' trends of the last sixty years (what I call the 'immanence movement') from the so-called 'death of God' movement to 'secular theology' to New Age thinking in the 1970s and 1980s. I probe the ways in which these strands of theological thinking reflect a more general tapestry of popular religiosity that have served to legitimate neoliberal hegemony and hold it firmly intact once challenged. Chapter 8 ('Endings') takes a stab at the urgent question of what lies beyond the horizons of neoliberalism. It proposes that it is not the case, contrary to Margaret Thatcher's infamous remark, that 'there is no alternative'. On the contrary, there is a certain 'eschatology of neoliberalism' of which we already have glimpses of as an 'alternative' in the writings of figures such as Emmanuel Levinas and what I call the new politics of 'personalism'.

As Marx and Engels famously wrote in *The German Ideology* in 1845,

> the ideas of the ruling class are in every epoch the ruling ideas, i.e. the class which is the ruling *material* force of society, is at the same time its ruling *intellectual* force. The class which has the means of material production at its disposal, has control at the same time over the means of mental production.[6]

As we shall see, the ruling class of the present era is the so-called 'knowledge class' – what in the first chapter I have named the 'corporate-university-financial-information complex'. It is a class that controls *both* the means of 'material' production (which is now essentially 'virtual') in the form of the global 'symbolic economy' of digitised media, computerised investment and currency transactions, an increasingly credentialled lifelong learning and professional service industry, and a vast intellectual cognitive and communicative machinery that rigorously defines and enforces a new 'global-civic' moralism of self-criticism and self-denial ostensibly aimed at the good of all humankind, all the while ruthlessly grinding down the dignity and physical livelihoods of workers of all races, cultures and ethnicities. Neoliberalism is not in any way now the old-style 'capitalism' of Marx's day. In fact, the word 'capitalism' as a synonym for neoliberalism may be highly misleading.[7] It is indeed what Marx and Engels named the 'ruling intellectual force' of our contemporary era. Ironically, it is the very neoliberal ideology that often invokes 'social justice' terminology in order to impose the opposite agenda than classical Marxism once envisioned. It is the true wolf in sheep's clothing, and it must be unmasked for what it is so that a radical and hitherto unenvisioned political and ethical path forward can be charted.

One final point, however, needs to be made in response to one or more advanced readers of the manuscript. The book strategically and deliberately goes up against the conventional view that neoliberalism is more or less an economic ideology that is thoroughly anti-statist and underpinned by the kind of 'free market fundamentalism' espoused by Reagan and Thatcher in the 1980s and politicians such as Rand Paul and Paul Ryan thirty years later. Such a view, according to this reading, naturally aligns itself with social conservatism, nationalism, political reaction and even military oppression, as the case of the Chilean regime of Augusto Pinochet from 1973–1990 exemplifies. The same caricatured image of neoliberalism, favoured by many academics and theologians such as Adam Kotsko,[8] persists largely because of a failure to grasp that it is a form of cultural hegemony far more than it is a system of economic administration. It is not atomic individualism, or 'libertarianism', so much as the new progressivist corporatism that employs the marketing mechanism in the service of invisible forms of social transformation that defines neoliberalism.

The watershed for much of the budding analysis of neoliberalism as a 'progressivist' rather than a conservative enterprise is the writings of Foucault, on which this book heavily relies. One critical reader of the manuscript has posed the question (one that has been tossed about in the last decade) as to whether Foucault himself was a neoliberal sympathiser, and thus whether reliance on him to make my case does not constitute some sort of circular argument. The most notable repositories for the idea that Foucault himself was some kind of crypto-neoliberal are, of course, books by Mitchell Dean and Kaspar Villadsen as well as Daniel Zamora and Michael Behrent.

In their extensive and detailed examination of Foucault's later lectures, Dean and Villadsen offer a brief that the former, especially over the last decade, has served as something of a shill for anti-statist rhetoric, which in turn is associated with neoliberal proclivities in political theory. They go so far as to make the claim that Foucault was primarily a 'political theologian' because he valorised civil society, the 'extrastate domain' of human allegiance and activity, over direct state intervention. According to Dean and Villadsen, 'this extrastate domain is epitomized by creativity, value-based discussion, and new forms of political activity located in either domestic or transnational civil society'.[9] Valorisation of this domain can only arise out of a distinct

Christian theological legacy that views the state as what Saint Paul named a *katechon*, a 'restraining' power that keeps in check the human capacity for evil-doing until Christ returns and establishes the kingdom of God on earth. Dean and Villadsen imply that such 'state phobia' with its religious provenance (a connection that Foucault through his anatomy of early Christianity's rigorously 'ethical' approach to politics, evidenced in the formation over the centuries of what he dubbed the 'pastorate') has always functioned as the conceptual threshold for the romanticism of libertarian thought and the market fundamentalism of both classical liberal and neoliberal economics. Hence, our critics insinuate, any Foucauldian study of the phylogeny of neoliberalism is merely gilding the lily.

This sort of criticism, however, depends on a sharper reading of Foucault's own strategies and motivations than I think is permissible, one of which even the authors themselves has their own doubts. It only makes sense if one accepts the premise that the valorisation of civil society is a uniquely 'Christian' idea. Scholars such as Abdulaziz Sachedina have convincingly shown that regard for the importance of civil society harks back to early Islamic thinking,[10] while others have traced the same idea back to ancient China.[11] There is hardly any question that suspicion of the state apparatus as the linchpin of political authority has its promptings in the early Christian tenet that only Jesus Christ could be addressed as 'Lord', but the link with neoliberal models of governance is sketchy and circumstantial at best. What I argue, in fact, is that the reverse is true. Neoliberalism is not so much the heir to historically entrenched attitudes of 'state phobia' but, as Brown has so elegantly put it, a 'stealth revolution' that injects the cancerous chromosome of statist control of mind and body into the healthy genome of global civil society. Neoliberalism, therefore, amounts to a secret, but highly effective 'hostile takeover' of tradition-hardened spiritual configurations of morality, society and politics by secular and decidedly anti-religious elements. Its deceptive tactics and means of self-representation lend it a profile conforming ironically to what Christian radicals and reformers throughout the generations have branded as the *anti-Christ*.

Zamora's and Behrent's critique is more transparent. It becomes obvious in the opening pages that the authors are unhappy with Foucault's account of the origins of neoliberalism because it does not fit within the conventional Marxist orthodoxy that makes class conflict the determinative factor. Zamora and Behrent maintain that Foucault's 'failure' lies precisely in his successful analysis of postwar European society as having tamed the rough beast of economic inequality through the active measures of labour-friendly social democratic governments. It was only at the close of this era of relative prosperity that Foucault, in Zamora and Behrent's opinion, was able to switch over from the familiar historical-materialist reckonings of a century of Marxist scholarship to a more diffuse cultural hermeneutics that coincidentally opened the door for identitarian paradigms of human emancipation, and that have by now become fixated within the discourse of critical theory. 'The tragedy of Foucault's thought', they conclude,

> is that the conceptual tools he had so skillfully deployed to shine a withering critical light on postwar society proved distinctly less trenchant when directed at the emerging neoliberal order – the contours of which, at the moment of his untimely death in 1984, Foucault could only have glimpsed in the vaguest of terms.[12]

Zamora and Behrent suggest that perhaps we need to go back to a more standard form of Marxist class analysis in order to rectify Foucault's short-sightedness when it comes to 'the despotism of capital' after the collapse of the Soviet Union. This recommendation is commendable and should indeed command the assent of scholars. But tackling the problem of neoliberalism is not, and has never been, a binary choice, where one either selects the 'hard' option of reducing contemporary neoliberalism to the classical Marxist specimen dissected in all four volumes of *Capital* or the 'soft' preference for delineating structures of domination and oppression as simply coterminous with inherited socio-cultural formations, gender significations and value lattices. It is a mistake to read Foucault's later lectures as nothing more than a riff on, or lavish orchestration of, his very well-known schema of political control through 'power/knowledge' rather than the more obvious methods of state coercion. There is far more of a discontinuity between the younger and older Foucault than his Marxist adversaries will acknowledge.

In fact, it is my contention (which I do not consistently address in this work, only because it does not seem at all necessary) that it is Foucault's analysis alone, as refined three decades subsequently by key feminist theorists such as Fraser and Brown, that can provide leverage for peeling back the interpenetrating layers of neoliberal hegemony that have hardened into place over time. Neoliberalism is a stranger animal than any conventional template for theory can furnish an account of. The problem with our standard academic accounts is that they are the product of a sophisticated pattern of confirmation bias. We see only what we want to see in the *Gestalt* that is neoliberalism today. Our failure as academics to see clearly can be deduced straightaway from our own profound complicity in the perpetuation of the neoliberal empire itself. For it is an empire that sustains itself not so much through jack-booted domination of our bodies as through the clever manipulation of our unconscious desires and the flattery of our collective educated egos. We have without doubt met the enemy, and it is ourselves. That perhaps may be the most difficult in reading this book in the manner that will finally allow the scales to fall from our eyes when it comes to the question of neoliberalism.

I   Towards a Genealogy of Neoliberalism

People know what they do; frequently they know why they do what
they do; but what they don't know is what what they do does.

Michel Foucault, *Madness and Civilisation*

The Crisis of Representation

In *Force of God* I argue that the current global crisis of liberal democracy is a
'crisis of representation', a commonplace inspired by, it not directly attributa-
ble to, the early Foucault. In some ways this statement is both tautological
and gratuitous. The question of liberal democracy, so far as we understand it
historically, is all about the problem of 'representation'. Contrary to Rousseau's
effort to radicalise social contract theory with his postulate of the *volonté
générale*, or 'general will', which as many critics have rightly noted can be
easily misconstrued as an argument for totalitarian control of all features of
society (the Nazi *Gleichschaltung*), we have now lived through almost three
centuries during which political theory, epistemology and theology have
been aligned around the late Medieval trope of a reflexive relationship
between words and things. The trope of an intimate correlation between
words and things – *verba* and *res, les motes et les chose, Wörter und Dinge* as
the framework for what in the history of philosophy has come to be known as
'correspondence theory' – harks back to ancient Athens, where democracy
was born. The ancient crisis of democracy ultimately derived from the struggle between Socrates and the Sophists, between Platonism and the cheap
kind of conceptual relativism associated with a crude nominalism, that the
latter hawked in the agora.

These epistemological debates, persisting in some guise for millennia, have
never been esoteric preoccupations for closeted thinkers disengaged from the

'practical' affairs of Western political theory. They are founded on a measure of commensurability between *to logos* and *ta onta*, between an ordering of speech in accordance with what we consider to be reliable markers of reference between what we say and what we experience. Such a linguistic ordering in a primordial way is also inseparable from the articulation of 'law' or *nomos*, the very architecture of common life which for eons has been severed from its instinctual signalling of collective solidarity, its *Blut und Boden* tribalism. The common life demands an account that is given within the discursive formations that are appropriate to its age, its *episteme* in Foucault's terminology. It is unsustainable without the power of *logos*, on which even the most rudimentary form of the *polis* is founded.

Foucault begins his famous 'archaeological' enquiry entitled *Les Mots et Les Choses* (in English, *The Order of Things*) with the recognition that all representational systems or forms of 'knowledge' – and by extension all social and political speculation – are dependent on reliable and consensual methods of classification. 'Our culture', he writes,

> has made manifest the existence – of order, and how, to the modalities of that order, the exchanges owed their laws, the living beings their constants, the words their sequence and their representative value; what modalities of order have been recognised, posited, linked with space and time, in order to create the positive basis of knowledge as we find it employed in grammar and philology, in natural history and biology, in the study of wealth and political economy.[1]

But what happens when this reflexive, or reflective, relationship breaks down because of the episodic and involuntary intermixing of cultures, grammars and conventions of discourse, as we have seen in terms of thoroughgoing social breakdown and disorder resulting from the geographical dislocations of peoples as well as mass migrations, such as the *Völkerwanderung* that changed the face of Europe entirely from the late fourth through the eleventh centuries?

The political crisis and the representational crisis turn out to be conjugate and dependent variables with each one thoroughly interwoven with the other. The upshot is not only a new language and new expressions of *nomos*. This sudden, *disarticulation* of the reflexive relationship between 'words and things' is experienced in terms of what Foucault terms 'heterotopia', an increasingly disjunctive or 'deconstructive' method of dealing with and denoting what is the most familiar furniture of everyday reality. In the political and social, such a disarticulation has profound practical consequences. It can be easily construed as strife and chaos. What we are witnessing today is not only the climax of a long-burgeoning crisis of liberal democracy itself but the tremors of a gigantic break-up of an international system of previously well-functioning ideals and values that are as much cultural and political as they are economic. The global crisis of political democracy, therefore, emanates from the jumbling of categories used in the machinery of the most 'sacred' referencing systems that delineate fundamental world views and constitute the semiotic cement of human solidarity, the idioms of 'justice', the language of God, or the discursive norms for how we talk meaningfully about the 'political' as a whole.

Everything is up for grabs. Multiculturalism, for example, undermines the sense of identity that hitherto had been the bedrock of national consciousness. Amid the so-called 'clash of civilisations', therefore, even so-called 'human rights' are relativised and regarded in certain instances as merely 'Western'. They can be contrasted, for instance, with the 'Islamic' take of what it means not only to be human, but also to have such 'rights'. Instead, they are regarded as 'colonial' or 'Orientalist' constructs that must be unmasked as mere ideologies.[2] This new kind of taxonomy is in many ways, as Foucault has made clear, the outgrowth of a new philosophical sophistication about the strategic role of language. Just as Jacques Lacan took structural linguistics and used it as a psychoanalytic boring device to lay bare the inevitability of scission, fracture or 'lack' in the imagined unity of desire and enunciation, so Foucault was able to see through the subterfuge of formal logic and the belief in a 'universal' structure of communication to demonstrate how the so-called 'linguistic turn' in late modern philosophy was but a subtle testament to the long-brewing crisis of representation. Foucault's early explorations of the close relationship between history, language and knowledge become his later semantic operating system for the analysis of post-industrial society. In essence, Foucault's approach in such works as *The Archaeology of Knowledge*[3] and *Madness and Civilisation*[4] morphed slowly into a powerful cultural-hermeneutical collection of tools for mapping and diagnosing the symptomatology of what has come to be known as 'neoliberalism'.

The Concept of Neoliberalism

The concept of neoliberalism is one that has arisen, especially since the end of the Cold War, as both a general economic descriptor and a quasi-political and critical-theoretical notion for explaining the nature and effects of globalisation. In his lectures at the Collège de France delivered from the late 1970s to his death in 1984, Foucault was, as scholarly consensus shows, the first to identify the underlying forces and factors that we now know as neo-liberalism. During his slowly evolving historical study of the transition from what he called 'the disciplinary society' to the advent of 'biopower' Foucault deftly made us aware that the forms of social control and political authority in the post-industrial period cannot be merely reified as some kind of axis of 'power/knowledge' without examining their *semiotic* makeup; that is, the way they function in a garden variety context as *interoperable sign-processes.* Even 'economic' processes can no longer be taken apart in the way they were in Marx's day as mere 'dialectical' or *material* phenomena. They must be seen as modalities of *linguistic rule-making* which both precede and provide the final shape for the 'objects' of political criticism and cultural change-making.

Why does any of the foregoing really matter? Ever since the summer of 2016, world events have proven tumultuous and unnerving for the proverbial 'global elites' who, according to the newly fashionable discourse, comprise the minions for what is alternately termed 'international capitalism' or 'neoliberalism'. The election of Donald Trump as President of the United States and the shock of the Brexit vote in England during that year set off a squall line of on-the-spot, overwhelmingly reactive commentary all across the ideological spectrum, ranging from a briefly vocal self-confidence on the part of an amorphous fringe constituency known as the 'alt-right' (which one writer has defined as 'a motley crew of sub-cultural political identities' consisting of 'conservatives, identitarians, dissidents, radicals, outcasts, anarchists, libertarians, neo-reactionaries, and other curious political form-ations')[5] to the kind of anti-egalitarian hysteria epitomised in James Traub's rant in *Foreign Policy* that 'it's time for the elites to rise up against the igno-rant masses'.[6] At the same time, there have been tentative, and often fumbling, efforts to cast what is happening in more encompassing, analytical terms than merely slinging in the familiar, thought-stupefying clichés about dark, atavistic insurgencies fired by 'racism' or 'populism' or 'nativism' or 'national-ism' or even 'fascism'. Predictably, these diagnoses have been couched in the jargon of neoliberal economism – wage stagnation, income inequality, the outsourcing of manufacturing, the domination of elections by 'big money', insufficient government spending on education or job retraining, etc. And the cultural side of the equation, manifested in anti-immigrant sentiment among the working classes in both Europe and America, is routinely blamed on the inherent character defects of the insurgents themselves – their parochialism, their entitlement, their 'white privilege', their ignorance, their social and moral backwardness, their susceptibility to demagoguery, and on and on.

The economic dislocations that are allegedly causing what French far-right party leader Marine Le Pen, while campaigning with signature bluster, termed a 'populist spring' (invoking obviously false analogies to what happened in the Middle East starting in 2011) have not all of a sudden become apparent, even to the 'experts' or to the populace at large. They have been visible and full blown since the financial crisis of 2008 and were even predicted by some savvy economic seers since the turn of the millennium. The conventional wisdom that it was the lack of 'real income growth' following the Great Recession that has all at once ramped up popular frustration belies a more subtle and diffuse structural dynamic within the global order that these knee-jerk economistic explanations are incapable of bringing to light. Radicals, along with those who call themselves 'progressives' these days, are accustomed to laying the blame for the crises, injustices, and social and political dysfunctions of our time at the feet of two rough beasts that are alternately named as both 'capitalism' and 'neoliberalism'. Often, the two are rhetorically conflated as one. The problem with this conflation, as the key theoreticians of the latter such as Foucault and David Harvey have repeatedly showed us, is that the former historically from Smith through Marx onwards has functioned largely, although not exclusively, as an economic construct, whereas the latter is a term saturated with various unrecognised political significations and hidden intentionalities, thus betraying its hybrid nature. 'Neoliberalism' is not a term that can be simply interchanged with 'capitalism', a word to which Marxism gave a kind of overdetermined set of connotations, and which is becoming less and less useful as a descriptor, other than to name the obvious, a complex and expansive worldwide webwork of markets and financial mechanisms that drive them.

Neoliberalism is really not about economics, but about *values*, instantiating them in almost invisible routines of symbolic exchange that have profound economic effects. The 'economic' facade of neoliberalism, as we are beginning to realise, is a merely contingent manifestation of what Foucault dubbed the biopolitical means of 'governmentality'. Ever since Adam Smith we have derived the familiar types of political organisation from economic means of production and distribution (as implied in the eighteenth-century concept of 'political economy'). Thus a vigorous conversation about neoliberalism requires in many ways, as Maurizio Lazzarato has made clear, an investigation into the value-sources of our social and economic condition – a good, old-fashioned, Nietzschean 'genealogy of morals'. According to such theorists as Foucault, Harvey and Lazzarato, neoliberalism (taking into account their different degrees of emphasis) amounts to a configuration of power relations in an expressive articulation of embedded social valuations which, in turn, frequently employ the rhetoric of economism – and economic 'well-being' – both to mask the reality of elite domination and to exploit the humane instincts of those who are dominated. In short, *homo neoliberalismus* only wears the colourful costumes of classical *homo economicus*.

Like L. Frank Baum's Wizard of Oz, *homo neoliberalismus* is a grand illusionist who exploits our willingness to be enchanted by what Nietzsche called the 'highest values' for the provision of our ultimate servitude. Every historical form whereby this articulation is made manifest consists of what Foucault called a *dispositif*, an 'apparatus' whereby power, knowledge, discourse and personal inclination are mobilised and intercalated to produce such a magic theatre of signs, what Michael Lerner has termed without irony the 'politics of meaning'.[7] Neoliberalism is the munificent politics of personal meaning in the late era of consumer capitalism that masquerades as an old-style conservatorship of economic interest (consider the unrelenting electoral mantra of preserving the 'middle class'), while relentlessly encumbering through an endless financialisation of the private wherewithal and assets (credit cards, mortgages, student loans, taxes) that become the sole 'property' of banks, hedge fund managers and 'crony capitalist' allies within government.

The double-sided *dispositif* of the Middle Ages was both the castle on the hill, protecting town and manor against the armies of rival feudal lords, and the cathedral with its massive stone fortifications to shelter the unity of the holy Catholic faith against the predations of the devil. In the industrial era it was the factory with its mobilisation of productive power, presumably safeguarding the social order against want and idleness. During the twenty-first century it has become the corporate-university-financial-information complex, leveraging some of the most impalpable and efficacious strategies of Foucauldian biopower to guarantee globally diverse populations not just the democratic dream of infinite opportunity, self-improvement and personal advancement, but a redoubtable rampart against what James Joyce described as the 'terror of history'. These defences are not merely virtual. They involve real weaponry, routinely to protect entire populations as has been the case in large part of most Western military interventions since the 1950s. To quote Foucault: 'Wars are no longer waged in the name of a sovereign who must be

defended; they are waged on behalf of the existence of everyone.'[8] The idea
that wars can be pursued simply for conquest, or to shield sovereignty from
whatever threatens it for whatever reason, defers now to a conviction that
blood and treasure must be expended only for some higher, irrevocable
'humanitarian' purpose, to which the occasional United Nations interventions authorised by the Security Council consistently call our attention.
Kantian morality in its more diffuse guises of global polity becomes the invisible template for a new *universalistic* biopolitics rotating around the Foucauldian
double axis of 'power/knowledge'. The same holds true for 'domestic struggles'
and the challenges of civil society, where actual armaments are only deployed
in the most extreme instances. The vast taxing, regulatory and welfare apparatus of the state replaces classical *raison d'état*, and the new 'governmentality' of
neoliberal biopower whose coercion is primarily 'discursive' supplants the
disciplinary systems of the moribund industrial era. The power of 'moral
shaming', which in an earlier era was available only to political and social leadership with its privileged access to broadcast communications, now is extended
to the masses through social media, and who, while believing themselves to be
masters of their own opinions, dutifully carry out the 'soft-coded' value imper-
atives of the neoliberal hegemony.

As Foucault so brilliantly disclosed in his Collège de France lectures, the
advent of biopolitics in the modern age is the result of a long, sequestered, yet
inexorable evolution of the valorisation of what he calls the 'pastorate' in
Western culture. For Foucault, relying more on Nietzsche than many of his
contemporary readers are wont to acknowledge, the pastorate are the custo-
dians of what the latter famously dubbed the 'moral-Christian' metaphysics
that has suffused Western epistemology from Plato forward. The pastorate
encrypts the real in terms of a signifying praxis of ethical responsibility for
the lowly, the mediocre and the ordinary, all the while elevating the 'priestly'
function of guilt assignment and assuaging in such a manner that curial
power is perpetually reinforced and multiplied.

The Revival of the 'Pastorate'

This peculiar 'revaluation' of values, which according to Nietzsche can be
traced back to the Christian Church in its earliest instantiations, elevates
confession over innocent vitality, abnegation over self-affirmation, systemic
social distributions of Hegel's 'unhappy consciousness',[9] with its irremediable
guilt psychology that is endlessly absolved and administered by way of

spiritual triage by the pastorate itself. Foucault writes that from the late Middle Ages all the

> struggles that culminated in the Wars of Religion were fundamentally struggles over who would have the right to govern me, and to govern them in their daily life and in the details and materiality of their existence . . . This great battle of pastorship traversed the West from the thirteenth to the eighteenth century, and ultimately without ever getting rid of the pastorate.[10]

Once the promise of heaven dissolves into the various secular heterotopias for the 'pursuit of happiness' from the Enlightenment onward, the pastoral oversight of spiritual credits and debits is transformed into the benevolent biopolitics of the liberal state.

In short, the battle for democracy, starting with the English Revolution in the 1640s ,was both an insurgency against the clerical 'pastorate' as the proto-structure of biopolitics in the West, and at the same time a campaign to install new mechanisms of biopower in the form of various 'republics of virtue', such as Cromwell's Protectorate, Robespierre's National Convention and even Lincoln's authoritarian redesign of the federal government around militant Christian nationalism during the American Civil War. Bismarck's *Staatssozialismus*, though not an obvious example of democratic biopolitics, can be added to this list, inasmuch as it laid the groundwork for the full governmental *appareil* of the secular pastorate in the twentieth century.

But what Foucault misses, according to Lazzarato in his analysis of the genesis of the biopolitical apparatus, is how the 'virtuous' and 'humanitarian' secular democratic state, which deliberately sought to replace the political *imago* of the Catholic Church as the guarantor of what today we would term 'social justice', was founded on a grand economy of both debt and indenture. One can of course read Dostoevsky's parable of the Grand Inquisitor in this register. Drawing his arguments from on-the-ground study of workers and employment trends, Lazzarato is perhaps the first, genuine critical theorist of the 'knowledge-based economy'. Lazzarato has devised the notion of 'immaterial labour' as the key instrument of exploitation throughout the neoliberal order. For Lazzarato, capitalism from its beginnings has always been founded on expropriation, i.e. 'capture'. Whereas nineteenth-century capitalism expropriated the labour of the working class, the post-industrial, neoliberal order has expropriated the future financial capacities of Richard Florida's new 'creative class' through an ever-expanding apparatus of debt and financialisation.[11]

In his book *Governing By Debt* Lazzarato describes the present-day private university – in particular, the American university – as the primal scene of exploitation in the same way that the factory could be characterised as such in the nineteenth century. 'In the production of knowledge', Lazzarato writes, 'class division no longer depends on the opposition between capitalists and wage-earners but on that between debtors and creditors. It is the model the capitalist elites would like to apply to all of society'.[12] But this debt, which he calls the 'debt of life', is founded as well on a cultural and socio-psychological agency of capture which neoliberalism exploits quite effectively. Debt and guilt are interchangeable signifiers in this process, as the dual meaning, for example, of the German word *Schuld* implies. The university 'expropriates' the individual self-worth as well as the financial assets of the new, highly-educated 'indentured servant', which the neoliberal order simultaneously demands becomes a responsible 'global citizen', one who is constantly 'sensitive', self-conscious and prepped to make amends for their privileged status vis-à-vis multitudes of disenfranchised 'others' (while donating to grand political and social causes) through constant re-education, personal reinvention, and a willingness to sacrifice for the greater good in ways that ultimately benefit primarily the ruling elites of the world.

The uneducated – the now obsolete menial labourers who still inhabit the economically faltering knowledge societies – are cast as the moral scapegoats in the same way that people of colour were throughout the colonialist and industrial eras, as David H. Freedman notes in his caustic article in *The Atlantic* entitled 'The War on Stupid People'.[13] Because these 'useless', uneducated holdovers from a bygone era of industrial production have frequently retained the chauvinism and biases that were systematically employed to set them against other wage earners in previous generations, the same divide-and-conquer strategy has now been ruthlessly engineered by the neoliberal elites themselves to camouflage the reality of the new system of exploitation, which casts its net over peoples of all colours. Just as Marx called religion the 'opium' of the masses a century and a half ago, so excessive types of secular, idealistic political crusading – what in hip parlance these days is known as 'virtue signalling' – could in many instances be considered the heroin of the degreed classes. As various writers have emphasised in recent months, the promise of neoliberalism was always that worker sacrifices, including the break-up of unions, longer working hours, deferred employment through a commitment to higher education, would 'lift all boats', as the saying went, and usher in a new era of productivity and prosperity. While productivity has increased, prosperity has not to any significant degree, and it is those who are the bottom of the economic food chain who are the ones who are showing the first, real signs of rebellion.

Although such an 'economy' had been interwoven for centuries with the 'pastorate' itself – a phenomenon that when driven to excess by the Renaissance popes helped to spark the Protestant Reformation – there was always within all variations of Christianity the built-in breaker of Jesus's ethical and spiritual teachings of the Sermon on the Mount. In other words, the pastorate in its 'cure' of bodies and souls was always compelled to temper the pain of debt with forgiveness. Secular biopolitics as the heir to the pastorate has never had such a constraint. In fact, according to Lazzarato, the biopolitics of the neoliberal order is incorporated at its very power centres on the dispensation, regulation, perpetuation and discursive dissimulation of indebtedness. In *The Making of Indebted Man* Lazzarato shows how under neoliberalism the 'subjectivity' of a caring society is alchemised through the magic of political rhetoric into a thoroughly instantiated and embedded system of personal liability and fief-like servitude. 'It is debt and the creditor-debtor relationship that make up the subjective paradigm of modern-day capitalism, in which "labour" is coupled with "work on the self", in which economic activity and the ethico-political activity of producing the subject go hand-in-hand.'[14] Such 'work on the self' can be the entrepreneurial praxis of what in popular lingo is known as 'self-help' and 'motivational' training, which is usually geared to some kind of profitable economic enterprise.

That, of course, is not to be confused with Weber's notion of a 'worldly asceticism', which characterised the Protestant ethic as the moral template for early merchant capitalism. The latter modality of 'work on the self' was always, to employ Kant's famous terminology, enjoined strictly by an 'imperative of pure practical reason'. It had no utilitarian end in view whatsoever. It was what today we call 'de-ontological'. It amounted to a striving for 'holiness' and was purely soteriological. In contrast, the neoliberal version of self-entrepreneurship never relied on any strategy of seeking after righteousness. It was always a quest for personal satisfaction. In a word, it was the foundation, as Daniel Bell noted over a generation ago in his *Cultural Contradictions of Capitalism*, for a broad, socio-psychological shift from a morality of maximised productivity and deferred gratification to incentivised self-indulgence – i.e. the inverted 'imperative' to consume that lubricates the wheelworks of consumer capitalism nowadays on a global scale.[15]

In line with Harvey's assessment it becomes easy to see that the imperative to consume cloaks itself in the 'evaluative' *patois* of personal freedom, the very generative grammar of neoliberalism with its honey-tongued celebration of 'rational actors' making choices that ultimately confirm the wisdom of 'markets'.[16] But, as Lazzarato points out, 'the debt economy is characterised not only by antiproduction but also by what we might call antidemocracy'.[17] He cites the way in which the Greeks in the summer of 2015 were subjected to ferocious austerity measures by both the International Monetary Fund and the European Union. Harvey, a well-known historian as well as theoretician, stresses that neoliberalism was always a system of co-optation or, as Gilles Deleuze and Félix Guattari call it, an 'apparatus of capture'.[18] In a nutshell, neoliberalism has captured the moral passions and sentimentality of educated cultural progressives in the developed world to advance the causes of the new planetary 'captains of industry'. According to Harvey, neoliberalism was launched in the 1970s as a counterpunch by economic elites against the ascendancy of the 'social state' in the postwar era that forced upon them income redistribution through taxation and the effective enfranchisement for the first time of organised labour. As he writes, 'an open project around the restoration of economic power to a small elite would probably not gain much popular support. But a programmatic attempt to advance the cause of individual freedoms could appeal to a mass base and so disguise the drive to restore class power.'[19] Neoliberalism picked up and preyed upon the street cries of political radicals for the loosening of restrictions by the state on moral behaviour as well as more individual autonomy and 'grass-roots' control of social and educational institutions. The ubiquitous New Left slogan of 'freedom now', expropriated from the traditions of Western liberal political economy itself, became the basis for what Nietzsche would call the 'revaluation' of all organisational value-standards and norms for evaluation.

The Function of 'Schuld'

At the same time, neoliberalism hybridised these libertarian proclivities with the new-found rage for 'social justice', building upon the realisation among the swelling numbers of the college educated that the historic ideals of liberty and equality had been severely compromised by the concentration of state power since the early twentieth century. In Harvey's words, 'neoliberal rhetoric, with its foundational emphasis upon individual freedoms, has the power to split off libertarianism, identity politics, multiculturalism, and eventually narcissistic consumerism from the social forces ranged in pursuit of social justice through the conquest of state power'.[20] The result, Harvey argues, was the creation of a new more 'socially conscious', meritocratic ruling class which, particularly after the collapse of Communism, employed various political 'wedge issues' to gain political dominance and gradually economic hegemony, which became the adhesive for its new, expanding global empire. The financial crisis of 2008 was indeed the output of predatory lending practices. But it was also promoted by both the Clinton and Bush administrations as a strategy for increasing home ownership among previously marginalised groups – a classic tactic of neoliberalism. The fact that the banks, which had sponsored this predatory lending, were immediately bailed out by the very government that had backed them (unlike in previous crises where financial institutions took the hit), under the pretext of forestalling the social chaos that its very practices had engendered, illustrates how by this juncture in history the apparatus of capitalism was now totally controlled by left-leaning rather than conservative political interests.

Neoliberalism seduces with the promise of freedom but ends up disenfranchising those who are caught up within it while slapping on the irons of debt servitude. In the end, according to Lazzarato, it can only 'govern the economy through drastic limits to democracy and a no less drastic drop in the expectations of the governed'.[21] Lazzarato draws on the anthropology of Nietzsche to make the case that the substitution within the neoliberal order of the much vaunted mechanism of exchange – so-called 'democratic capitalism' – for the debt regime is the direct outcome of this seduction. There is no 'zero point' from which economic relationships historically ensue. They all begin with initial conditions of dependency and domination.

The concept of economic exchange, in mirroring the fiction of the social contract, assumes a voluntary set of primal social relationships, when in fact the universal, abject condition that Freud described as 'hunger and love', or basic need and extravagant desire, inevitably prevents the possibility of any original equilibrium as fantasised by the classical political economists. The neoliberal 'social state', pretending to overcome all historical disequilibrium to the extent that it claims to regulate the means of production while distributing fairly and justly the fruits of collective labour, becomes a 'total' system of 'capture' – i.e. 'expropriation' in the traditional, Marxian sense – of the lives and livelihoods of those who are inscribed within it. The cycle itself is self-sustaining. In *Governing By Debt* Lazzarato argues that the 'democratic' promise of future consumption by the neoliberal state betokens a crisis that 'does not reveal a mere economic failure but rather a breakdown in the political relationship between appropriation, distribution, and production. Growth cannot pull us out of the crisis, only new principles of appropriation, ownership, and production can.'[22] The growth of the system is inseparable from the growth of the state and its *undemocratic* machinery of capture.

Interestingly, Lazzarato in the second chapter of *Governing By Debt* singles out the American university as the ganglion of the neoliberal debt-capture-expropriation machine. He characterises the university itself as 'the model of the debt society'. According to Lazzarato, 'the American student perfectly embodies the condition of the indebted man by serving as a paradigm for the conditions of subjectivation of the debt economy one finds throughout society'.[23] The fact that almost 70 per cent of students graduating from American universities have financed their education through loans, and many with enormous sums, means that even the most highly sought-after forms of employment are but glorified versions of nineteenth-century menial labour where every day workers, as the old song goes, got 'another day older and deeper in debt'. The federal government, or the private banks whose student lending operations are secured by the government with no possibility of default, literally becomes the 'company store' to which the worker owes his or her 'soul'.

As Lazzarato stresses, 'students are indebted before entering the job market and stay indebted for life'.[24] But this conjuration of a new 'universal' class of chattel where the master-slave relationship is no longer one of personal ownership but a lifelong fealty towards the state itself does not arise from the traditional workings of indenture. 'Students contract their debts by their own volition: they then quite literally become accountable for their lives and . . . they become managers.'[25] They are not, as in the old paradigm of indenture, merely struggling to survive or feed their families. They are challenged all the way from grade school onwards to be all that they can be, to fulfil their lives by doing some greater public good. In Foucault's terms they are 'entrepreneurs of the self', who believe they are commissioned to add value not only to their own lives, but to others'. Unlike the monks of yore who took vows of poverty, chastity and obedience, they are joyfully pledged instead to a life of indebtedness, profligacy and self-seeking all the while under the powerful illusion that they are maximising 'human potential' while relying on the neoliberal state to establish justice.

'Capitalism', as Marx and the earlier generations of political economists understood the word, was precisely the apparatus of the 'capture' of the value of the worker's labour in the guise of 'surplus value' manifested in assembly-line machinery, real-estate housing factories and of course the speculative price of tradeable securities. Marx in many ways did not deviate that much from the theoretical framework of figures such as Smith and Ricardo. What distinguished 'Marxism' in its earliest iterations was the recognition of the invidious fallacy of an economy founded simply on 'exchange' and its epochal insight that capital accumulation means 'expropriation', a sophisticated strategy for reconfiguring Proudhon's celebrated remark, derived from Rousseau, that 'property is theft', as well as a cognizance that all economic relations at even the most primitive level are the augmentation of a system of domination. The inevitable and merciless logic, therefore, of capital accumulation as the engine of class differentiation and class conflict in the nascent industrial age became the cornerstone of the Marxian dialectic.

The *Nomos* of the Earth

But neoliberalism from the outset was, strictly speaking, a conscious effort to give capitalism a 'human face' by mitigating the human exploitation and suffering Marx had so trenchantly diagnosed in the 1840s. At the same time, neoliberalism was really a *coup d'état* masquerading as 'democratic' reform. Germany's 'Iron Chancellor' Otto von Bismarck was the one who first envisioned its basic 'biopolitical' operating system, seeking to foil incipient proletarian insurrections with such innovations now taken for granted as rudimentary pensioning and the creation of the 'common school'. The Great Depression forced the hand of *Sozialstaat* planners by requiring that similar kinds of anti-insurgency measures also be plied in the fiscal and monetary spheres. John Maynard Keynes, whose grand designs were focused not on transcending but on 'saving capitalism', therefore became the shadow architect of neoliberalism with his revolutionary theories about regulating the business cycle in order to reduce economic risk and, especially, with his programmes of artificially stimulating consumption in times of downturn through deficit spending. Although present-day, pop political economists such as Paul Krugman have emphatically denied the historical ties between Keynesianism and neoliberalism, the historical record speaks for itself.

The nascent consensus of historians of the Great Depression seems to be that the first tangible successes for Keynesian economics were registered not by the Western democracies but by the National Socialists, thus cementing the dubious co-determination from World War II onwards of prosperity and militarisation in the rise of the proverbial 'warfare-welfare state'.[26] It is no accident that President Lyndon B. Johnson, the prime mover of the greatest military build-up since World War II, was also the champion of the 'Great Society'. Nonetheless, it was the gross excess of warfare spending on the futile Vietnam adventure over a decade that overstimulated the economy and led to the runaway inflation of the 1970s which, according to Harvey, was the real occasion for the acquiescence to the policies of neoliberalism.

Ronald Reagan's infamous 'supply side' economic policies, though it was shot through with the polemics of classical economic theory, was actually the next major innovation in neoliberal 'governmentality' by dint of its mainte-nance of the now permanently instantiated Keynesian stimulus to consumer spending from military outlays, while privatising many government services, which simultaneously began the process of shifting income distribution away from the 'middle class' towards corporate-government power brokers. The belief that Reagan and his conservative successors somehow 'curtailed' federal influence over the economy is one of the greatest urban legends of the last quarter-century. Reaganism merely reallocated priorities. The same can be said of Barack Obama's policies from a different angle. According to Lazzarato, 'neoliberalism represents a new stage in the union of capital and the state, of sovereignty and the market'.[27] The transition from nineteenth-century 'liberalism' to nineteenth- and twentieth- (and twenty-first-) century 'neoliberalism' is nothing more than going 'from wanting to govern as little as possible to wanting to govern everything'.[28]

The penchant to 'govern everything' is built into the debt-fuelled demand system of neoliberalism, and it is the very leaven, according to Lazzarato, of the growing authoritarianism wherever the imposition of market economies once promised instead the expansion of human rights and personal free-doms. It is not accidental that the same word – i.e. 'liberal' – used commonly to characterise state-directed moral 'compassion' is the same word baked into the very term neoliberalism. What distinguishes neoliberalism, as Lazzarato shows in an earlier work entitled *Signs and Machines*, is that it makes capitalism into a 'semiotic operator' where real economic conflicts are suppressed by the machine-like processes of cultural differentiation that both forge imagined identities and foster endless divisions which are then 'managed' by the purely discursive politics of the centralised state, including state-influenced media (i.e. what is loosely termed 'identity politics').

As Lazzarato observes, 'enslavement does not operate through repression or ideology. It employs modeling and modulating techniques that bear on the "very spirit of life and human activity".'[29] Such 'machinic enslavement' (a 'Truman show', or Baudrillardian 'hyperreality', of unacknowledged associations, triggers and extremely subtle moralising prompts and cues) 'formats the basic functioning of perceptive, sensory, affective, cognitive, and linguistic behavior'.[30] In sum, neoliberalism captures through the barely perceptible codifying processes of ubiquitous 'humanising' education and media while formally demanding that every 'good citizen' commit to the 'higher values' incarnated in the 'soft' governance of the neoliberal state.

In 1950 Carl Schmitt, the *éminence grise* and founder of the intellectual discipline we have now dubbed 'political theology', wrote in the aftermath of the catastrophe of the 1940s, just as the new 'cold war' between the two superpowers of America and the Soviet Union was rapidly intensifying, that both a new geopolitics and what Deleuze would term a 'geophilosophy' were in the works. Such a new global *episteme*, he argued, was the inexorable expression of the appearance of an unprecedented, new topography of value and meaning that radically redistributed the familiar signs and markers of both truth and power. Schmitt, in fact, anticipated by almost three decades Foucault's observation in *The Birth of Biopolitics* that the formulation of the principles of law (*nomos*) are ensconced from the very beginning at the 'site of truth'. Schmitt dubbed this new topography the *'nomos* of the earth'. 'Every new age and every new epoch in the coexistence of peoples, empires, and countries, of rulers and power formations of every sort, is founded on new spatial divisions, new enclosures, and new spatial orders of the orders.'[31] This spatial reordering cannot in any manner be factored out of the linguistic, or sign, systems employed to rationalise it. *Nomos* means 'capture', and the 'enclosures' of labour, labour-value, life-value and livelihood which these semiotic 'machines', as Lazzarato designates them, systematically carry out determine how we will envision such a redesign of human relationships *in toto*.

Towards the end of *The Nomos of the Earth* Schmitt posits three possible outcomes in the gradual emergence of this new signifying topography. The first would be the outright victory of the Western democratic *nomos* – what throughout the Cold War was somewhat tendentiously referred to as the 'free world' – or, more darkly, the triumph of Soviet Communism. The second would be the 'expansion' of the historically dominant European *nomos* which, according to Schmitt, began with the discovery of the Americas in the seventeenth century and now includes the United States. The third would be a 'combination of several independent . . . blocs', the so-called 'multi-polar' international order that has been described since the fall of Communism as either an ideal or a nascent reality.[32] To a certain extent, all of these envisaged *nomoi* have simultaneously come to pass, but what Schmitt did not of course foresee was the way in which such a new '*nomos* of the earth' would be the product of digital communications technologies that would have been complete science fiction in 1950. Neoliberalism has become the current *nomos* of the earth, and it is not founded on the projection of military power and political influence so much as on the power to capture value through the machinery of sign-making.

What Kurt Appel has called the 'new humanism' that challenges the false humanism of neoliberalism is one of the central items on our agenda.[33] The kind of humanism Appel describes recognises the fragility and abjectification of the *real* global condition of peoples who inhabit this *nomos*, while calling for a Christian theological as well as an ethical (in a Levinasian sense) commitment to pull back the Grand Wizard's curtain so that the truth of our collective existence is finally exposed. We will offer a prognosis of what possibly lies beyond the horizons of neoliberalism in the concluding chapters of this work. But first we must examine relatively recent historical events as well as bring to bear some fine-honed (we might even say 'surgical') tools of critical theory and analysis that will illuminate the present as well as the immediate future.

2 Progressive Neoliberalism and its Discontents

> . . . 'the people' is not something of the nature of an ideological
> expression, but a real relation between social agents. It is, in other
> terms, one way of constituting the unity of the group.
>
> Ernesto Laclau, *On Populist Reason*

Populists and Cosmopolitans

THE ELECTION OF Donald Trump to the presidency of the United States in November 2016 not only stunned the world, it also ignited a ferocious debate within the political left, internationally as well as in America, over the causes and implications of the surprising turn of events. At first the narrative was defiant and oppositional. Trump had supposedly been elected because of an upsurge in white racism, 'ethno-nationalism', xenophobia and a brute and mindless 'populism' which the candidate himself had encouraged, according to the narrative. Yet Trump was only the first swallow of a new populist spring. The United Kingdom's Brexit vote the previous summer had shown that the malaise was not confined to the United States. 'Populist' revolts evident in the outcome of national elections followed swiftly over the next two years in countries as far-flung and diverse as Austria, Italy, Hungary, Poland, Brazil, Germany, Sweden, France, Turkey, India and Mexico.

Yet, as America's 2017 presidential inauguration day approached, strains of self-rebuke and mutual recrimination began to surface among American and global neoliberal elites, even while claims that the election itself had been manipulated by the Russians through online hacking and dark subterfuges of many kinds, including 'fake news' and private influence-peddling, remained the dominant form of scapegoating. One of the more forceful lines of critique was offered by political philosopher Nancy Fraser in *Dissent*, the well-known and long-established left-wing magazine for intellectuals. Fraser proclaimed that the election of Trump was undeniably the outcome of, and the electoral pushback against, an unspoken and long-evolving secret alliance between the interests of global capital and the leftist elites themselves, what she branded as 'progressive neoliberalism'. Referencing planetary trends and ideological shockwaves that had commenced the previous summer with the successful 'Brexit' decision by voters in the United Kingdom, Fraser declared that, 'In every case, voters are saying "No!" to the lethal combination of austerity, free trade, predatory debt, and precarious, ill-paid work that characterise financialised capitalism today.'

But Fraser went on in the article to say something even more controversial, and, to perhaps the majority of her readers and admirers, something counterintuitive and seemingly outrageous. Trump's 'victory', she opined,

> . . . is not solely a revolt against global finance. What his voters rejected was not neoliberalism *tout court*, but *progressive* neoliberalism. This may sound to some like an oxymoron, but it is a real, if perverse, political alignment that holds the key to understanding the U.S. election results and perhaps some developments elsewhere too. In its U.S. form, progressive neoliberalism is an alliance of mainstream currents of new social movements (feminism, anti-racism, multiculturalism, and LGBTQ rights), on the one side, and high-end 'symbolic' and service-based business sectors (Wall Street, Silicon Valley, and Hollywood), on the other. In this alliance, progressive forces are effectively joined with the forces of cognitive capitalism, especially financialization. However unwittingly, the former lend their charisma to the latter. Ideals like diversity and empowerment, which could in principle serve different ends, now gloss policies that have devastated manufacturing and what were once middle-class lives.[1]

Her position, of course, provoked immediate recoil with counterarguments that were inevitable. Twelve days later Johanna Brenner insisted that there could be no such thing as 'progressive neoliberalism'. After all, neoliberalism had been a bogey word for the anti-globalisation left for almost two decades. Brenner pulled off the familiar gambit of attacking Fraser and her line of critique as a smokescreen for its own form of covert reactionary politics.

> By shifting the analysis away from the capitalist class offensive that ushered in the neoliberal order, and which is primarily responsible for the US

political drift to the right, Fraser ends up attacking "identity politics" in favor of "class politics." While her conclusion is that of course the left must embrace anti-sexism and anti-racism, her analysis implies the opposite – she's clearly suspicious of multiculturalism and diversity.[2]

To which Fraser herself replied that Brenner had misunderstood what she was doing. The real question on which she was focusing, Fraser insisted, was the issue of 'hegemony', a term with a venerable legacy in Marxist theory, specifically with the twist given by Antonio Gramsci.

Gramsci had argued that in a multicultural society, economic hegemony is often achieved by 'idealist' intellectuals, who mask their bourgeois interests by foisting a world view on the working class that serves to exploit the latter in the interests of the former. Such exploitation as well as structures of dominance are maintained through a transcendentalist kind of moralising that conceals the flagrant class interests of the 'idealists' themselves.[3] Gramsci termed this process the 'manufacture of consent'. Following up on Gramsci's argument, Fraser stressed that

> ... neoliberals gained power by draping their project in a new cosmopolitan ethos. Contra Brenner, the point is not to dissolve 'identity politics' into 'class politics'. It is to clearly identify the shared roots of class and status injustices in financialized capitalism, and to build alliances among those who must join together to fight against both of them.[4]

This kind of debate continues to move forward with various shadings and contingencies, although most Western liberals have a very difficult time perceiving themselves as unaware 'neoliberals' in the kind of invidious sense that Charles Hugh Smith has railed about on his blog.[5] The transformation of 'class politics' into 'identity politics' was a shift that took place almost a half-century ago with the advent of the New Left in the late 1960s and what came to be called, for the most part by its critics, as a form of 'cultural Marxism' influenced by Herbert Marcuse and the later Frankfurt School.

What made Fraser's stance timely and noteworthy was a recognition, shared by mainstream sociologists, that the radicals of that period long ago grew up and became the 'establishment' and thus unconsciously enabled the transformation itself, which today many take for granted.[6] What the New Left of olden days proudly characterised as a strategy of self-affirming 'revisionism' – precipitated ironically by the realisation of feminists within what was called 'the Movement' that they had been hoodwinked by a certain 'manufacture of consent' to the hegemony of male leadership – had devolved over the years into a new global, 'hegemonic' progressivism that remained blind to the very economic 'contradictions' (as classical Marxists would say) that the long-germinating ideological shift had gradually opened up.

It is not just coincidental that 'cosmopolitan' was a familiar term of derision among orthodox Marxists before and after World War II, aimed at those in their ranks whom they considered ideologically soft and who they believed were in covert league with the 'capitalists'. It is ironic that decades after the collapse of Marxism as an international political force – and even much longer after the end of Stalinism when the word was commonly employed – that the same kind of long-forgotten reproach should suddenly surface again. But there is more than meets the eye in the cry of cosmopolitan elitism. And, despite offering a courageous and insightful analysis of what perhaps is truly taking place these days on a global scale, Fraser seems to be missing something important – i.e. what I would identify as the inextricable religious dimension of neoliberalism, 'progressive' or otherwise.

Joshua Ramey has caught a glimpse of what this religious dimension might well be when he brands neoliberalism as a 'politics of divination'. Ramey has compared the 'market fundamentalism' of historical neoliberal theories, first advanced by the Austrian economist Friedrich Hayek, to a form of intellectual sorcery.

> The argument . . . that . . . markets alone can resolve the problem of how to construct social life in the face of unforeseeable contingencies . . . is a perverse and disavowed colonization of archaic divination rites, the rituals through which human cultures, on the basis of chance, have perennially sought for more-than-human knowledge.

According to Ramey, his 'book attempts to prefigure a decolonization of divination beyond neoliberal authoritarian capture of the powers of chance'.[7]

Ramey's argument is both clever and subtle, but it is based more on an ingratiating trope that largely serves to essentialise the dual neoliberal obsession with the overly mathematicised method of explanation and forecasting, along with the phenomenon of rampant financial speculation, that brought down the world economy in 2008 through the creation of opaque special investment vehicles (in the latter case what has with snarky disdain been named 'casino capitalism'), than it is on the general social, political and cultural formations that Fraser seeks to expose. Ramey spends more time than is probably necessary massaging this trope in order to explore the familiar terrain of contemporary market and monetary theory without really penetrating, apart from financial mechanisms, the systemic relations at both the surface and deep levels, which Fraser tries to set before us. Contra Ramey, it is not magic but *morality* that, strangely, has contributed to a gaping income imbalance and inequality between the proverbial 'one per cent' and the rest, which became a shibboleth with the Occupy movement and was confirmed through the famous studies of the French economist Thomas Piketty.[8] How do we begin to understand how this dynamic has unfolded?

One must start with Mark Lilla's observation in the opening section of his highly discussed book *The Stillborn God* that in this age of smug secularity 'we are no longer in the habit of connecting our political discourse to theological and cosmological questions, and we no longer recognise revelation as politically authoritative'.[9] Throughout the book Lilla maps the interlocking patterns of political rationality within Western thought alongside sundry religious ways of perceiving and thinking. Lilla is not by any means the first theorist to make these connections, but he is perhaps the most concise and comprehensive among those who have undertaken this project. Lilla's underlying thesis is that we cannot have a serious political philosophy without a tacit *political theology*, and that the 'war' on political theology in the name of a new secular reason, which began in the seventeenth century and found its initial voice in Thomas Hobbes's *Leviathan*, has led us into a contemporary wilderness of confusion. If, as Schmitt famously wrote, all political statements turn out to be disguised theological statements, then modern political thinking has lost both its heft and its bearings. Lilla's project, when the book came out right about the time of the great financial collapse, was far more diagnostic than prescriptive. And its lack of any discernible anodyne rendered its impact less effective. It is easy to disbelieve the doctor's diagnosis if the doctor does not advise a remedy.

Nietzsche and Critical Theory

But Lilla was remarkably clear-sighted in his view that if the theological groundwork of Western politics had fatefully withered away, then the vacuum would have to be filled by a pure politics that served the very purpose of theology. The venerable and ancient form of *odium theologicum* had evolved into an *odium politicum*. It is no accident that the totalitarian political monstrosities of the twentieth century – fascism and Stalinism – were thoroughly and decidedly anti-clerical as well as, especially in the latter instance, anti-Christian. And it is no less curious that contemporaneous with the decline of religious belief in America's 'post-Christian' or 'post-evangelical' twilight, partisan rancour, vilification and zealotry has grown at an almost equal pace. Nietzsche, whose iconic saying 'God is dead' (in German, *Gott ist tot*, a deliberate word play) has been grossly misunderstood by even those most fashionable theological types who flaunt it as a brand label, was even more prescient well over a century ago. Nietzsche's *Nachlass*, i.e. his unpublished literary remains consisting mostly of thought sketches, future book outlines, notes and unfinished aphorisms, is shot through with observations about why what elsewhere he contemptuously characterises as the 'Christian-moral view of the world' has given rise to a general European culture of 'decadence' that is careening on its way to catastrophe.

Nietzsche, of course, foresaw the coming of World War I (what those who lived through it named 'The Great War' and even 'Armageddon') as the inexorable outcome of such decadence, whose inner secret is an overspreading and debilitating condition of *nihilism*. Nietzsche's theory of nihilism, functioning as the conceptual centrepiece from so many of his well-known ideas about God's death, 'priestly' or 'herd' morality, decadence, *ressentiment* and the so-called 'last man', is unfortunately only haphazardly elaborated or developed in his published works. But it sprawls in detail across the opening sections of his *Nachlass*, formally published in 1930 under the seemingly arbitrary title of *Der Wille zur Macht* ('The Will to Power'). The theme of nihilism, which in many ways can be regarded ironically as a more comprehensive reckoning of Nietzsche's thought, has tremendous ramifications for the crisis of the Western imagination in a vein similar to what Lilla underscores. In addition, a close reading of Nietzsche can help to clarify what possibly Foucault was pressing towards – insofar as the latter was indebted intellectually to the former – in singling out the Christian 'pastorate' as the occasion for the metamorphosis of the political into the *biopolitical*. It will also succeed in charting our genealogy of neoliberalism as a structure of *valuations* as much as an economic terrain. In short, we may not be too far off the mark in claiming that Nietzsche's diagnosis of the nihilistic predicament of modernity also anticipates the current political crisis which has been associated with a break-up of the neoliberal world order.

Nietzsche opens *The Will to Power*, composed in the 1880s, with the following prophetic lines: 'What I relate is the history of the next two centuries . . . the advent of nihilism. This history can be related even now, for necessity itself is at work here. This future speaks even now in a hundred signs, this destiny announces itself everywhere.'[10] As with the death of God announced by the madman in Nietzsche's parable, such an 'event' is still unfolding to this very day, while its indices are many, even if the meaning behind the markers remain yet undeciphered. Nietzsche concludes the opening paragraph:

> For why has the advent of nihilism become necessary? Because the values we have had hitherto thus draw their final consequence; because nihilism represents the ultimate logical conclusion of our great values and ideas – because we must experience nihilism before we can find out what value these "values" really had.[11]

Most admirers of, as well as commentators on, Nietzsche train their sights on his appeal for a 'transvaluation of values' through a mobilisation of the will to power. Few, however, really pause to sift through and seriously analyse Nietzsche's critique of the historical Western value system, which he set forth in his *Genealogy of Morals*. Nietzsche's entries in the *Nachlass* can be regarded as a highly nuanced elaboration of his insights from the *Genealogy* with an added, distinctive attentiveness to the process by which these values have over time self-immolated, resulting in the 'tremendous event' that is the divine demise. Perhaps Nietzsche at the end of his life had come to recognise that he was on track of something with a magnitude and consequence that even he himself was only beginning to appreciate.

In his proclaimed *reversal of Platonism* Nietzsche offered the seminal observation that all forms of philosophical idealism constitute in some measure a moral judgement. It is no accident that the word Plato himself chose to denominate ultimate reality was *to kalon*, 'the good'. But what exactly is 'moral judgement' in the strict philosophical sense? Almost a century before Nietzsche, Kant had formulated it as an act of will that subsumed a concrete aim under a general principle of 'pure reason'. Relying on the two, somewhat competitive terms for 'will' in German that are missing in English (*Wille*, or deliberative agency versus *Willkür*, or arbitrary volition), Kant refined many of the tacit assumptions within the tradition of Western moral philosophy. Only *Wille* can be the basis of a moral decision, because it has an end in view. However, a truly 'good' will, according to Kant, is not founded on a particular end or purpose that one seeks to accomplish, but one that wills something 'for its own sake' in accordance with the strict principle of *universalisability*.

If a 'moral judgement' is judged to be 'moral' at all, it must be valid in the same circumstances for every conceivable rational being making the same judgement. Or, as it is phrased in Kant's famous, *first* formulation: 'Act only on that maxim through which you can at the same time will that it should become a universal law.'[12]

But Kant, who formulated this universal demand as part of his so-called 'practical philosophy' that was designed to reconcile the transcendental and cognitive methods of the natural sciences, set forth in his earlier *Critique of Pure Reason*, with the doctrine of moral obligation anchored hitherto largely in the theological argument for divine revelation, could not escape what might be called the 'valuation trap'. Without delving into all the complexities and technicalities of both Kant's argument and Nietzsche's critique, we can reiterate Nietzsche's own point that any fabrication of a 'universal' concept must of necessity prescind from the welter of existing and divergent intuitions of what such a thing might look like, thus prioritising what the former called the 'ought' as opposed to the 'is'. Later both Marx and Freud characterised the tendency to reify such an *ought* as the unconscious creation of an 'inverted world', what came to be regarded as the theory of *ideology*. The goal of any critical philosophy – and by extension what later came to be known in the early twentieth century as 'critical theory' – is to 'unmask' these ideological constructs and reveal them for what they are, i.e. collective self-deceptions that turn our gaze away from what we cannot bear to acknowledge in its own right for the sake of an 'other world' (what Nietzsche termed the *Jenseits*, the 'beyond') which, although thoroughly unreal, seems far more congenial.

From the standpoint of both Nietzsche and critical theory, humankind had never really stopped confusing Plato's 'shadows of the cave' with the real. The true 'idols', therefore, are the ones Plato believed a philosopher could see once a mind was lighted by the sun, the transcendent idols he named *eidoi*, which we translate as 'ideas' in the epistemological realm and 'ideals' within the framework of moral philosophy. It was Nietzsche's genius to fathom the *singular genealogy* of universalistic thinking as a whole, regardless of whether it be 'practical' or 'theoretical', in accordance with Kant's framing of the basic notion. But, unlike the critical theorists who followed him, Nietzsche was not so sanguine about the ability of philosophy to see through itself and apprehend its own inherent idolatry. As the prophets of ancient Israel realised, idolatry is always more subtle and fugitive than we are accustomed to presuppose. But such idolatry does have a built-in tendency to corrode and, like certain oak trees that hollow out as they age, finally collapse on account of its own flimsiness. That is what Nietzsche implied when he insisted that nihilism means 'the highest values devalue themselves. The aim is lacking; "why?" finds no answer.'[13]

The self-devaluing (*Entwertung*) of the 'highest values' is an unavoidable by-product, according to Nietzsche, of the phenomenon of moral rationality itself. The 'death of God' is but a gripping, pictorial instrument for enforcing our awareness of this process. 'We see that we cannot reach the sphere in which we have placed our values; but this does not by any means confer any value on that other sphere in which we live; on the contrary, we are weary because we have lost the main stimulus. "In vain so far!"'[14] Even though Nietzsche is famous for presumably blaming the death of God and the advent of nihilism on Christianity, it should be noted that he regarded the problem as endemic to Greek thought itself. In fact, he notoriously decried Christianity simply as a commodified form of the latter. Christianity is 'Platonism for "the people"', he quipped in the preface to his *Beyond Good and Evil*.[15] Nihilism is not strictly the unalloyed remainder of a degenerate moral philosophy, but the destined outcome of the ancient effort to ground ethics in reason itself, as Kant had magisterially done. 'The faith in the categories of reason is the cause of nihilism. We have measured the value of the world according to categories *that refer to a purely fictitious world*.'[16]

This thesis of Nietzsche's, perhaps because it remained undeveloped as well as seemingly incidental to the typical summary of what we might term Nietzsche's peculiar 'critical' perspective, is far more consequential than many realise. Gilles Deleuze, however, in effect unravels Nietzsche's supposition at great length in *Difference and Repetition*.[17] Valuation, for Nietzsche, is a strategy of both discrimination and affirmation. But in the exercise of moral judgement only one component, that of distinguishing, is enabled. We might call this element the 'critical' one, inasmuch as it differentiates, which is an essential aspect of human cognition as a whole. But differentiation alone leads us to manufacture new 'ideas' or 'types' which take on a life all their own. That is the point Aristotle emphasised in his *Categories*, which is one of the chief reasons that logic has always dominated the other subfields of philosophy, even metaphysics. It is inherent in the positing of a 'kind', or genus, to differentiate itself and thereby proliferate 'specific' instances of the same.[18] As Benjamin Whorf noted, this momentum towards 'specific differences' is genetically embedded within the subject-predicate structure of Indo-European languages, of which not only Greek but most Western philosophical languages are cognate iterations.[19]

As Nietzsche makes clear, the impulse towards differentiation brings alongside the temptation towards comparison. And with ever comparative differentiation one makes a valuation, mainly a negative one. Thus, morality as a kind of Pharisaic commemoration of the fact that one is 'not like other men' arises. At the same time, it is those who form the 'gigantic mass' (*die ungeheure Menge*) who have not distinguished themselves in any notable way from others who control, so to speak, the discourse of morality. The 'mass man', or 'mass woman', cannot predicate or affirm anything unique about themselves. In Nietzsche's parlance they lack the positive 'will to power'. Their 'will' aims only to be conformed to an abstract, universal and 'rational' ideal that is always pragmatically out of reach. It remains, like the kingdom of heaven, forever *transcendent*, on the 'other side' of the existing world. But in their impotence to achieve this abstract (what Hegelians and Marxists would dub 'alienated') aim, they are bent on fiercely judging others – particularly those who are exemplary in their status and accomplishments – as morally suspect. It is a deflection, or transference, of their own consciousness of failure. Democratic egalitarianism, therefore, for Nietzsche becomes the exemplar of what he terms the 'herd' mentality with its corresponding moralism. It is a mentality both perpetuated and legitimated by a 'Christian-moral' metaphysics of existence which constantly feeds on its own dynamism of comparison, resentment and blaming the 'other'. The 'solution', for Nietzsche, lies not in any refinement of the basic Platonic-Christian-Kantian prototype of rational and moral discrimination, but in letting go of all such comparison entirely, the strategy which he labels as going 'beyond good and evil'. Nietzsche's 'philosophy of the future', as he named it, would amount to utilising difference not as a method of comparison with the covert aim of blaming and shaming, but to *affirming difference as difference* – in other words a 'metaphysics' of difference itself. That, of course, is what Deleuze as a disciple of Nietzsche undertook to map out in his own lifelong philosophical project.

In the socio-political realm Nietzsche foresaw 'nihilism' as the permanent condition of 'mass society'. The modern *populus* 'unlearns modesty and blows up its needs into cosmic and metaphysical values'.[20] One calls to mind not merely the incendiary 'yellow journalism' of the late nineteenth century, but the obsessive and ineffectual posturing and rage-choking partisanship and paranoia that dominates the hour-to-hour political news cycle. The incessant parsing of every sound bite or gesture by public figures into some sort of outrage or scandal, the amphetamine-like delirium that social media offers its bored and addicted users to vent constantly about every reported injustice or offence that comes to their overstimulated field of attention, the ceaseless 'trolling' of contrived as well as obvious malefactors, manifests itself as an ongoing multi-media theatre of the absurd that most darkly bears out Nietzsche's glimpse of what was indeed coming from the standpoint of his own day and age. In the face of this 'twilight of the idols', Nietzsche notes, we substitute frenetic moralising and rhetorical, as opposed to material, activism for religious discipline, cultivating the profile of what today has come to be known mockingly as the 'social justice warrior'. 'One attempts a kind of this-worldly solution' for problems on which we used to rely on God almost exclusively. That is not, according to Nietzsche, heroism but 'decadence'. 'Believing one chooses remedies, one chooses in fact that which hastens exhaustion.'[21] Morality appears as a 'great sense of truthfulness', but it turns out in reality to be little more than a perverse kind of 'sentimentality'.[22] Or, as Nietzsche puts it acidly, 'the instincts of decadence should not be confused with *humanness*'.[23]

Wendy Brown's Critique of Neoliberalism

What do these musings of Nietzsche have, in fact, to do with the question of neoliberalism? Far more than would be evident to most of the many Nietzsche admirers today, who hail his ruthless vivisection of popular Christian credulity, while in the same breath adhere to the same 'decadent' moral convictions which the nineteenth-century prophet of nihilism saw as the outcome of Christianity itself. 'The time has come', Nietzsche wrote, 'when we have to pay for having been Christians for two thousand years'.[24] What does that comment imply? To answer that question, we need to follow the trajectory outlined by both Lilla and Fraser. Fraser writes passionately about the self-delusion of a faux neoliberal 'left' that calls itself the 'resistance', but is not resisting neoliberalism at all. In fact, in its frenzied moralising it is firming up what it claims to be resisting.

It is a movement that pretends to be morally superior in championing the 'marginalised' and the oppressed, but in truth knows only how to shame, blame and complain, all the while demonising the 'deplorables' just as it morally privileges itself and romanticises the global exploiters who, as Fraser puts it, peddle the '[unholy] alliance of emancipation and financialisation'. That is a perhaps a polemical condensation of the general argument that Wendy Brown makes in what she dubs the 'stealth revolution' of neoliberalism. The 'stealth' factor has been the appeal to 'progressive' or 'humane' rather than acquisitive impulses, the laying of the egg of an exploitative cowbird in the nurturing nest of an indigenous progressivism among the educated elites that purports politically to instantiate on a global scale the 'Christian-moral view of the world'. Think of the creation of failed states in Libya and Iraq under the banner of promoting human rights. Think of galloping income inequality and wage immiseration under the unfurling moral banner of borderless economies and the perpetuation of subsistence labour through unrestricted immigration, once more by bringing down the moral hammer against 'xenophobia'.

In what she identifies as the 'changing morphology of *homo oeconomicus* and *homo politicus*', Brown underscores how neoliberalism seeks with its superior, 'cosmopolitan' authority to put to rout the foundational, Rousseauian inspiration about the sources of democratic politics, where 'we are free, sovereign, and self-legislating only when we join with others to set the terms by which we live together'.[25] In neoliberalism the terms of sovereignty are no longer set by the *demos*, but by the demands of capital itself, which masquerades as the guarantor of the social 'welfare' of all who may find their way within its borders, not just 'citizens'. It would appear counterintuitive to the progressive mind that 'emancipation' can be a straightforward subterfuge for profiteering, but that indeed is precisely how 'socially conscious' capital actually operates. The young Marx called out the sham of Hegel's argument that the political subject is only self-actualised through participation as a citizen of the Prussian state by dismissing it as merely touting (in Brown's phrasing) a 'ghostly sovereignty' that lacks a body because of the condition of alienated labour. Then a genuine – as opposed to a *faux* – radical nowadays would be one who sees through the deceits of global neoliberalism by recognising that its self-proclaimed 'emancipatory' project is impossible save for an entrenched, international 'precariat' routinely exploited and morally browbeaten by the corporate-financial-educational complex in order to advance the aims of worldwide economic domination by a self-serving, and self-limiting, minority.

The pivotal construct for this kind of subterfuge, if one reads Brown correctly, is what has come to be called 'human capital'. The grandiloquence of such an expression turns on the association of human agency and achievement with the classical idea of accumulated personal wealth. But, in reality, it is but one more instance of extracted, 'surplus value', as Marx understood the word 'capital'. Such a surplus is not the fruit of one's own labour, but a contracted debt to whoever provided the wherewithal for the augmentation of such 'value'. Since the phrase 'human capital' is most readily associated with the pursuit of higher education (which is necessary both to acquire and to advance in stable employment), the very euphemism can be decoded, following Lazzarato, as the amassing of student debt, which continues to bear interest that can rarely be paid off in a timely fashion. Brown's contribution to this discussion, however, consists in her *sui generis* account of how human capital under a neoliberal regime is transposed from what Marx termed 'alienated labour' into a pathology of *expropriated self-worth*. The standard 'progressive' narrative concerning the genesis of neoliberalism usually portrays it as the fruition of the Anglophone political heritage of competitive individualism, and the original association of the adjective 'neoliberal' with the revived libertarian morality of the late 1970s and 1980s as well as the free-market fundamentalism of the Reagan and Thatcher administrations of that period.

The extended argument of Francis Fukuyama's *The End of History and the Last Man*, that famous paean from the early 1990s to 'democratic capitalism' and the universalising of the global market economy, laid out what came to be commonly regarded as the ideological markers of the neoliberal outlook.[26] But the emergence of the so-called 'millennial generation' from 2000 onwards, with its supposed 'altruistic' passion for social responsibility, combined with President George W. Bush's appeal for a 'compassionate conservatism' that was soon succeeded by Barack Obama's vision of a new co-operative and peaceful global commonwealth, gave many observers the false sense that the moral tide of Western civilisation was on the verge of turning. Something else, however, unexpectedly occurred. At the same time as the official rhetoric, and in large measure even the international policy apparatus, did in fact replace the deep grammar of competitive individualism with the discourse of international 'accountability' towards others, the trend towards greater income inequality and the amassing of capital under the auspices of a tiny elite of global financiers became – paradoxically – ever more pronounced, especially after the collapse of an international banking system.

According to Brown, the shift took place alongside the increasing inoperability of the economy as a whole, which cannot be blamed for obvious ideological reasons on the vast, new disequilibrium between productive wealth and labour capacity. Instead appeal must go out for a new type of 'responsibilized human capital', rallying under the banner of 'sacrificial citizenship'.[27] As Brown stresses with her longer historical view than many critics of neoliberalism bother to extend to us, the golden age of liberalism melded the duty of an 'active' citizenship with the economic dogma of *laissez faire* and the glorification of the rationality of 'self-interest'. The imperative within the economy to reduce both wages and benefits in order to preserve the destabilised system from collapsing is masked by a certain high-minded extolling of public virtue, and of course one that fosters the comforting belief that one is aiding the marginalised of the world. In effect, Kant's grand moral commonwealth or 'kingdom of ends', once instrumentalised through an actual cosmopolitan politics functioning as the cultural sidecar to global capital, can be singled out retrospectively as the formal template for what today we understand as neoliberalism.

Whereas conventional nationalistic responses to moments of privation have valorised the violent sacrifice of the 'other' through war or conquest in the name of preserving the purity of the *Volk* (the essential impulse in recent centuries of proto-fascist, fascist and neo-fascist movements), the neoliberal pedagogy has switched the emphasis to the 'sacrifice of oneself', not for transitory reasons of patriotic solidarity in the face of threat from an external enemy, but as an open-ended commitment to spiritual or 'intangible' forms of self-improvement that simultaneously improve oneself and (at least ideally) 'others'. As Brown puts it, such a gesture is 'above all a sacrifice *for* rather than *to* something or someone'.[28] The originally moral or political idea of self-sacrifice thus becomes strictly 'economistic' in Brown's words. And, playing out in the midst of the Great Recession, 'rage' that was 'appropriately directed at investment banks' was 'redirected into a call for shared sacrifices undertaken by their victims. This would seem to be exactly the logic that Occupy was seeking to expose and reverse in its attempt to hold the banks, rather than the people, responsible for creating an unsustainable debt-based economy.'[29]

Brown's book went to press just before the global populist pushback against neoliberalism became a daily news feature, and one of its greatest drawbacks is that while it is 'right on', for key reasons it remains only *half-right*. Brown quite cannily documents the long-developing dynamics, not just economic but also cultural, of neoliberalism in this latest phase of what Karl Polanyi called the 'great transformation' of the modern period.[30] What she seems to miss is that the kind of 'entrepreneurship of the self', which Foucault traced back to the Christian ideal of the 'pastorate', can be expressed not just through the personalistic vector of self-improvement and spiritual formation (the latter's 'care of the self') but also through the corporate, institutional and bureaucratic matrices that regulate, sustain and ultimately validate it. In other words, Brown's take on the 'pastorate' is almost exclusively about the 'sheep' and not about the system of 'shepherding', which Foucault so astutely and extensively catalogued. She remains blinkered on what we might call a true 'neoliberal' (as opposed to a classic 'liberal') assumption that the ideology of what she calls 'responsibilism' trickles down from certain institutions and their symbolic machineries that are invested à la the Marxian mechanism of an ideologically 'inverted world' in concealing their own true interests in maintaining the fiction of a globally 'engaged' citizen. Especially with the millennial generation on the scene now, the outmoded baby-boomer mentality of 'looking out for number one', once the watchword of the 1970s and 1980s 'Me Generation', has now morphed into the ironic formula of *self-actualisation through sacrificial citizenship,* which she exposes as a neoliberal subterfuge. In brief, Foucault's model of 'governmentality' requires an existing, and to a large degree sacralised, *government,* – a distinction that is crucial to grasping neoliberalism as a thoroughgoing transformation of the classic liberal *politeia.*

Neoliberalism's 'Ironic Spectator'

The psycho-political tenor of the distinctive, millennial legitimation of neoliberalism has been sketched by Lilie Chouliaraki in her book *The Ironic Spectator: Solidarity in the Age of Post-Humanitarianism.* As Marx pointed out almost two centuries ago, the ethico-religious correlate to global capitalism is romantic *cosmopolitanism.* In the digital age such a cosmopolitanism is perpetuated through online news and social media, which offers us a 24/7 intensive peephole into the sufferings, misfortunes and calamities wrought upon our fellow human beings. Thus, cosmopolitanism is no longer what Kwame Appiah refers to as a two-fold position – 'universal concern' and 'respect for legitimate difference'.[31] Rather it has morphed into a Baudrillardian 'hyperreality', an instantiation of the ill-defined and open-ended *humanitarian imaginary.* The conventional bourgeois imaginary, Chouliaraki notes, was energised by 'pity', a moral category which Nietzsche ruthlessly associated with the 'decadence' of popular democracy. However, the new elite, cosmopolitan sensibility is characterised instead by 'irony', a pseudo-engagement that is not even emotional, but relies on the projection through the lens of sublimated moral outrage of our own sense of isolation, purposelessness and emptiness into the open spaces of 'theatricalised' human suffering.

As Chouliaraki remarks,

> irony is not simply a cultural sensibility characteristic of our times. It is also an ambivalent political project firmly grounded on the neoliberal 'spirit' of capitalism – a politics that, in seeking to maximise the commercial and technological efficiency of the imaginary, risks transforming our moral bonds with vulnerable others into narcissistic self-expressions that have little to do with [genuine] cosmopolitan solidarity.[32]

Thus, the digitised, neoliberal magic theatre of promiscuous, politicised affrontery, which only the god of governmentality can save us from, has managed to stupefy us with this *faux* enactment of planetary empathy and compassion.

The Populist Internationale

But in what way exactly has this process succeeded in 'undoing the demos'? Brown has at times been criticised for pushing a romanticised view of democracy, one that particularly ignores the fact that the transformation of *homo politicus* into *homo oeconomicus* is mainly the consequence of the rise of what Jodi Dean terms 'communicative capitalism', which has shape-shifted considerably since the end of the last millennium on account of ubiquitous 'informatisation'.[33] Brown's book, published prior to the events of 2016, furthermore fails to address the 'populist' reaction to neoliberalism on a world scale that has been gaining steam since that year. Aside from the fraught and tangled question of whether the expression 'populism' is actually the best choice to label what has been happening not just in America, but also in Europe and countries as diverse as Turkey, India, or the Philippines, we need to examine from the standpoint of theory whether invocation of the word aids us to a certain degree in unravelling what is clearly a seismic shift in nominally 'democratic' politics in opposition to the neoliberal order. The prevailing theoretical rhetoric has been to conflate populism with caricatures of fascism, but this gambit, often motivated by a certain cosmopolitan and elitist bias, tend to ignore the fact that populist regimes, once installed, do not necessarily eliminate 'democracy' as commonly understood, but often reinforce the power of the *demos* as a majoritarian instrument of political control without abolishing the electoral process (which fascist regimes invariably do).

At the same time, they are not at all immune from corrupting the electoral process itself, but so too are 'minoritarian' systems of elite governance. As South American political philosopher Ernesto Laclau in a landmark treatise makes clear, populism as a movement emerges out of what is ostensibly a democratic *politeia* from the outset. It is a symbolic and polemical *redistribution* of what has been represented hitherto as the *populus*, or the 'people'. That is why populism can alternate between 'left-wing' and 'right-wing' constituencies. According to Laclau, 'populism requires the dichotomic division of society into two camps – one presenting itself as a part which claims to be the whole' through a calculus of 'antagonistic division of the social field' along with 'the construction of a global identity out of the equivalence of a plurality of social demands.'[34] Besides functioning as a redistribution of the ideal content of representations of democracy by and large, populism also has the effect of *sorting out* in a quite different fashion the methods of signification within democratic politics as a whole. Thus, it is a major alteration in the makeup of what Claude Lefort famously has termed *le politique* as a condition for the performance of *la politique*.[35] The 'people' hence rediscovers itself 'by finding the common identity of a set of social claims in their opposition to the oligarchy'. Likewise, 'the enemy ceases to be purely circumstantial and acquires more global dimensions'.[36] For Laclau, populism is not primarily a 'movement' but a 'political logic'.[37] It is essentially a 'new hegemonic game', inasmuch as a new 'people would require the reconstitution of the space of representation through the construction of a new frontier'.[38] Elsewhere, Laclau terms populism a 'contamination of the universality of the *populus* by the particularity of the plebs'.[39]

The use of the term 'contamination' is slightly tendentious here, because the kind of 'logic', or 'rationality', Laclau charts in his book does not differ much from what Marx and Engels rely on in *The Communist Manifesto* to make the case that the 'proletariat', or industrialised working class, has become historically a 'universal class'. Laclau, of course, situates himself within the Marxist tradition. Even though *plebs*, or the underclass of citizens (excluding foreigners and slaves), are opposed in classical political theory to the *populus*, or those who have the proper status to govern, largely through their ownership of property, it has only a legal rather than a political meaning. At the same time, *plebs* is roughly equivalent to the Greek *demos*, which in ancient Athens was denied any political weight except in the negative sense of that which might threaten the sanctity of the *politeia*. The very modern notion of 'democracy' implies the conceptual transmutation of what was previously politically *excluded* into the very 'universalising' force of the political itself. One could easily argue that 'populism' is indeed, strictly speaking, what has been 'undone' by neoliberalism, and therefore is not theoretically the bane of democracy but its consummation.

But the underlying issue is not simply a semantic one. What Brown, and in a more limited way Laclau, is driving at is a recognition that the 'economisation' of the political has had immense consequences that still remain largely invisible. Critics of 'populism' rightly emphasise that historically it has led routinely to racial, ethnic and even religious policies of exclusion – at times virulent and violent. An explanation is not difficult to ascertain. Laclau demonstrates that the 'antagonistic' rationale of populism is predicated on an expansion of the notion of the *populus*, now incorporating what was formerly the *plebs*. But this expansion tends to 'empty' the content of the political itself, and the logic of inclusion yields to the logic of antagonism. A strange type of political metonymy emerges. What was concrete (i.e. those excluded by a false equivalence between the elites and the *demos*) now becomes an abstract universal (i.e. the 'people'), and certain segments of the abstract *populus* are *mutatis mutandi* concretised as 'alien', or excluded. Populism habitually re-inscribes often overlooked, ignored or disempowered elements of this false abstract universalism of 'democracy' (for instance, certain minorities or outsiders) as *discrete others* who somehow pose a menace to the *vox populi*. Muslims in the West after 9/11 are an obvious example of how this subtle art of populist demonisation functions. But so too is the uneducated slice of the native white *demos* in the minds of the Western educated classes ever since the election of Trump.

The literature on what we know as 'populism' is extremely nuanced and extensive, and it is not our business here to take a stab at surveying or summarising it while in pursuit of some measure of precise phraseology. Most of the leading theorists of neoliberalism tend to ignore the issue of populism, which has been around for almost a century and a half. Perhaps their penchant for sidestepping the issue can be accounted for by the fact that 'populism', like 'neoliberalism', has been used in a vast assortment of ways by political theorists and commentators together. Furthermore, to make the construct intelligible at all requires that the investigator contextualise its usage. Because 'populism' does not have an easily decipherable referent in the preponderance of situations, it has become, according to Laclau, an 'empty signifier' (although Jacques Lacan's label 'sliding signifier' might be more appropriate, since the word is not at all meaningless, only conspicuously adaptable to competing circumstances).

As most theorists agree, the one common attribution of the word as routinely used is its unique reliance on a polarisation of political discourse, one that makes a dialectical division between the 'people' and the 'elites'.[40] The content of both dialectical expressions oscillates from one setting to another. The other area in which analysts seem to have achieved a provisional consensus is in characterising the rather fraught relationship between populism and 'democracy'. The former almost invariably claims an affiliation with the latter, while the latter frequently disavows the former. The nub of the controversy can be found in the conundrum which sparked our own enquiry – i.e. the 'crisis of representation'. According to Jan-Werner Müller, 'populism is neither the authentic part of modern democratic politics nor a kind of pathology caused by irrational citizens. It is the permanent shadow of representative politics.'[41]

Populism and the Failure of Representation

What Müller appears to suggest in this statement is that populist grievances are more often than not the direct outcome of a burgeoning sentiment that the 'representational' system has either failed or is fraudulent. Modern political philosophy since its inception in the sixteenth century has consistently grappled with the problem of representation. The definition of the social compact hinges on this very conundrum, which is why Müller proposes that populist agitation is 'really just another way of saying that some sort of new social contract is needed'.[42] Rousseau's effort to circumvent the failure of representative politics in postulating a theory of sovereignty based on the 'general will' may be tabbed as the ultimate 'populist' solution. Indeed, Rousseau-style appeals to not just the semantic, but the *ontological*, priority of the *demos* can be found in much populist rhetoric. As Cas Mudde and Cristóbal Rovira Kaltwasser expound the dilemma, the *populus* in 'populism' does not necessarily connote the people as a whole, but the 'pure people'. The purity of the authentic – as opposed to the putative – demos is contrasted with the 'corrupt' elites, whoever they may be.[43] At the same time, 'purity' does not in any way always imply racial supremacy, nor ethnic homogeneity, the authors note. The multi-racial, or ethnically heterogeneous, character of so much Latin American populism – e.g. Venezuela, Peru or even Mexico – belies the assumption, favoured these days by Western academic elites, that racism and populism automatically go together, according to the same authors. As we shall see, the recent racialisation of populism, which was historically more a mustering of 'class' demands than anything else, has served as a convenient canard for neoliberal elites to dismiss, or morally ostracise, populist reactions to their own hegemony.

At the same time, the racialisation of the populist demographic has gone hand in hand with the ideological masking of structural racism by the very processes of economic 'entrepreneurialisation' and 'responsibilisation', which Brown so aptly documents. As Eduardo Bonilla-Silva in his searching, empirical enquiry into what he calls 'racists without racism' has shown, not only a persistence but also a deepening of racial discrimination in the post-Jim Crow period turns out to be the unvarnished effect of the cumulative legacy of social and educational advantage attached to the historically dominant racial caste in America (so-called 'white privilege'). Ironically, progressivism and unacknowledged white privilege, along with the handicapping of racial minorities, are apt to go hand in glove with each other, because the former is more likely to call attention to the behavioural or expressive peculiarities of the white underclass, while downplaying its own overwhelming stake in maintaining the cultural expectations, and social configurations, that hold back people of colour. In other words, the educated elites start out with a disproportionate share of 'social capital' which they are able to augment to the detriment of both the white and non-white working classes. Since in the neoliberal economy culture is the most valuable form of currency, de facto discrimination against those who lack it happens to be even more severe. As Bonilla-Silva stresses,

> the wages of whiteness are not equally distributed. Poor and working-class whites receive a better deal than their minority brethren, but their material share of the benefits of whiteness is low, as they remain too close to the economic abyss. Hence, white workers have a powerful reason to exhibit more solidarity towards minorities than whites in other classes.[44]

Bonillo-Silva also cites empirical data to show that, 'contrary to those who hold the "commonsense" view on racial matters, racial progressives are more likely to come from working-class backgrounds'.[45]

The pushback of populism against neoliberalism worldwide (not just in America) cannot be localised, or regionalised. Nor can it be simply racialised, although racial prejudices, whether innate or an epiphenomenon of labour exploitation, without doubt do figure in the populist equation from time to time. Finally, it cannot be said that populism follows a definitive trajectory of nationalist, socialist or of course ethno-racialist grammars of political soli-darism. There is no 'populist internationale' analogous to the workers' internationale of the nineteenth and twentieth centuries. But populism is also far more than a 'performance style'. It is a symptomatology without evident symptoms, one that builds upon the increasing confusion in many cultural and linguistic venues about the relationship between *homo politicus* and *homo oeconomicus*. In that respect, it is perhaps the most salient marker of the 'crisis of representation' at a planetary level. But before we explore the epistemic character of such a crisis, we need first to take a close look at how such a crisis is intimately associated with the present-day *mediatisation* of the political *tout ensemble*.

3   Mediatic Hegemony: The Kingdom, the Power, the Glory and the Tawdry

The media's the most powerful entity on earth. They have the power to make the innocent guilty and to make the guilty innocent, and that's power. Because they control the minds of the masses.

Malcolm X

A Brief History of 'Governmentality'

IN *THE KINGDOM AND THE GLORY* Giorgio Agamben lays out in the opening sentence a project that will take Foucault's theory of 'governmentality' to a new level. 'This study', he writes, 'will inquire into the paths by which and the reasons why power in the West has assumed the form of an oikonomia'. It 'locates' itself within the ongoing genealogical investigations that Foucault initiated in the 1970s, Agamben says, 'but, at the same time, it also aims to understand the internal reasons why they failed to be completed'. Foucault was unable, Agamben suggests, to acknowledge that 'the shadow that the theoretical interrogation of the present casts onto the past reaches well beyond the chronological limits that Foucault causes, as if a more primordial genetic rank would necessarily pertain to theology'. In fact, according to Agamben, it can be traced all the way back to the very 'onto-theological' template for all Western thought itself, the *three-in-one Godhead*.

Agamben announces in his opening statement that he aims to go beyond Foucault's fixation on the clerico-confessional management of both the language and psychology of salvation compressed into the latter's notion of the 'pastorate', which becomes the groundwork for the theory of 'biopolitics'. He argues that he wants to

> show instead how the apparatus of the Trinitarian oikonomia may constitute a privileged laboratory for the observation of the working and

articulation – both internal and external – of the governmental machine. For within this apparatus the elements – or the polarities – that articulate the machine appear, as it were, in their paradigmatic form.

Agamben proposes a few sentences later that the question of *oikonomia*, which means of course 'household' in Greek and from which we derive both the terms *economy* and *ecology*, is ultimately about the essence of 'power' in the Western context. The metaphysics of 'economy' is, in crucial but somewhat opaque respects, paired with the seemingly 'antinomical' (Agamben's term) construct of 'sovereignty' in the absolute sense that Carl Schmitt analysed in the 1920s.

> The double structure of the governmental machine, which in *State of Exception* (2003) appeared in the correlation between auctoritas and potestas, here takes the form of the articulation between Kingdom and Government and, ultimately, interrogates the very relation – which initially was not considered – between oikonomia and Glory, between power as government and effective management, and power as ceremonial and liturgical regality, two aspects that have been curiously neglected by both political philosophers and political scientists.[1]

For Agamben, both Schmitt and Foucault serve as the double axis today, much like Kant and Hegel in the nineteenth century, for an investigation of the political. In addition, the analysis of the political is impossible without consideration of its embedded *theological* substrata, a famous argument which Carl Schmitt advanced almost a century ago, but which has only been applied for all intents and purposes (as Agamben points out) heretofore to the notion of exceptionality (*Ausnahmezustand*) without due regard for the increasingly relevant concept of *proportionality*. This question, which perhaps amounts to a Derridean *aporia* or 'undecidable', harks all the way back to Plato and the beginnings of Western philosophy itself. It also trenches on the question in early Christianity of the significance of 'law', or *nomos*, within the larger scheme of what the Greeks named *dikaiosyne*, or 'justice'. Is the law strictly situational (i.e. does it apply only, as Paul asked, to those who like the Jews are 'under the law'), or is it truly 'universal' in the way that Kant's 'practical reason' later formulated it (i.e. valid for all persons from all cultures and polities at all times in the same set of circumstances)?

Simply stated, is 'justice' ultimately *retributive* or *distributive*? And who can, or *should*, administer it? If justice is founded merely on sovereign, or divine, decree, then the appropriate 'political' configuration is doubtlessly *autocracy*. If justice is all about *ratio*, or proportional allotment (Simonides's 'rendering to each person his due'),[2] then it must be subject to what contemporary theoreticians would term 'administrative' or 'managerial' reason – in other words, the logic of bureaucracy and the subtle play within the biopolitical venue of 'power' alongside 'knowledge', as Foucault understood it.[3] The latter would also be the prevailing semiotic coding mechanism for present-day *democracies*. How does one, therefore, assess *real*, as opposed to imagined, power in accordance with the paradigm of 'governmentality' that Foucault initially sketched out? And what would be the theological *episteme*, as Foucault might call it, within which this process unfolds?

Agamben notably argues that the paradigms of both sovereignty and *oikonomia* derive straightaway from 'Christian theology' – on the one hand, a 'political theology which founds the transcendence of sovereign power on the single God', and on the other hand, an 'economic theology, replacing this transcendence with the idea of an oikonomia, conceived as an immanent ordering – domestic and not political in a strict sense – of both divine and human life'.[4] The theological provenance of both transcendent sovereignty and an 'immanent ordering' is the Trinitarian formulation at Nicea. Trinitarianism historically can be seen as a compromise to reconcile the Caesaro-papal instincts of Christianity's new imperial benefactor Constantine, who sought to unify the empire under one common faith, with the 'pastoral' apparatus that the underground and previously persecuted church had already achieved with its remarkable, organisational prowess over nearly three centuries. The Trinitarian formula was also a sophisticated outworking in both a political and philosophical context of the inherent 'incarnational' synthesis of pagan and Jewish thought that was articulated from 50 to approximately 65 AD by the apostle Paul. Apart from such a synthesis, Christianity would not only have failed to develop over time, especially after the debacle of the Jewish War in 70 AD, but it would also have proved inadequate as a true 'state religion' designed to hold the fractious and centrifugal forces of a decaying Roman Empire together, a project which successive Caesars prior to Constantine had unsuccessfully attempted under the guise of an innovative form of unitary 'solar monotheism'.[5] The prestige of the militarised Roman state had already been in decline since the disasters on the frontiers a century earlier. Hence, Constantine needed a new, religio-symbolic order that embraced the pieties of the already sprawling and largely literate clerical classes that were saturated with Christians. The Christianity of antiquity from the outset was what Foucault terms 'governmental', and it came to be secularised – especially in the France of the seventeenth and eighteenth centuries as well as Prussia during the nineteenth century. Prussia invented through the ministrations of the Lutheran *Landeskirche* what has come to be known as 'state socialism'. Genealogically, the Prussian prototype of a secularised clerical state governance, centred on the university and its 'faculties' along with the military and a cartelised financial system dating all the way back to the Middle Ages, was the seed plot for the growth of what currently we recognise as a larger 'neoliberal' order, not to mention Bernard Stiegler's 'cognitive capitalism' or Peter Drucker's 'knowledge society'.

From *Oikonomia* to Biopolitics

So far as Agamben is concerned, the 'biopolitical' administration of the world is authorised by the idea that the divine is, in effect, a triple functionary, as first enunciated per scholarly consensus by the Church Father Irenaeus of Lyon in the latter half of the second century, with his claim that the Godhead is one in reality but manifests through three different functions, or operations.[6] Whereas Irenaeus understands the 'economic' administration of the Triune God to entail the work of the Son as well as the Father and the Spirit, Agamben is concerned mainly with the first and third persons of the Trinity. But what makes *oikonomia* unique, according to Agamben, is that it mirrors *not* the sphere of sovereignty that informs the *politeia* (that is, 'the political') but the *household*. Broadly conceived, *oikonomia* in the Aristotelian setting has only to do with the conduct of personal or family affairs – dealings between master and slave, father and children, husband and wife – that are completely set apart from, and impenetrable by, the *polis*. Whereas in the modern 'republican', or bourgeois, setting the household would be regarded as a kind of monadic prototype for civil society – and in Hegel's 'philosophy of right' for the rationality of the state *tout court* – in the Athenian environment it would be envisioned paradoxically as the very penumbra of the political. Therefore, how would the 'economic' model of human relationships be gradually given separate but equal importance with 'despotic' sovereignty? The result would be a Christian 'political theology' that would ultimately leave its unmistakable 'signature', as Agamben puts it, on the modern secular world, while perhaps becoming what Schmitt would describe as the 'nomos of the earth'?

It is a commonplace among historians that the Christian *ekklesia* evolved during and throughout the pre-Constantinian era as a kind of shadow state, purposed for the general 'care of souls', filling an enormous social as well as spiritual vacuum which the militarised and overly politicised *imperium* was completely derelict in executing. The role of the Christian pastorate, therefore, became its own kind of Aristotelian 'household' writ large and inscribed – despite the recurrent antagonism of the imperial authorities – within the 'cosmopolitan' expanse of an increasingly unwieldy – and ungovernable – empire. After the 'conversion' of Constantine, the dialectics of *polis* versus *oikonimia* throughout the Mediterranean world resulted in an unparalleled moment of *Aufhebung*, which has persisted into the present.

At the same time, if 'politics' and 'economics' are now separate, yet theoretically *inseparable*, in the guise of what we have come to call 'political economy', and if these two modalities of 'administration' have been fused ever since the age of Constantine by a dominant *political theology* of both God and government as necessarily sovereign (yet simultaneously 'caring' and concerned for the general welfare), what does that portend for the present and evolving 'globalist' configuration of polities and peoples, one in which once independent ethnicities, the pith of national sovereignty ever since the seventeenth century, have been replaced with the new transnational empire of fluid markets and nomadic capital? This new empire is no longer defined by disciplinary structures of hegemony and authority as much as by the swarming and 'sliding' signifiers (in Lacan's sense) that constitute digital communications and the infinitely rarefied specimens of financial transactivity? Such indicators, following the academic conventions of the last decade or so, delineate much of what has come to be known as 'neoliberalism'. And the new planetary regime that carries its name has come to be invested with a certain disrepute, even among those who are visibly as well as invisibly its agents of influence and benefactors.

At a very superficial level, this new global demesne of etherealised capital, which as we have seen derives its power from the pseudo-ethical imperative of a 'socially conscious' consumerism that will 'save the planet', resembles the ancient ideal of *Romanitas*. Such an ideal can be summed up simply as collection of higher 'humanist' values on which citizens of the empire relied in order to justify morally and culturally their brutal subjugation of the far-flung multitudes. It was similar to the British coloniser's fiction of their 'civilising mission' throughout the nineteenth century. But this kind of 'humanism', which the Romans invariably contrasted with the pervasive 'barbarism' that they were convinced had to be conquered and pushed back from its borders, was ultimately inadequate to keep the empire together. It inexorably fell prey to a kind of regional warlord-ism stoked by the increasing reliance of the regime on non-citizens, or what today we would describe as 'stateless' mercenaries, to maintain peace and order amidst a widely dysfunctional political, as well as steadily collapsing economic, system.

What the Christian *oikonomia* provided was a different form of governance, what today we would call 'soft power' through the mediation of a compelling new *symbolic* ensemble of instrumentalities and agencies. In Agamben's view the power wielded by the 'pastorate' in this new clerical economy derives from what he calls a politics of 'glory'. Such a politics is immanently inscribed within the social order to the extent that it encompasses the entirety of those who are not mere *subjects*, but also those who are claimed by, or theorised as coming under the authority of, the lordly realm. The Medieval legal figment of a 'Holy Roman Empire' could not have been elaborated over the centuries without this curious sort of *pastoral postulate*. In Roman times this privilege of invoking such a principle was accorded only to the narrow circle of those holding 'citizenship'. But the early church rendered it 'transcendental' in the sense that it promoted a novel style of 'subjectivity' through baptism into, and participation within, the *body of Christ*. In other words, because of the pastoral postulate Christians were constituted as more than simply *political* subjects. They were incorporated *soteriologically*, rather than strictly civically, into a 'kingdom not of this world'.

The Instrumentality of Glory and the Origins of a Symbolic Economy

Augustine, writing during the decades of imperial prostration in the early fifth century, first laid out the general theory of such dual subjecthood in his *City of God*. But while he, like Paul, looked for the reconciliation of these 'two kingdoms' only at the moment of an eschatological finale, his ecclesiastical imagination laid the groundwork for the revival of the Constantinian synthesis during the high Middle Ages and eventually for the rise of a *novum ordo seclorumn* in the late modern period. The question of 'glory' as 'the uncertain zone in which acclamations, ceremonies, liturgies, and insignia operate', for Agamben came to be transposed from the sacerdotal to the symbology of secular politics overall.[7]

Agamben writes:

> glory is the place where theology attempts to think the difficult concilia-
> tion between immanent trinity and economic trinity, theologia and
> oikonomia, being and praxis, God in himself and God for us. For this
> reason, the doxology, despite its apparent ceremonial fixity, is the most
> dialectical part of theology, in which what can only be thought of as
> separate must attain unity.[8]

The instrumentality of 'glory', which was used routinely by both kings and
clergy up until the early twentieth century and became the flash point for the
kind of sectarian conflict that eventually morphed into anti-clerical political
revolutions, served as the precursor, according to Agamben, for the *aestheti-
cisation* of mass politics that found its most demonic expression in the various
totalitarianisms of the twentieth century. 'We find here, as we find at the
hidden root of all aestheticisms', Agamben notes, 'the need to cover and
dignify what is in itself pure force and domination'.[9] But this 'aesthetic'
subterfuge can also be understood in terms of the virtualisation of politics
through both earlier and later forms of media and the manipulation of what
once were material interests through the idealising mechanisms of such a
'symbolic economy'.

The idea of a purely symbolic economy was advanced during the 1970s by a
lesser-known French post-structuralist theorist named Jean-Joseph Goux, at
roughly the same time as Foucault began his decade of lectures at the Collège
de France. It is Goux's overarching approach – adapted from Marx's analysis
of the fetishism of commodities in Book I of *Capital* as the generative principle in the formation of surplus value – which helps us frame a broader theory
of neoliberalism as *global governance by purely semiotic operators*. These
operators, or 'signifiers', are not so much a cover for pure force and domination as they are *the force of domination itself*. Goux relies on Marx's
observations about how commodification serves as an anticipation of the
ultimate epiphany of alienated labour under the aspect of money. Political
economy, not only for Marx but for a number of his predecessors, comes
down to the issue of how value is created. In Marx's final analysis, such value
constitutes different transmutations, or 'crystallisations', of labour as
commodities, culminating in their 'dazzling money form'.[10] Commodification
progresses through the increasingly obscure alchemy of the market exchange
mechanism. In order for commodities to be exchanged their 'values' must be

compared by some kind of rational set of criteria. But the commodities themselves cannot serve as a basis of comparison. Their values are merely 'relative' to each other.

Thus, there must emerge a general principle for comparing the relative values of commodities, a 'value of values', so to speak, or what political economy designates as a 'general equivalent'. The brandishing of the general equivalent requires that we excise the value of the labour that went into making it, yielding a more recondite form of value containing nothing more than 'abstract labour'. Marx writes that 'the body of the commodity that serves as the equivalent, figures as the materialization of human labor in the abstract, and is at the same time the product of some specifically useful concrete labor'.[11] The money form of the commodity becomes the very *prima materia* for the accumulation of 'surplus' labour value (*Mehrwert*) from which all historical variants of 'capitalism' spring. The general equivalent, or the 'money form', thereby becomes the sorcerer's apprentice that sets in motion an endless procession of formal correlations ('simulacra', as Jean Baudrillard calls them), converting material inputs into immaterial regalia. This 'virtualisation' of concrete value through commodity production, especially in the money form, is also the occasion for class conflict and exploitation, according to Marx.

Marx, of course, in his fidelity to Hegelian dialectics believed that over time this process would bring about the ripening of multiple, inherent 'contradictions' in the system, leading to its eventual breakdown and the onset of revolution. But what Marx did not foresee was the way in which the virtualisation process itself, including what Lazzarato terms 'immaterial labour', could be further virtualised and consequently commodified, bringing into being the brave new world of today where 'knowledge' is not a simple condition for the manufacture of usable 'things', but a thing to be produced and valued for itself, which is what we really have in mind when we prattle on about 'knowledge workers' and the 'knowledge society'.[12]

Goux explains how this kind of transformation takes place: 'instead of the relation, in which symbolicity is constituted; instead of exchange, through which subjects, in partially reversible fabric, can metabolize the signifiers that constitute them – the symbolic freezes into a rigid mediation that dominates them'. Furthermore,

> if the symbolic relation introduces a *third entity*, a mediating element, by which the ceaseless floods of the imaginary are absorbed . . . a symbolic

counteraction, operating like a forced currency, blocks the balancing
process and dispossess subjects of their own activity, through the symbolic
functions of the state, money, the concept.[13]

Thus the contemporary 'crisis of representation' can be understood as
fundamental to the very translation of *politeia* into *oikonomia*, or at least the
beginning of a recognition that they are interchangeable somehow at an
ontological level. The introduction of the primordial intuition of value as
'exchange value', which defines the 'economic' paradigm as a whole, demands
this shift in our perception.

The Neoliberal Moment

Nevertheless, it is not only money that presents itself as the new face of
tyranny in serving to 'dispossess' subjects of what is properly their own
through the apparatus of symbolisation, virtualisation and de-materialisation.
If, as most analysts agree, the virtualisation of finance had a lot to do with the
Great Recession that started in the fall of 2008, the digitisation and proliferation of personalised media has been a driving force in the degeneration of
politics into low-grade civil war. Standard critiques of neoliberalism, especially since the instant media sensation that came to be known as the Occupy
movement in September 2011, have focused on the heightened maldistrib-
ution of wealth and traced the current malaise to a revival of a predatory
capitalism not seen since the 1890s. But a more recent body of literature has
focused on the hegemony of the symbolic economy itself. Many of these
writers have drawn attention to the co-dependency of such an economy with
what we might term *consumptive consumerism*. Wendy Brown, perhaps fore-
most among such theorists, characterises the way in which these symbolic
economies expropriate not only a person's labour, but their very value and
self-worth. They force us to become 'entrepreneurs of the self', an expression
coined by Foucault which Brown leverages extensively in her argument that
neoliberalism transforms everything into capital, especially the kind of
'personal capital' that thoroughly reconstitutes individual self-worth as
professional identity in keeping with socially enforced criteria of symbolic
comparison. Brown writes:

> The figure of the human as an ensemble of entrepreneurial and investment
> capital is evident on every college and job application, every package of

study strategies, every exercise, every new diet and exercise program. The best university scholars are characterised as entrepreneurial and investment savvy, not simply by obtaining grants or fellowships, but by generating new projects and publications from old research, calculating publication and presentation venues, and circulating themselves and their work according to what will advance their value.[14]

One might add that contingent knowledge workers, the so-called 'precariat', should not be considered 'entrepreneurs' of the self in the true sense. They are better described as contractors of the self, where the relentless pursuit of accumulating 'personal capital' utterly fails to yield any kind of financial wherewithal whatsoever.

At the same time, what these strategies of both cultural and economic analysis – which prove to be intimately intertwined when it comes to the critique of neoliberalism – tend to miss is the determinative role of media. As the pioneers of critical theory within the so-called Frankfurt School during the first half of the twentieth century realised, the 'holy alliance' of culture and capital, which achieves its Gramscian-style synthesis in the evolving figurations of social control through not only mass media platforms but also individualised digital communication, is the real dark matter that needs to be illuminated by the light of reason. The politics of mediatisation need to be reviewed in light of the mediatisation of politics, and that is where Agamben's claim that modern communications provides an aura of 'glory' for democratic politics, where pomp and pageantry no longer suffice, turns out to be suggestive, even while it remains rather obscure. According to Agamben, Schmitt's rule that politics rests on a monarchial declaration of sovereignty – or at least a constant condition of inimicality (the 'friend/enemy distinction') analogous to the state of exception – only works within an autocratic setting.

Rousseau's notion that sovereignty in a formal sense can also be engraved within the *demos* is not necessarily compatible with Schmitt's deduction of political power. Likewise, Rousseau's contention that democratic sovereignty has an historical warrant, insofar as it invokes contra Hobbes a certain commensurability of the political with life the state of nature ('man is born free, but everywhere he is in chains'), presses us towards accepting the 'economic' model of governance. Such a move is consistent with the kind of providential calculus concerning the rise and fall of human societies implied in Adam Smith's metaphor of the 'invisible hand', and it constitutes an epochal shift in the rudimentary representation of 'political economy' as a whole.

Agamben perhaps takes Rousseau further than he would have otherwise been willing to go. One of the essential tensions in the eighteenth-century theory of the social contract turns out to be a tug-of-war between the ideal of collective cohesion founded in the 'general will' and the need for some kind of supersensible legitimation of democratic sovereignty. With the latter goal in mind, Rousseau came up with the heuristics of a 'civil religion'. Rousseau's formulation of such a civil religion can be found towards the close of *The Social Contract*: 'there is therefore a purely civil profession of faith of which the Sovereign should fix the articles, not exactly as religious dogmas, but as social sentiments without which a man cannot be a good citizen or a faithful subject'.[15] These 'social sentiments' can only be buttressed by the weight of the symbolic. The potency of the symbolic, or what Agamben terms 'glory', has its avatars in the era of democratic egalitarianism with what Guy Debord famously named the 'society of the spectacle'. Agamben writes that:

> If we link Debord's analysis with Schmitt's thesis according to which public opinion is the modern form of acclamation, the entire problem of the contemporary spectacle of media domination over all areas of social life assumes a new guise. What is in question is nothing less than a new and unheard of concentration, multiplication, and dissemination of the function of glory as the centre of the political system. What was confined to the spheres of liturgy and ceremonials has become concentrated in the media and, at the same time, through them it spreads and penetrates at each moment into every area of society, both public and private. Contemporary democracy is a democracy that is entirely founded upon glory, that is, on the efficacy of acclamation, multiplied and disseminated by the media beyond all imagination. (That the Greek term for glory – *doxa* – is the same term that today designates public opinion is, from this standpoint, something more than a coincidence.) As had always been the case in profane and ecclesiastical liturgies, this supposedly 'originary democratic phenomenon' is once again caught, orientated, and manipulated in the forms and according to the strategies of spectacular power.[16]

It is not entirely clear what Agamben has in mind with this analogy with the phrase 'efficacy of acclamation'. The analogy with regal pomp and circumstance implies that the media somehow manages only to lionise, and thereby legitimate, the formation of sovereignty within the modern *demos*. However, it becomes immediately apparent, once we read just a little further in this concluding reflection of Agamben's *The Kingdom and the Glory*, which admittedly is not as developed or well-formed as it should be, that he is alluding to Jürgen Habermas's theory of 'communicative action'. Habermas's recipe for democracy as founded on the inherent rationality of communicative, or deliberative, power is well known. As Habermas declares in *Between Facts and Norms* (1996), 'all political power derives from the communicative power of citizens'.[17]

Habermas grounds this assertion in what he dubs an 'illocutionary' construct of rationality – something akin, more 'Platonist' in its origins, to what Derrida came to call the 'New Enlightenment' – 'when language is conceived as universal medium for embodying reason'.[18] The maintenance of linguistic coherence as a 'postmodern' version of the classic *political logos*, resident within the systems or communicative transaction and symbolic exchange comprising the new cosmopolitan *agora*, fosters in our present-day 'lifeworld' (to invoke Habermas's own expression) the conditions for both democratic participation and the commitment of citizens to some form of the 'common' or 'public' good. For Agamben, this preservation of Habermas's 'knowledge-constitutive interests' through the cultivation of a pluralised, yet intelligible fabric of shared discourse is *not*, however, to be established pragmatically through the intervention of the academic disciplines, especially philosophy. Such a higher, *governmental* role for 'critical theory' was always the aspiration of the Frankfurt School, and can perhaps be traced all the way back to Plato's own call for rule by 'philosopher kings'. It can, at least, be linked to some of the inclinations of Frederick the Great during the eighteenth century in his dream of a Europe commandeered by 'enlightened despots'. Frederick sought to replace the hegemony of the clergy with that of professors, an episode in the evolution of the social imaginary that inspired to a certain degree the founding of the Prussian state system of universal education, which would indirectly nurture a 'virtuous' citizenry.

The 'glory' of the democratic and 'holistic' state in the view of Agamben is

founded on the immediate presence of the acclaiming people, and the neutralised state that resolves itself in the communicative forms without subject, [are] opposed only in appearance. They are nothing but two sides of the same glorious apparatus in its two forms: the immediate and subjective glory of the acclaiming people and the mediatic and objective glory of social communication.[19]

According to Agamben, 'glory' in this regard demonstrates 'its dual aspect, divine and human, ontological and economic, of the Father and the Son'. Following Habermas's distinction, it can be construed as *mediating* both 'the people-substance and the people-communication'.[20]

Bernard Stiegler's Critique of Political Economy

But what if Agamben were dead wrong, and what if his notion of mediatic 'glory' has metastasised, as we are seeing increasingly nowadays, has turned out instead to be the *tawdry*? What if this 'tawdriness' were in fact the inevitable 'cash-out' of the symbolic economy itself, of an appalling but spectacular climax to the ongoing virtualisation of both labour and capital in a latter-day, gargantuan immolation of both meaning and signification whereby the 'crisis of representation' becomes a global catastrophe of the political itself? What if the linguistics of 'communicative reason' had now morphed as in some kind of insidious mutation of its own semiotic genomes into a hyperpartisan 'hate machine?' How could that even happen? In order to answer that question, we must begin to pay heed to Bernard Stiegler's urgent call for a 'new critique of political economy' that understands the linguistic process in keeping with both Plato's and Derrida's reading *pharmakon* as both 'poison and remedy'. Stiegler's brilliant analysis of the problem, published in 2010 at a time when the current sordid state of politics was lamentably but a small, lowering cloud on the horizon, calls into question the very sentimental assumptions about the connections between democracy, discourse, rationality and mediatic expression, which Agamben together with Habermas have dangled in front of us. 'We thus have pure cognitive labour power utterly devoid of knowledge with cognitive technologies', Stiegler writes.[21] 'The cognitive elites' are 'deprived of their own logic and by their logic – a logic reduced to a calculation without remainder as well as to a market of fools'.[22]

In order to achieve a better grasp of what Stiegler intends with such a comment, we need to flesh out his larger perspective. For *A Critique of Political Economy* pulls together many of the threads of his extensive, earlier writings to revive a call for a critique of capitalism in the twenty-first century that takes up from what Marx left undone in the nineteenth century. Stiegler set forth these remarks in the immediate wake of the worldwide economic crisis that began in the fall of 2008 but became manifest in 2009. In the first chapter, entitled 'Heads Buried in the Sand: A Warning', Stiegler makes the case that both the Keynesian 'stimulus' to what was supposed to have engineered recovery from the Great Recession and the digital automation of industry that is proceeding apace 'is the translation of a moribund ideology, desperately trying to prolong the life of a model which has become self-destructive'.[23] At the same time, Stiegler is not merely advancing some cheap, hackneyed version of rhetoric against *capitalism* per se. It is the distinctive new kind of capitalism – i.e. 'cognitive capitalism' – that is bringing the crisis to a head. Cognitive capitalism constitutes an economic as well as a social apocalypse of the virtualisation process, the beginnings of which antedate electronic media by two and a half millennia. The overarching philosophical dilemma we have dubbed the 'crisis of representation' is centred on the technical issue of *hypomnesis*, or the exteriorisation of memory, Plato identified in the *Phaedrus* as the danger posed by writing. Plato's preoccupation was the loss of direct access to the real, a position Derrida in *Of Grammatology* characterised as 'ontotheological'.

Writing, Plato insists in the latter section of the *Phaedrus*, is anti-philosophical because it offers us 'learning rather than wisdom' (σοφίας δὲ τοῖς μαθηταῖς δόξαν),[24] and philosophy is of course the pursuit of the latter. Such 'learning' is mere 'semblance' (*doxa*), and even though it provides expanding opportunities for the elaboration of new discursive connections, it fosters an amnesia of the thing itself, as Heidegger was fond of pointing out, through the production of incessant *re-presentations* (or if we wish instead to use Baudrillard's terminology, we can say the 'precession of simulacra'). Such re-presentations are, if we want to use a current cliché, a form of 'fake presence'. And it is 'presence', or *ousia*, in the Platonic tradition that constitutes the authentic object sought through philosophical enquiry. As a student of Derrida who in turn criticised the Socratic discomfort with writing as a 'potion' (*pharmakon*) that simultaneously 'poisons' the well of wisdom while 'remedying' the affliction of forgetfulness, Stiegler ironically seems to side with Plato. But his Platonic sympathies have little to do with a preference for ontology. The crisis of representation derives from the manner in which 'learning' (*mathesis*), or the spatio-temporal coding and archiving of what was once knowledge by acquaintance, comes to reify the hypomnetic process as the human essence itself.

Thus, the invention of 'writing', which by Stiegler's reckoning is but a convenient trope for *hypomnesis* as a whole encompassing everything from symbolic logic to electronic bits and bytes, sets in motion an historical juggernaut careening towards a 'transhuman' future. *Hypomnesis* is what we really mean by 'capital' as a rendering of Marx's 'alienated labour', and it threatens to eclipse us all as 'artificially' intelligent machines that not only eliminate jobs but even human intimacy (think the latest, uncannily human 'sexbots' that are creeping into the market). The difference between 'wisdom' (*sophia*) and 'learning', or 'science' (*mathesis*), is what Stiegler calls *savoir faire* versus *savoir vivre*. Science and technology furnish only 'know-how' (*savoir faire*), engendered from experiences brought about through manipulation of the human environment using symbolic tokens and apparatuses.

Relying on terminology harking back to Edmund Husserl, Stiegler refers to this mode of sign-production as 'tertiary retention'. Tertiary retention is the key to *hypoamnesis*, because it gives impetus to a wider process Stiegler dubs 'grammatisation', a convoluted but inexorable and irrepressible historical movement for which the development of writing is only the first instantiation. In other words, grammatisation – encompassing everything from manuscripts and their dissemination to the even more sophisticated use of numbers and formal protocols for ciphering equivalencies to abstract reasoning on the part of both *homo sapiens* and computing machinery – consists in the *commodification of truth* itself. The commodification of labour, as Marx understood it, is merely one moment in the unfolding of a much greater and consequential trendline. 'Alienated labour' is simply a harbinger of the eventual extinction of what it means to be human, which relies on *savoir vivre*, 'knowing how to live'. A genuine 'critique of political economy', for Stiegler, cannot be separated from the critique of human knowledge overall.

Stiegler insists that this extreme stage of alienation conceals a genuine crisis of capitalism. We might add that it appears as well to be the watermark of neoliberalism itself. 'The capitalist economy strictly speaking *no longer works*', Stiegler contends, 'because it wants the psychic individualism to be self-detected, to become the "entrepreneur of the self," without collective individuation, but rather through a collective disindividuation orchestrated by marketing', which Stiegler says includes both the so-called 'conservative revolution' of 1980s and the present post-millennial phase of global, corporate neoliberalism.[25] The Foucauldian notion that contemporary culture is a form of *self-entrepreneurship* whereby our alienated *self-knowledge* now becomes a kind of high-octane fuel that powers the capacious neoliberal mode of operation, of course, has been the *pièce de résistance* for Brown's analysis. Brown is the first to recognise that neoliberalism is not merely a tendentious set of economic principles, but a 'a form of normative reason remaking the state, society, and subject, generating social policy, positing truth and a theory of law'. It is, in effect, 'a revolutionary and comprehensive political rationality, one that draws on classical liberal language and concerns while inverting many of liberalism's purpose and channels of accountability'.[26]

Brown stresses that neoliberalism subtly stands on its head the classical liberal values emphasising personal freedom by summoning such grandiloquence to perform the task of constraining the social agent to the *unfreedom* of self-entrepreneurship in the name of the vast, collective good – what she terms 'responsibilism'. Responsibilism never prescribes an objective, person or idea to which is nevertheless always 'responsible'. One can never do enough, because there is always infinitely more to do. Responsibility is unbounded; it is forever committed to an imperceptible 'elsewhere'.

Cognitive Capitalism and the Crisis of Neoliberal Hegemony

The idolatry of cognitive capitalism, which seduces both of our instincts for self-validation and helping others, is founded on an ethic of 'knowledge, thought, and training' that are 'valued and desired for their contribution of capital enhancement'.[27] It should be noted that contrary to latter-day sentimentality of today's 'bohemian bourgeoisie' that is fond of parroting Marxist slogans from the cubicle of a tech firm offering exorbitant salaries and benefits, or from the comfort of an oak-panelled university office where 'revolutionary' ideology is not matched by the commitment to taking authentic political risks, the real neoliberal power complex is no longer vested in the likes of Ebenezer Scrooge, the Koch Brothers, nor even the legendary 'military industrial complex'. Instead it accrues to the captains of the new 'knowledge industries', allied with intelligence agencies and vast, government bureaucracies, which leverage the infrastructure of electronic communications networks more and more to manage and regulate the content of information flow and their formatting into usable snippets of insight. The new planetary space of cognitive capitalism (it is actually, he insinuates rather cryptically, a type of 'mafia capitalism'), according to Stiegler, becomes a vast desert of 'pure calculable exchange' wearing the deceptive mask of 'socially conscious' enterprise. It becomes a type of transnational, postmodern, post-Christian, secular 'superego', as Emmett Rensin has called it,[28] that exploits in its own unique style the consumerist 'will to nothingness', as Nietzsche would have described it.

Stiegler is not, however, an unrepentant pessimist. Like Marx, he offers his own eschatological vision, which we will explore in some of the passages that follow. But what is absent in Stiegler – and to a large degree in the growing chorus of critics as well as diagnosticians of the deeper 'logic' of neoliberalism – is the way in which this novel type of 'political rationality' is driven by and large by mediatisation itself. In other words, how does Agamben's mediatic 'glory' alchemise into the basest illustration of the 'tawdry'? In order to answer that question, we must examine another core concept of Stiegler's, what he in a very plain-spoken manner identifies as 'stupidity' (*bêtise*).[29]

Stiegler views his calling as a renewal of the task defined by Horkheimer and Adorno in *Dialectic of Enlightenment* and detailed at the height of World War II, that of courageously investigating how the Age of Reason had metastasised into the pseudo-politics of totalitarianism, where 'public life has reached a state in which thought is being turned inescapably into a commodity and language into celebration of the commodity'.[30] The commodification of thought and language, for Stiegler, is far more complicated than what the Frankfurt School interpreted as the descent of reason into unreason, the 'reversion' of *logos* to *mythos*, as manipulated cunningly through fascist propaganda. It is the baleful outcome of the triumph in all spheres of *hypomnesic technology* and its very 'interiorisation' in both conscious and unconscious life. 'What is occurring, on a scale and in conditions that were hitherto inconceivable', Stiegler writes, 'is the effect of what Gramsci described as a cultural hegemony that de-forms reason – reason understood in Enlightenment terms as that historical and social conquest that now seems to decompose so rapidly into rationalisation'.[31]

In his *Prison Writings* from 1929–35 Gramsci himself had foreseen this evolution with his observation that Hegel's 'ethical state' as the embodiment of moral and cultural reason (favoured by liberal democrats) had fallen victim to the same kind of 'fetishism' that Marx ascribed to the logic of commodification. This fetishism marks usurpation of what Gramsci called the 'philosophy of praxis' by the cultural and linguistic apparatus exercised through popular communication techniques appropriated by the rising class. Writing at that juncture in the history of Europe when fascism had supplanted class consciousness with what the Frankfurt School had recognised as a hostile takeover of the *collective unconscious* under the sway of the 'culture industry', Gramsci discerned that hegemonic relations in twentieth-century society were neither political nor economic so much as they were *semiotic*.

In that respect Gramsci was the one, long before Stiegler, to cognise how any 'revolutionary' seizure of the means of production could not be separated from the means of *culture production*. Moreover, such a seizure, if it were

MEDIATIC HEGEMONY | 67

possible at all, would have to depend on a new kind of *communicative internationale*, which through a universal dictatorship of the cognitive proletariat would upend the system of semiotic control in accordance with which Foucaultean biopower resolves itself into the most insidious subterfuges of *logopower*. 'Every relationship of "hegemony"', Gramsci contends, 'is necessarily an educational relationship and occurs not only within a nation, between the various forces that comprise it . . . in the entire international and world field'.[32]

It is significant that Gramsci alluded in his notebooks to the emerging hegemonic role of journalism, which he characterised as a contingent of 'pocket-geniuses', which pretends to be 'holding the whole of history in the palm of its hand'.[33] But Gramsci was naturally unable to anticipate the digitisation of both news and entertainment media where the 'manufacture of consent' was boosted exponentially by an explosion, if not the amalgamation, of digital communication and commerce, especially what we now know as 'social media'. In social media, Stiegler's 'tertiary retention' desiccates not only lived experience but the spiritual fabric of human relationships, an electronic *bellum omnium contra omnes* that has become the strange and eminently hostile 'twittering' virtual universe we know as politics in this day and age. The *demos* is 'undone' by this global apotheosis of grammatisation and mediatisation. It comes apart under pressure from a proliferation of not only 'fake news' but 'fake agencies' of the electronic sort that cull, peddle and feature what we are supposed to know through marketising algorithms and hyperbots that exercise their own seamless, yet invisible, control over the new 'symbolic milieu' (Stiegler).

Stiegler himself calls for an insurrection against this pervasive alien dominion of a machinic 'deep state' that might be fomented somehow through a recovery of the intimacy of wisdom itself, the wisdom of the body, of classical *mnemosyne*, of philosophy as the *philia* of *sophia*, something akin to Alain Badiou's notion of *love* itself as a revolutionary praxis, or 'truth procedure'. Such an insurrection requires the severance, according to Stiegler, of 'the interface between the technical system and social systems' and the 'economic system'. The upshot would be what he calls *l'économie de contribution* ('the economy of contribution'), which unfortunately he does not specify in any detail. Knowledge must be valued for its own sake, or at least for social flourishing. Such a society would be anti-consumerist.

In an interview with a representative of the Macif Foundation, Stiegler comments:

This model [of the society of contribution] rests on investment and citizens taking responsibility. It differs from Fordism because it depends on de-prolaterisation (sic). For Marx, the workers are proletarised when their expertise is replaced by the machines that they serve. In the 20th century it was the consumers who were proletarised and we lost the old knowledge. Proleterisation isn't financial poverty, but the loss of knowledge. Consumers do not produce their own way of living, which is now prescribed by the big corporate names.[34]

Although Stiegler's solution sounds vague and not a little utopian – and certainly does not have the 'critical' transformational perspective we would expect perhaps from such incisive social and political theorising – it steers us in a direction from which the broader critique of neoliberalism often shies away. The crisis of neoliberal hegemony comes down to a crisis of liberal democracy stemming from the crisis of representation that can be tracked all the way back to the end of the *Aufklärung*. It is a hollowing out of the political, caused by the passage of dialectic into a highly *undialectical* planetary *economism of algebrarically codified and commodified desire*. The same process is spurred on by the sophisms of marketing (in contradistinction to the production of exchange values on the market itself), where the sublimation of drives in the traditional Weberian analysis is transmuted into what Herbert Marcuse called 'repressive desublimation', according to which 'the progress of technological rationality is liquidating the oppositional and transcending elements in the "higher culture"'.[35] The fundamental challenge of the new era is to recapture the sense of 'real presence' in both our language in our social relations and in our politics. In order to demonstrate how we may go beyond the 'hyperreal', or 'more real than real', spell of the neoliberal symbolic economy, we have to consider how its own epistemology actually works.

4   Killing Us Softly: On Neoliberal 'Truth' Protocols

> Every established order tends to produce the naturalisation of its
> own arbitrariness.
>
> Pierre Bourdieu

The Utopia of Exploitation

IN A PRESCIENT and prophetic essay in the newspaper *Le Monde* during the
last month of 1998, the famed French social theorist Pierre Bourdieu laid out
a disturbing vision – long before the concept of 'neoliberalism' had emerged
as anything beside a somewhat esoteric construct among political scientists – of where the tidal currents of globalisation were taking us. The essay
was provocatively titled 'The Utopia of Exploitation – The Essence of Neoliberalism', and it brilliantly laid bare *avant la lettre* the imperceptible stimulus
behind the post-Cold War growth of the new global economy in a way that is
only becoming apparent nowadays. What makes his brief essay not only
insightful but epochal is that it was formulated at a time when the integration
of the world through global market forces and monetary consolidation was
perceived among the international elites as 'the end of history' (in the immor-
tal words of Francis Fukuyama). Bourdieu, however, glimpsed with surprising
clarity the more enmeshed pathology which it would take theoreticians and
policy-makers alike more than a decade to unravel.

The basic problem, according to Bourdieu, was the conversion of *homo
politicus* into *homo oeconomicus*, anticipating Brown's formula. 'As the dominant discourse would have it', Bourdieu writes, 'the economic world is a pure
and perfect order, implacably unrolling the logic of its predictable consequences, and prompt to repress all violations by the sanctions that it inflicts,
either automatically or – more unusually – through the intermediary of its
armed extensions', such as central banks, the International Monetary Fund,

stock exchanges, etc.[1] However, he asks, what if this vision of bettering the lot of all humankind through the economist 'logic' of open markets and unimpeded capital flows were not a kind of 'utopian' construct, which in practice was destined to becoming a dystopian nightmare comparable to the failed grand collectivist projects of the twentieth century?

As a sociologist Bourdieu discerned in the neoliberal pipedream the same ruthless epistemological fixation that Hannah Arendt had connected to the origins of totalitarianism – the complete deracination of both persons and entire peoples, the mobilisation of 'masses' rather than 'classes', as the latter diagnosed the situation after World War I. As Arendt herself wrote:

> 'totalitarian' movements are possible wherever there are masses who for one reason or another have acquired the appetite for political organisation. Masses are not held together by a consciousness of common interest and they lack that specific class articulateness which is expressed in determined, limited, and obtainable goals. The term masses applies only where we deal with people who either because of sheer numbers, or indifference, or a combination of both, cannot be integrated into any organisation based on common interest, into political parties or municipal governments or professional organisations or trade unions. Potentially, they exist in every country and form the majority of those large numbers of neutral, politically indifferent people who never join a party and hardly ever go to the polls.[2]

For Bourdieu, they still exist today, and the process of deracination – what globalisation theorist Thomas Hylland Eriksen has called 'disembedding'[3] – has become a latter-day kind of planetary petri dish for the fomentation of the soft totalitarianism that characterises the tentacular neoliberal regime.

At the same time, this process of disembedding succeeds masterfully, Bourdieu argues, in 'severing the economy from social realities', from all historical and synchronically immanent networks of human reciprocity and signifiers of common solidarity. But such a posthumanistic invasion into all spheres of this new 'desert of the real', as the language of the movie *The Matrix* describes it, is not due primarily, as the mythology of today's alienated 'knowledge workers' would invariably have it, to some juggernaut of predatory 'capitalism' per se. It comes down to a *transeconomic* logic, a veritable *mathesis*, i.e. an unquestioned inferential system grounding our sense of the *real* that is older than capitalism itself, one that while sustaining the process of capital formation is intrinsic to the transmutation of the capitalist economy under neoliberalism. It is the same 'logic of late capitalism' (Frederic Jameson's expression) that has produced the financialisation of both the 'forces of production' and the 'relations of production' in Marxist phraseology. It is a 'tutelary theory' which, though ubiquitous, turns out to be a 'pure fiction'. It is, according to Bourdieu, the 'pure fiction' that reality itself, let alone 'social reality', can be mathematised as 'pure theory'. The explanation is simple. 'In the name of a narrow and strict conception of rationality as individual rationality, it brackets the economic and social conditions of rational orientations and the economic and social structures that are the condition of their application.' In addition, 'this "theory" that is desocialised and dehistoricised at its roots has, today more than ever, the means of making itself true and empirically verifiable. In effect, neoliberal discourse is not just one discourse among many. Rather, it is a "strong discourse" – the way psychiatric discourse is in an asylum.'[4]

The Problem of 'Veridiction'

The economic machinery of neoliberalism, which almost collapsed in 2008 because of the global economic meltdown, has been driven by this 'strong discourse'. But it should be noted that when writing this essay decades earlier, Bourdieu was not making a simple case against the kind of runaway financialisation that spurred the global crash of 2008. Nor was he simply denouncing the deregulation of banking and other methods of monetary chicanery that was all in vogue during that period. His critique was far more holistic, if not encyclopedic. The discourse of neoliberalism, he stressed, was but the pragmatics of a hegemonic protocol for 'truthfulness' (what Foucault had dubbed 'veridiction') that had been gaining ascendancy in the West for centuries. Such a protocol has been 'so strong and so hard to combat only because it has on its side all of the forces of a world of relations of forces, a world that it contributes to making what it is'. The protocol, which can be loosely summed up in the notion of *scientism*, 'does this most notably by orienting the economic choices of those who dominate economic relationships', while augmenting them with 'its own symbolic force to these relations of forces'. Scientism as an epistemological conviction, Bourdieu insists, has over the centuries been fatefully 'converted into a plan of political action, an immense political project' that 'aims to create the conditions under which the "theory" can be realised and can function: a programme of the methodical destruction of collectives'.[5]

The upshot is a brave, new Darwinian 'world of struggle' that renders permanent a 'structural violence' that is simultaneously subtle and almost invisible. One example of this can be found in the Centre for Disease Control's June 2018 alarming report that there had been a 30 per cent increase in suicides in half of US states (with all but one showing a rise) since the turn of the millennium, and that over half of those who had taken their own lives did not have a previous mental health condition.[6] Almost half of those who committed suicide had a 'relationship problem', and in another 28 per cent of cases the major factor was substance abuse. Such data confirms the insuperability of such an 'infernal machine' founded on a calculus of the pure efficiency of markets, which through the total destruction of intersubjective fidelities and communal loyalties touts in various, unspoken ways in what Bourdieu calls a 'race to the abyss', a seductive egalitarian logic, one that appears to proliferate 'difference' and abolish it at the same time by fostering the cloud cuckoo land conceit of a singular utopian – and therefore completely abstract – oneness of humanity as well as the anarchic ecstasy of release from every political constraint, all under the 'sign of freedom'. The historic emancipatory politics of anti-capitalism thus falls victim to its own passion to strip away the cultural and biological concreteness of human institutions and their behaviour dispositions – what Bourdieu famously terms their 'habitus' – and merges almost imperceptibly with the neoliberal project itself. The *enragées* themselves become the unwitting shock troops of the new 'posthuman' forms of capital that expropriate what is left of human value, turning the gold of human affect into the dross of ceaseless 'social justice warfare'. It is Marx's theory of commodification applied to the emancipatory trajectory overall.

Alain Badiou in his theory of the subject as that which operates outside the strictures of formal ontology, which he identifies with mathematics, has undertaken to chart a method of disruption, if not insurrection, against the machinic logic of neoliberalism. Without actually employing the term 'neoliberal', Badiou makes his own 'strong' case that any effective resistance to the regime of mathematical elaboration necessitates a new thought-procedure that is *generative* rather than reflective, an undertaking whereby 'truth' ceases to be a mode of verification but a certain kind of 'generic procedure' that brings to light what were previously 'indiscernible' structures that can no longer be considered ontological but *evental*. Philosophy at the same time ceases to be both 'speculative' and 'analytic', but functions instead as a means of *intervention*. The 'mathematico-logical revolution of Frege-Cantor', as Badiou stresses in his introduction to *Being and Event*, therefore, gives way to the 'theoretico-practical orientations of the modern doctrine of the subject', which disclose themselves as not only 'clinical', but eminently 'political'.[7] It is this 'subjectivisation' (as opposed to the Cartesian *subjectivity*) of truth that can make possible, Badiou suggests, the 'soteriological' moment when, as Marx anticipated, philosophy would no longer 'interpret' the world but change it.

Subjectivisation as the agential discharge of a generic procedure rips open the fabric of the age-old *mathesis univeralis*, separates *logos* from logic, being from event, what Deleuze would term *haeccity* from intensity. 'As such, subjectivisation is that through which truth is possible',[8] Badiou writes. It makes truth possible, because it substitutes the 'militant' for the mere spectator. Neoliberalism has turned us all into spectators, albeit angry and conflicted ones, in an orgy of self-inflicted violence resulting from epistemic indecisions as the prevailing condition of Debord's 'society of the spectacle'. Truth, however, always has a militancy about it, and that is because it creates new solidarities through 'fidelity to the event', where hitherto all fidelities and solidarities had been de-constituted through the abstraction process that goes hand in hand with *the ontology of pure numeracy*. Numeracy itself, as Badiou argues, reduces the structured, or relational, system of multiples to the 'count-as-one', the commodified – or, as we used to say, 'atomised' – individual.

Such an individual corresponds to Robert Musil's *Der Mann ohne Eigenschaften*, 'The Man Without Qualities', a soulless 'difference engine' (Deleuze) of passionless, but pointless, discrimination of the world around him, a highly cultivated and intellectually adept automaton who barely passes for a self-conscious personality and for whom everything from libidinous urgings to patriotic sympathy resolves itself into the kind of computational nirvana, expressing itself through what Nietzsche labelled the 'passive nihilism' of the *fin de siècle* era. The *Man Without Qualities*, of course, is an intricate literary masterpiece that sets the collective psychological as well as literary mood on the eve of the great catastrophe of 1914. Could *homo neoliberalismus* be our contemporary version of Musil's character with the exception that his apotheosis as a pure *matheme* of calculative rationality now finds its parallel in the cubicle-confined 'knowledge worker' of Silicon Valley rather than in the jaded, overeducated *Mann von Stand* ('man of position') in the waning days of imperial Vienna? Could, as in the 1914, the once-vaunted grand empire of digital dominion also be on the verge of unravelling and collapsing?

The New 'Mathesis Universalis'

One of the failures of theorists in seeking to comprehend the full scope of neoliberalism is the tendency to focus almost exclusively on postulated economic predations and the commission of wrongs involving distributions of wealth. But, as German sociologist Wolfgang Streeck observes, 'capitalism denotes both an economy and a society, and that studying it requires a conceptual framework that does not separate the one from the other'.[9] In other words, it is impossible to separate social relations from economic structures. What many critics of neoliberalism overlook is that their own methods of social, or cultural, critique unconsciously presuppose the very 'late capitalist' frame of reference which they invariably denounce. According to Streeck, capitalism must *not* be studied primarily as an 'economic system'. The mathematisation of economics, which in many respects was responsible for the crash of 2008, has been the long-haul consequence of the classical, nineteenth-century doctrine that social interactions, including commercial behaviour, could be modelled somehow after Newtonian laws of motion. But, as Weber sagely realised, and which he explored in detail in his *Protestant Ethic and the Spirit of Capitalism*, commercial behaviour is but a subset of general social patterns and constraints of conduct, which in turn are enmeshed with metaphysical commitments and religious convictions.

Capitalism, therefore, can be in a certain measure considered a grand sort of Bourdieuian *habitus*, a codifiable and transpersonal assemblage of motives, practices and affective relationships that work themselves out in terms of quantifiable transactions that can be surveyed by the social sciences, and that are routinely regulated not only by law but by customs as well as social norms and expectations. The capitalistic 'habitus', as Weber described, stems from a certain anxiety initially consisting in the psychological mirror effect of a harsh and demanding theology, but it becomes gradually 'secularised' to take the form of an ever-expanding dynamo of 'creative destruction', as Joseph Schumpeter called it, that puts all bonds of human affiliation, dependence and fealty in question while threatening to dissolve and erase them. Thus, the consumerist ethos of seeking fulfilment for every multiplying desire for new and different experiences as well as objects follows naturally upon the original 'productivist' obsession that Weber associated with the religious world view of early modern merchant societies. But consumerism does not merely involve an obsession with 'things'; it may also be described as an obsession with 'differentiation'.

Streeck analyses how the logic of capitalism itself succeeded in manufacturing the Deleuzean 'difference engine', which came to serve within two decades after the end of World War II as the *lingua franca* within Western culture of a wholly unprecedented regime of abstraction and commodification. Following standard economic history, Streeck describes how the rapid urbanisation of both Europe and America in the 1920s gave strong impetus for the production and purchase of new durable goods, such as the automobile and the washing machine. In order to foster a functioning financial infrastructure for the new industries built around mass production of durables along with 'Fordist' methods of labour discipline and organisation, the captains of industry both pioneered and promoted the unprecedented – and until recent times morally suspect – institution of consumer credit.

It was, of course, as Liaquat Ahamed notes, the fatal combination of consumer credit expansion and the enforcement of low interest rates aimed at making it easier for the victors in World War I to pay off their massive sovereign debts during the same period that was the fuel for the stock market crash of 1929 and the plunge into the Great Depression.[10] Once the next cataclysm that was World War II pulled the Western economies out of the Depression, the delicate balance of Fordist productivism and Keynesian policies of 'stimulus' orchestrated by central governments to keep consumer buying on an upward trajectory helped nurture the approximately two-decade 'golden age' of rising prosperity from the late 1940s to the end of the 1960s. But, as Streeck emphasises, that economic growth track stalled eventually, as do all spurts in the capitalist life cycle, and a drastic new configuration for the development of the system was sorely needed. Hence, there began 'a desperate search for a new formula to overcome what threatened to be a fundamental crisis of capitalist political economy'. The solution lay in accelerated product differentiation – and even to a significant extent in the differentiation of services, which increasingly were now becoming the core of the new systems of 'production'. According to Streeck, 'capital's answer to the secular stagnation of markets for standardised goods at the end of the Fordist era included making goods less standardised'.[11] And this rapid, *strategical* plan for differentiating goods and services (ironically, at the very time when 'difference' emerged as the ideological watchword among the cognitive elites in advanced societies) became the turbine for the new 'symbolic economy' of digital communications based mainly on marketing, media and advertising.

As Streeck notes, 'marketing discovers, but typically also develops consumer preferences; it asks consumers what they would like, but it also proposes to them things they might be prepared to like, including things they never imagined could have existed'.[12] The difference engine of the mass of transpersonal and somatological 'desiring machines', which Deleuze and Guattari saw as the key to undermining capitalism through valorising the 'schizophrenic' substratum of all human experience, was expropriated almost immediately during this period by the capitalist apparatus itself. The result, Streeck argues, was the advent of a novel kind of 'sociation through consumption'. It was highlighted by

> the sheer extent of the commercialisation of social life that aimed to save capitalism from the spectre of saturated markets after the watershed years. In effect, what firms learned in the 1970s was to put the individualisation of both customers and products at the service of commercial expansion. Diversified consumption entailed hitherto unknown opportunities for the individualised expression of social identities. The 1970s and 1980s were also a time when traditional families and communities were rapidly losing authority, offering markets the opportunity to fill a fast-growing social vacuum, which contemporary liberation theorists had mistaken for the beginning of a new age of autonomy and emancipation. The possibilities for diversified consumption and the rise of niche markets, with the accelerated obsolescence they inflicted on first-generation consumer durables, also helped to motivate renewed work discipline, among both traditional workers and the newcomers to paid employment, not least the women.[13]

Interestingly, the same period marked the normalisation, at least within the academic sector, of the politics of 'liberation' which came to be fortified by the innovation of identity theory. Identity theory, mistakenly branded by its conservative critics as 'cultural Marxism' (it only retained in a bare-bones way any kind of 'Marxist' colouration because of its preoccupation with historical forms of 'oppression'), followed to the letter the differential logic of the new consumer capitalism, inasmuch as it 'created' wants – in this case, new demands for political action to redress claims of injustice through social exclusion. Identifying both the unrecognised position of exclusion and the demand for action fuelled the difference engine. According to Streeck,

> the vast variety of alternative possibilities of consumption in affluent post-Fordist markets provides a mechanism that allows people to conceive of an act of purchase – concluding, as it often does, a lengthy period of

introspective exploration of one's very personal preferences – as an act of self-identification and self-presentation, one that sets the individual apart from some social groups while uniting him or her with others.[14]

Under neoliberalism, 'solidarity', particularly among the educated elites, acts as a symbolic operator for not only self-identification, but for self-exaltation, all the while stoking the appetite for further differentiation of one's passions and purposes. The total vacuity of one's own sense of selfhood is propped up by the differential logic of ever more rarefied fault-finding assuaged in time by the 'messianic' fantasy of being able to solve the problem through a strange combination of compassion and outrage.

Streeck's greatest insight is that 'communities of consumption', as he dubs them, can be completely virtual rather than material. And, as the 'symbolic economy' increasingly metastasises into a dense traffic in affect-loaded ideas rather than tangible goods and services powered by corporate interests with the tools and financial wherewithal to manoeuvre people's better angels into serving their worst instincts, 'communities of consumption are much easier to abandon than traditional "real" communities', while social identities become structured by weaker and looser ties, allowing individuals to surf from one identity to the next, free from any pressure to explain themselves'.[15] In effect, the new stage of neoliberal hegemony gave rise not only to 'the high phase of globalisation' but 'the establishment of a cosmopolitan consciousness industry which discerned its opportunities for growth in turbocharging the expansionist drive of capitalist markets with the libertarian values of the social revolution of the 1960s and '70s and their utopian promise of human emancipation',[16] which in itself required the ongoing differentiation of who and what needed to be 'liberated'. Thus, late neoliberal capitalism also had to take on the mantle of a supreme moral authority that could no longer be justified through God or tradition. It required its own 'immanent frame', a set of discursive markers that would sanctify the economically productive behaviour of social actors in the transnational consumer economy. 'In the process', Streeck writes in a more recent article,

the technocratic pensée unique of neoliberalism became fused with the moral juste milieu of an internationalist discourse community. Its control over the airspace above the seminar desks serves today as operations base in a cultural struggle of a special kind, one in which the moralisation of a globally expanding capitalism goes hand in hand with the demoralisation of those who find their interests damaged by it.[17]

Streeck is even more tart and pronounced in his tracking of fashionable progressive politics to the neoliberal discursive juggernaut *tout court*. 'The cosmopolitan identitarianism of the leaders of the neoliberal age, originating as it did in part from left-wing universalism, calls forth by way of reaction a national identitarianism, while anti-national re-education from above produces an anti-elitist nationalism from below.'[18] In other words, the struggle over so-called 'ethno-nationalism' versus a more high-minded idealism of global 'citizenship' and a preference for the excluded can be boiled down to the interests of the global capitalist elites who seek to denigrate and shame the disenfranchised 'workers of the world' into submission. The notion of 'anti-national re-education' can without mincing words be construed precisely in the terms Marx had in mind in *The German Ideology*, namely, that 'the ideas of the ruling class are in every epoch the ruling ideas, i.e. the class which is the ruling material force of society, is at the same time its ruling intellectual force'.[19] Streeck himself turns the 'radicals' of today completely on their heads:

> Whoever puts a society under economic or moral pressure to the point of dissolution meets with resistance from traditionalists. This is because all those who find themselves exposed to the uncertainties of international markets, control of which has been promised but never delivered, will prefer the bird in their hand to two in the bush: they will choose the reality of national democracy over the fantasy of a democratic global society.[20]

The neoliberal 'fantasy' of global democracy, according to Streeck, corresponds to the libertarian air castle of 'democratic capitalism'. Streeck makes a convincing case that so-called 'market discipline' and democratic participation have been historically incompatible options. The touchstone for the romanticism of democratic capitalism, which Fukuyama blindly proclaimed to have triumphed once and for all with the collapse of Communism after 1989, was always the American experience of generalised well-being following World War II and the *Wirtschaftwunder* ('economic miracle') of Germany during the same era. The 'good times' that persisted during the postwar interval up until the runaway inflation of the 1970s, according to Streeck, were an historical exception rather than the rule. And they fostered a false confidence, as was the case also throughout the 1920s and the 1990s, that economic well-being was the inexorable output of *laissez-faire* policies. The article of faith was that 'truly free markets would in the long run deliver anyway, but must fail to deliver when distorted by politics'.[21]

On the contrary, it is 'politics' that has kept capitalism afloat, Streeck contends, insofar as the true, implied 'social contract' has always been to let markets go their merry way *only so long as* reciprocal political interests can be reasonably assured and broad economic needs and expectations met. The secret of success for a country like Germany in the late twentieth and early twenty-first century has been to make certain that the social contract is upheld at all costs – a formula first developed during the salad days of the newly formed German Federal Republic ('West Germany') under the name of 'ordoliberalism'. Nevertheless, maintenance of the social contract, which ever since John Locke has been the basic postulate of modern theories of democracy, becomes increasingly difficult when the logic of differentiation, as it does in post-industrial capitalism, holds absolute sway. The 'difference engine' is simultaneously political and economic. New constituencies must be defined and factored into the equation. Novel articulations of Carl Schmitt's 'friend-enemy distinction' as the very essence of politics must be undertaken, and ever more rarefied rumours of skullduggery and grounds for recrimination given an aura of plausibility. A frenzied 'reactive politics' of the kind witnessed largely in America, but also in other parts of the world, feeds the largely invisible, but wryly smirking neoliberal leviathan as it ravenously putrefies and engorges like some horrific strain of 'flesh eating bacteria' every bond of social connection, every ligature of mutual respect, every tendon of civility, and every filament of dignity.

'Deplorables' and the New 'Civilizing Mission'

Meanwhile, the only 'division of labour' remaining is that between the 'one per cent' and the digital infrastructure which they have totally appropriated for their own control of both the economy and the communication networks. Cable news with its 'trumped up' political scandals becomes the 'bread and circuses' of the failing neoliberal *imperium*, which keeps itself in power through (in Fraser's provocative phrasing) the 'the unholy alliance of emancipation with financialisation'.[22] Like the missionaries who invaded the 'dark continent' of Africa in the late nineteenth century along with adventurers and imperialist soldiers of fortune, today's educated, transnational elites are incapable of seeing themselves as complicit in plunder, only as righteous commanders of a new 'civilizing mission' to eradicate from the face of the earth the innumerable 'uncivil' and *un-cosmopolitan* behaviours and phobias among the masses of 'deplorables'.

Oliver Nachtwey's description of populist politics as a trend towards 'de-civilisation' perfectly illustrates such a neo-Victorian attitude. The only difference is that it is not the overseas 'natives' who resist 're-education' through the beneficent but iron hand of colonial governance, but the domestic natives themselves, the once prosperous middle classes of the Western nations who fail to understand that their moment has come and gone, that 'social progress had always created losers', and that it is now their turn to fall by the wayside while formerly disadvantaged groups are positioned in their stead under the wise and protective oversight of their cosmopolitan overlords. 'What unites these groups', writes Nachwey, is the 'negation of civilisation in practice in the name of an imagined Western civilisation'. The 'civilisation in practice', of course, happens to be the omnibus neoliberal hegemony.[23]

If you scratch a new cosmopolitan, what you will find under the skin is an old-fashioned colonialist, albeit one with slightly different prejudices, of course. It has been the nature of colonialism to view itself not as exploitation, but as a certain grim allegiance to some vital, though not necessarily congenial, higher moral mandate. As Joseph Conrad's character Marlow in *The Heart of Darkness* describes what Rudyard Kipling called 'the white man's burden':

> The conquest of the earth, which mostly means the taking it away from those who have a different complexion or slightly flatter noses than ourselves, is not a pretty thing when you look into it too much. What redeems it's the idea only. An idea at the back of it; not a sentimental pretence but an idea; and an unselfish belief in the idea.[24]

Here 'complexion' becomes culture and education. But the 'idea' remains the same, what post-colonial theorist Achille Mbembe calls 'commandment', a somewhat schizophrenogenic pairing of arbitrariness with an 'inflation of right'. Given the discrepancy between the rational state model familiar to the Western imperialists and the more temporalised, historically murky lattice-work of dominion and custom that had characterised traditional African societies for centuries, the colonialist 'methodology' was to exaggerate without any citation of precedent the 'rights' of the morally superior colonist over his or her subject. The 'inflation' of such right had little connection with legal argumentation or inference (as would have been the case in Western courts of law) and everything to do with an intuitive self-confidence that the colonialist was remedying the 'laziness', 'backwardness', 'superstition' and naturally the unproductiveness of the colonised. But in keeping with the kind of 'cultural logic' of capitalist efficiency that Weber discovered and Streeck harps upon, the colonialist was primary concerned with extracting measurable economic value from the colonised that could also be viewed as a kind of 'ethical' discipline in its own right. As Mbembe argues:

> Colonial arbitrariness notoriously sought to integrate the political with the social and the ethical, while closely subordinating all three to the requirements of production and output. Improving the lot of the colonized, and making equipment and goods (trade or non-trade) available to them, was justified by the fact that they were to be enrolled into the structures of production. For a long time, the preferred means of achieving that integration were, not freedom of contract, but coercion and corruption; social policies tried by successive administrations were heavily determined by normative and disciplinary concerns, and were, in fact, designed to alter the moral behavior of the colonized.[25]

The same 'arbitrariness' of neoliberalism (i.e. Streeck's 'moral juste') can be discerned in the manner in which the differential logic of a correspondingly inflated discourse of victimisation is constantly inflicted upon the middle classes with their 'traditional' values. Opposition to gay marriage becomes not only 'homophobia', but 'hate'. Suspicion of terrorist motivations, regardless of the circumstances, automatically become 'Islamophobia', which is then reinforced with the accusation of 'white supremacy'.

The tenability of these rapid-fire accusations against the moral probity, if not the humanity, of such conventional 'values voters' cannot be easily challenged or questioned, not merely because they are rarely formulated with sufficient precision or specificity to be tested, but because they reflexively trigger an already entrenched anxiety among the 'accused' that they are white Westerners who are somehow pre-eminently responsible for the dysfunctions of the global order. Like the pastorate of yore, the neoliberal 'guilt machine' has been devastatingly effective over several generations in creating a uniform narrative of secular damnation and salvation that seems unassailable. Economic predacity is constantly carried out and made to look legitimate through an invisible and discourse-saturated *biopower* wielded by countless bureaucratic officials, political representatives, state actors, financial magnates and 'thought leaders' who also happen to be the prime beneficiaries of the system as a whole.

Whereas in former days robber barons were not likely to speak out on behalf of the presumed 'conscience' of a society (Commodore Vanderbilt's celebrated quip 'the public be damned' immediately comes to mind), in the current neoliberal 'gilded age' we find everyone from hedge fund titans such as George Soros to social media tycoons like Mark Zuckerberg forever moralising about recompensing the marginalised and dispossessed, all the while swooping up millions, if not trillions, from the pockets of investors and consumers through their sundry subtle and not-so-subtle monopoly practices. As Fraser maintains in an updated version of her earlier *Dissent* article, 'progressive neoliberalism mixes together truncated ideals of emancipation and lethal forms of financialisation'. For the populations displaced or 'colonised' by this new rapacious form of administration, 'the injury of deindustrialisation is compounded by the insult of progressive moralism, which routinely portrays them as culturally backward'.[26] Fraser further insists that the absence of a genuine 'left' in the Western world has nurtured the dominance of a *faux* left (such as we saw in the electoral politics of both Bill and Hillary Clinton) that leverages the rhetoric of emancipation versus authoritarianism – or, with increasing hyperbole, 'fascism' – to entrench the neoliberal order. But, 'seen analytically', Fraser writes, 'liberalism and fascism are not really two separate things, one of which is good and the other bad, but two deeply interconnected faces of the capitalist world system'. She adds that 'although they are by no means normatively equivalent, both are products of unrestrained capitalism, which everywhere destabilises lifeworlds and habitats, bringing in its wake both individual liberation and untold suffering'.[27]

The combination of a secular moral triumphalism that relies on the 'arbitrary' enforcement of ever more arcane and differentialised claims about who are the 'oppressors' and who are the 'oppressed' in the pursuit of economic supremacy is hardly different from colonialism. So, one must ask why so many who are hypnotised by the spell of a predatory, 'progressive neoliberalism' cannot see through their own inanity, gullibility and duplicity? It is the same question John Hobson asked in his ground-breaking work at the beginning of the twentieth century on how colonialism had remodelled itself into the vicious, worldwide scramble for riches that came to be known as 'imperialism'. Hobson asked: 'why does Imperialism escape general recognition for the narrow, sordid thing it is?'[28]

Hobson's own answer was both surprising and timely. It is not the 'businessmen' who create the storyline but the 'politicians' who hide behind the skirts of the missionaries. He ticks off a whole slew of high-minded justifications offered at the time by leading spokespersons for imperialism, including the infamous King Leopold of Belgium who orchestrated around the turn of the century what amounted to sustained genocide in the Congo. Hobson describes these justifications, or what psychoanalysis would have termed 'rationalisations', as 'masked words'. The deception is not to be blamed on the guardians of morality, who are quite sincere and genuinely appalled by their experience of real 'savagery' at times among the indigenous peoples (in the same way that our present-day 'social justice warriors' are remissibly angered by racial slurs, bullying of the transgendered, or the social ostracism of law-abiding, naturalised immigrants or Muslims). It is the way in which this moral militancy, rooted in a clear conviction of what true saintliness and virtue might look like, is insidiously co-opted by worldly interests who redirect the march of Christian soldiers away from a battle for the soul and into a campaign to acquire diamonds and construct railroads (or to move blue-collar jobs to Asia). As Hobson declares, 'Imperialism has been floated on a sea of vague, shifty, well-sounding phrases which are seldom tested by close contact with fact.'[29]

The 'strong discourse' of neoliberalism has had a powerful effect in the transformation of the rhetoric of American exceptionalism into that of a transnational, or even anti-nationalist, cosmopolitanism. The use of such cultural indicators as 'race' has been one of its most useful tools. Such a change most obviously took place during the Obama years. Born of a white American mother and a black African father, Obama was able to play on the subliminal American belief that had evolved since the end of the civil rights movement that we had entered a 'post-racial' phase in our history (what Jodi Melamed designates as the tacit ideal of 'race as culture') in order to grease the skids for the acceptance – following upon the putative rejection by the electorate of the outgoing Bush administration's 'patriotic' military adventures overseas – of a 'post-national' era of cosmopolitan cultural hegemony where the machinery of global financialisation could finally take charge. It is no accident that the election of Obama simultaneously signified the seeming closure of an end of racial politics in America and the loosening of a financial and commercial regulatory steamroller that in the name of 'human rights' and the rectification of past wrongs inflicted on domestic minorities accelerated the prevailing trends towards income inequality in the new 'post-industrial' democracies. According to Melamed, who wrote the article prior to Obama's election but with an insightfulness that would apply throughout the subsequent decade, 'contemporary neoliberal multiculturalism sutures official antiracism to state policy in a manner that prevents the calling into question of global capitalism'.[30] Increasingly, this suturing was tied to the moral condemnation of the victims of de-industrialisation, who were doubly stigmatised for their provincialism, as Obama's notorious 'God and guns' remarks during the 2008 election brought to light, and for their theorised 'racism'. Such a stigmatised consciousness, comparable to what Ashis Nandy in his analysis of the long-simmering after-effects of Indian independence dubs the 'second colonialism',[31] was in large part responsible for the surprise election of Donald Trump in November 2016 from voters, who often lied to pollsters about their real preference out of fear of being morally disgraced for flouting neoliberal orthodoxy.

If neoliberalism, however, has leveraged the shame of historic racism to demonise its own 'throwaway people' in order to staunch any insurrectionary tendencies within their ranks, it has also through the process of epistemological abstraction and commodification of personal self-referentiality in manufacturing 'enterpreneurs of the self' made a desert out of the sphere of social relationships in ways that prevent the kind of 'real' resistance to the system. Organised resistance, let alone political activism of any kind, requires a matrix of perceived solidarity that is both material and spiritual, rather than merely polemical, or theatrical. Sustainable politics depends on a vision of concrete relationality that is both present and future. It cannot be rallied by screeching appeals for mobilisations and donations around the kind of ethereal and episodic affronts to human indignity that serve as the grist for perpetual social justice warlord-ism – and, to be sure, suffice as convenient agitprop for ensuring the political incumbency of neoliberal finance itself. In an age of globally distributed and detached 'entrepreneurial' self-fabrication the phenomenon of politics as usual transmutes itself before our eyes into a deep pathology, into a feckless idolatry that simply feeds the very beast that first 'disembeds' it, then devours it with barely a flutter of recognition. Neolilberalism, as the old tune from the early 1970s suggests, is 'killing [us] softly with [its] song'.

Neoliberalism's Sentimental 'Song'

The song of neoliberalism is a seductive as well as a sentimental one. The sentiment becomes incrementally extraordinary and captivating as a glittery fantasia all its own – a strange sort of 'eschatological' reconciliation of perfect Platonic ideality with seamless equity, the materialisation of Derrida's 'undeconstructible' justice in a secular rather than transcendental guise, the moral and juridical fulfilment of every guilty dream of finally setting right every act of offence or exclusion that has ever been committed, both genuinely and conjecturally, in the chronicles of civilisation. But it is also a song that has been around for a long time and has gone through innumerable songwriter-ly iterations. Ever since Descartes made his Faustian bargain with his 'mathematised' God in the *Meditations* to replace the surety of faith with the certitude *of clara et distincta perceptio*, the momentum of not only 'scientific' but also social and cultural change has been invariably in the direction of what we might term The Great Mathesis that gave us both the Great Recession and the 'Great Regression'. The latter development, as evidenced in both planetary populism and the culturally 'conservative' backlash that has been the most visible outcropping of it, follows its own kind of *non-differential* logic, as we will explain shortly. But these more recent *l'affaires des temps* are but the latest mutations in an historical dynamic that Daniel Bell forty years ago christened the 'cultural contradictions of capitalism'.

In his well-known book by that title, Bell set out to provide perspective for the social, cultural and political upheavals of the late 1960s that rocked much of the Western world. Bell framed his analysis, as we have done in Chapter 2, in terms of Nietzsche's diagnosis of the advent of 'nihilism' at the end of the nineteenth century. According to Bell, 'the source of this nihilism for Nietzsche was rationalism and calculation, a temper of life whose intention was to destroy "unreflective spontaneity"'.[32] Bell proposes that when Nietzsche compiled these prophetic jottings into his *Nachlass*, Western civilisation had finally begun to show a symptomatology which, in retrospect, could be characterised as a realised eschatology of the Cartesian *mathesis universalis*, which Marx himself had foreseen as early as the European revolutions of 1848 when he and Engels penned *The Communist Manifesto*.

> The bourgeoisie has through its exploitation of the world market given a cosmopolitan character to production and consumption in every country. To the great chagrin of reactionaries, it had drawn from under the feet of industry the national ground on which it stood. All old established national industries have been destroyed or are daily being destroyed. They are dislodged by new industries, whose introduction becomes a life and death question for all civilised nations, by industries that no longer work up indigenous raw material, but raw material drawn from the remotest zones;

industries whose products are consumed, not only at home, but in every quarter of the globe. In place of the old wants, satisfied by the production of the country, we find new wants, requiring for their satisfaction the products of distant lands and climes. In place of the old local and national seclusion and self-sufficiency, we have intercourse in every direction, universal inter-dependence of nations. And as in material, so also in intellectual production. The intellectual creations of individual nations become common property. National onesidedness and narrow-mindedness become more and more impossible, and from the numerous national and local literatures there arises a world literature.[33]

The 'cosmopolitan' character of capitalist production – Marx's diction for what today we would call 'globalisation' – is intimately tied with a certain mode of 'intellectual production', though we should acknowledge that Marx as an historical materialist tended to view the latter as 'superstrate' rather some kind of co-determinative process. It would take Weber to understand that these 'forces' and 'relations' of production that Marx identified as 'capitalist' were also bound up with a kind of immanent historical rationality that was already in place prior to the Industrial Revolution and would be, as Bell and others would later make the case, the internal inductive gearbox for what has come to be known as *neoliberalism*.

Without realising it, Marx saw that 'capitalism', as Streeck observes, was really a form of totalising 'cultural' production as well, insofar as it required the formation of *homo rationalis* as the basis of *homo oeconimus*. Bourgeois productivism as a universalised configuration of moral personality had already been theorised to a certain degree by Kant in his *Critique of Practical Reason*. As Bell put it, 'bourgeois capitalism sought initially to unify economy, character structure, and culture in a common frame'.[34] Ironically, that became the revived task of neoliberalism after the amoral bacchanal of the 1960s, but in a completely different way that managed curiously to hybridise the seemingly incompatible grammars of liberation and subjugation in order to restore the 'common frame'. For Bell (as well as for Weber), the 'common frame' prior to World War I can be summed up in a single word – *asceticism*. What Weber had spoken of as the 'worldly asceticism' of Protestantism (Weber's actual source material was the Calvinist tradition) became the rational moralism of the nineteenth century, which found its philosophical expression as neo-Kantianism on the continent and utilitarianism in England. Foucault's 'disciplinary society' presupposes this kind of cultural matrix.

The worldly ascetic ideal can be correlated, at least if we are to indulge in historical typologies, to a certain extent with classical economics and the principle of self-regulating market mechanisms. The 'discipline' of markets formally mimics the 'self-control' of the truly virtual individual. However, with the rise of marketing and advertising along with a mounting focus throughout the twentieth century on the stimulation of consumption, theorised as the crucial role of government in John Maynard Keynes's *The General Theory of Employment, Interest, and Money* in 1936, the 'common frame' began to shift. By the postwar period the logic of asceticism could no longer be maintained in the spheres of politics, culture or economy. Keynesianism as a strategy of 'rescuing' capitalism from the very 'contradictions' Marx had predicted in his theory of immiseration required that a new culture of consumption – where both unquenchable desire along with a boundless reserve of imaginative objects and merchandisable experiences posing as previously inconceivable 'wants' – be installed as the drivers of this new, largely 'symbolic' complex of social motivations. Resolving one set of contradictions, however, engendered them at a different level. These contradictions now, according to Bell, were no longer merely economic.

Bell staked out the real crisis of capitalism as the turbulent 1960s. The crisis coincided with the exhaustion of the 'modernist' aesthetic, which for approximately three quarters of a century had spawned a rebellious psychology of sexual, behavioural and artistic deliverance from the tyranny of bourgeois 'worldly asceticism'. Although modernism developed apace with revolutionary Marxism, it was founded on a parallel, but alternate, vision of what emancipation might genuinely betoken. Both modernism and Marxism drew upon what Paul Ricoeur termed the 'hermeneutics of suspicion', the intuition that all appearances deceive and that beneath the surface of seemingly obvious or manifest representations there subsists a disfigured world that the prevailing consensus either cannot see, or refuses to see. The supposedly 'real' world is a sophisticated lie, and the hidden world turns out to be the unrecognised truth of things. Whatever any 'critical theory' in its rudimentary application undertakes to uncover, it is always a matter of finding the cipher that can distinguish between what *actually is* and what merely *appears to be*, between the 'superstructure' of immediate representations (i.e. 'ideology') and the concealed 'substructure' that stares at us without dissemblance, between language and the *force* of the linguistic. The task of properly signifying this 'force', on which Hegel built his very architecture of dialectical rationality, was the challenge of modernism.[35] Modernism was *au fond* the project of demonstrating, as Nietzsche routinely remarked, that the *phenomenological was pathological*, although, as later epigones would try conversely to make the case, the pathological itself can be reinterpreted as redemptive.

Freud, Modernism and Critical Theory

That was basically the problem which Freud, one of the true paragons of modernism, confronted. Although Freud was popularly interpreted, especially in bohemian culture, as a prophet of instinctual liberation, the founder of psychoanalysis himself had a far more sardonic, and pessimistic, take on what he called the 'vicissitudes' of human drives in the history of civilisation. Freud was neither a bohemian nor a romantic primitivist, even though he was often extolled by the cultural avant-garde who inserted him into these categories. A clinical observer of the incessant promptings of *eros*, Freud understood from early on that civilisation itself was only possible if the 'life force' was somehow bent or deflected. After World War I, Freud began to advance under the influence of his student Sabina Spielrein the notion that there is a 'death drive' (*Todestrieb*) that is equally important and tends to override the 'pleasure principle' (*Lustprinzip*). In *Beyond the Pleasure Principle*, where he introduces for the first time the construct of the death drive, Freud associated it with the ego-function,[36] although by the time he published *Civilisation and its Discontents* a decade later he tended to conclude that as a covalent factor in erotic bonding it was somehow inscribed within the evolution of human solidarity itself.[37] The persistence of civilisation required the superego, according to Freud, to ward off the destructive impulses that were woven into the very libidinous attachments that hold human societies together.

Freud's real innovation in the epic of modernism was his recognition that just below the deceptively calm surface of what we term 'civilisational' values a titanic struggle between myriad creatures of the abyss is taking place, that *eros* and *thanatos* amounted to a secret *polemos* that might break out from time to time in rapturous or savage eruptions – or both. The mechanistic theories of human self-equilibration that prevailed throughout the nineteenth century could no longer remain plausible after both psychoanalysis and world conflict of the magnitude that was initiated on a lazy summer's day in August 1914 altered the very topology of Western thinking. Like Hobson's acid assault on the high-flown rhetoric and rationales for imperialist politics, these developments made the notion of any kind of 'civilizing mission' highly suspect.

Freud's Manichean 'metapsychology', of course, did not play well with the orthodoxy of modernism. But after the horrors and devastation wrought by the fascist regimes were fully laid bare from 1945 onwards, the double valence of *eros* had to be acknowledged, and it became the staple of the Frankfurt School of critical theorists who, now ensconced in New York after having fled Germany, were beginning to have an impact on the Western intelligentsia. The Frankfurt School was noted for its use of a certain penetrating *cultural hermeneutic* to either supplement or revise, depending on one's critical perspective, Marxist historical materialism. The Frankfurt School achieved special prominence for both its elevation of psychoanalytic insights as an instrument of social critique and for its recognition for the first time of the role of mass media in the formation of culture. What also distinguished the Frankfurt School was its insight that the category of 'alienation' – thematised by Marxist dogma in terms of the expropriation by capitalism of what is rightfully the worker's share of the productive value of labour – had to be reconfigured within the new array of historical circumstances as a *cultural pathology* as well. This cultural pathology, finally, had psychological roots, a tendency within the human organism towards self-alienation as a result of the death drive, what Erich Fromm – one of the Frankfurt School's more popular authors – denoted as an 'escape from freedom'.[38]

The Frankfurt School luminary who crystallised this line of critique at a philosophical level – one which, in fact, left a profound effect on the New Left radicals of the 1960s and 1970s – was Herbert Marcuse. In his *Eros and Civilization*, published for the first time in the mid-1950s, Marcuse in a rather erudite, and at times convoluted, fashion took hold of Freud's metapsychology of the instincts and parlayed them into a distinctive analysis of capitalist motivation in the postwar era. Marcuse's underlying thesis, which he would elaborate with increasing acuity in his subsequent writings, was that the modernist assault on the disciplinary regime of historical capitalism in vaunting the liberty of the instincts had now been co-opted by bourgeois rationality itself. Whereas in the Freudian model the 'necessity' of work as an instrumentality of civilisation in holding in check the disruptive tendencies of the drives themselves was taken as a means of balancing the reality and the pleasure principles, for Marcuse mass media, marketing and advertising had subtly and ingeniously turned the contradiction upside down (in Hegelian terms 'negated the negation'), and made the pursuit of pleasure part of what he termed the 'performance principle', or the maintenance of a new productivist ethic of working no longer for the sake simply of sustenance, but for enjoyments. In other words, consumerist capitalism demanded not self-discipline, but *self-realisation* (an early rendering of Foucault's self-entrepreneurship). In consumerist capitalism the 'work relationships which form the base of civilisation, and thus civilisation itself, would be "propped" by non-desexualized instinctual energy', Marcuse wrote. 'The whole concept of sublimation is at stake.'[39] In a word, it was the domestication of the forces Freud most feared that would save capitalism from the collapse Marx had once predicted.

In *One Dimensional Man* (1964), Marcuse termed this capture of *eros* for the sake of industrial productivity 'repressive desublimation'. Repressive desublimation was a strategy of taking the rejected, or *disowned*, representations of instinctual life that could not be reconciled with the demands of the superego and making them the furniture of a new kind of 'superegoic' system built around a performativity of guilty obsessions and pleasures, one which transmuted alterity into normativity.

> The vamp, the national hero, the beatnik, the neurotic housewife, the gangster, the star, the charismatic tycoon perform a function very different from and even contrary to that of their cultural predecessors. They are no longer images of another way of life but rather freaks or types of the same life, serving as an affirmation rather than negation of the established order.[40]

Or another way of phrasing it would be to say that the new commercial-saturated and techno-consumerist form of capitalism offered a mass-produced, *commodified* version of the alienated artist and intellectual, a pattern which was to become obvious after the Summer of Love in 1967 when the strange and hermetic 'beatniks' of San Francisco suddenly morphed into the media icons that came to be known as the 'hippies'. What David Brooks later would term the 'bohemian bourgeoisie' (or 'bobo') was born.

For Marcuse, the commodified cultural 'revolutionary' was the latest gambit of the surplus extracting machinery to neutralise all resistance to it. The bohemian bourgeoisie he wrote in *One Dimensional Man*, constitutes one more pinion in the transmission of

> a rational universe which, by the mere weight and capabilities of its apparatus, blocks all escape. In its relation to the reality of daily life, the high culture of the past was many things – opposition and adornment, outcry

and resignation. But it was also the appearance of the realm of freedom: the refusal to behave. Such refusal cannot be blocked without a compensation which seems more satisfying than the refusal. The conquest and unification of opposites, which finds its ideological glory in the transformation of higher into popular culture, takes place on a material ground of increased satisfaction. This is also the ground which allows a sweeping desublimation.[41]

Repressive desublimation greases the skids of a smoothly serviceable *biopower*, one expressed through a virtually invisible regime that derives its legitimacy by allowing the pursuit of ever more rarefied forms of 'happiness', including degrees of sexual libertinism that never would have been acknowledged, let alone countenanced, in prior generations. After a while there is no limit that has not been transgressed, no standard that has not been mocked, no measure of *jouissance* in the sense that Jacques Lacan meant it that has not become commonplace. The syllogism-like exigency of the 'categorical imperative' to shatter all moral and social inhibitions, which the process of cultural desublimation harnesses for the maintenance of consumer capitalism, reached its apogee with the maturing of the counterculture in the last quarter of the previous century. The normalisation of hedonism through the growth of a conventional, material culture that reflected the once, but no longer, *outré* lifestyles associated with an earlier underworld of 'sex, drugs, and rock 'n' roll' presented a challenge for late capitalism, whose own interior logic required an ongoing and ever more potent, if not addictive, commitment to the 'creative destruction' of the existing order in a way that had never been imagined before.

If the process of desublimation could no longer rely on a fascination with either *eros* or *thanatos*, while the modernist adage of *épater la bourgeoisie* ('shock the middle class') finally became irrelevant for cultural radicals because there was no one left to shock, the only remaining profitable strategy for disruptive change through milling outrage would turn out to be the very sort of priggish moralism against which the early avant-garde had set their face in the first place. The seeds were sewn once the bohemian bourgeois baby boomers, settling into middle age and abnormally anxious that their children might somehow not merely follow but exceed them in their youthful dalliance with excessiveness, invested in the kind of over-nurturing child-rearing practices that helped shape the stereotypical 'entitled' millennial. It was this reactivity that gave rise to proverbial 'helicopter parents' who hover over every emotion and activity of their precious offspring, and that has furnished the matrix for the prevailing, obsessional neoliberal 'ethic' of self-entrepreneurship. This is not to say that both generations did not equally share this character defect, but they tended to live out their sense of entitlement in significantly different ways. Whereas the boomers had focused almost exclusively on their own *personae* (in that respect they were true pioneers in the art of entrepreneurial selfhood), the millennials displayed a passion for championing 'social justice' without actually doing much that might actually put them at personal risk through an ever more refined and differentiated commitment to right all the perceived wrongs of the world. In that regard they truly became the generation whose epitome was Chouliaraki's 'ironic spectator'. The trend towards a cultural 'political correctness', a trait for which the millennials eventually became notorious, can best be understood, on the other hand, not as some strange behavioural or psychological anomaly on their part, but as the inevitable output of the progressive, intergenerational neoliberal *matheme* of 'making noise', as Bell sardonically phrased it. The only thing remaining to be trespassed against was the underlying *amor sui*, or 'love of oneself', that served as the *characterology of capitalism* itself writ large.

Capitalism and Cosmopolitanism

But even such an 'insurgency' could in a short while be handily inscribed within the deep logic of neoliberalism. Cosmopolitanism – and its corollary of anti-nationalism – with its valorisation of the rights of the 'other' over the rights of oneself was much better suited to the new age of global capitalism, which was at the same time inherently corporatist. William Whyte's 'organisation man' as the icon of America's Eisenhower-era business corporatist ethos could easily be refurbished and updated to yield the much-vaunted 'global citizen' of today who succours the interests of transnational businesses and governments while reaping enormous profits from pretending to be 'humanitarian' in a quest to save the planet from anything that might imperil it. The new 'millennial' (*pace* the 'progressive neoliberal') mentality might be formulated as the outright reversal of Gordon Gekko's infamous motto in the Reagan-era movie *Wall Street* that 'greed is good'. Speaking somewhat facetiously, we might fashion the new jingle of the Apples, the Facebooks and the Clinton, Inc.'s of the world as follows: *good is greedy*.

The upshot was what Fraser in her analysis of second-wave feminism describes as a 'resignifying' of previously emancipatory tokens and tropes within the grammar of neoliberalism. As happened with feminism over time, according to Fraser, emancipatory politics in the new millennium indulged in a seductive dance with – and eventually surrendered to – 'a capitalism so indiscriminate that it would instrumentalise any perspective whatever, even one inherently foreign to it'.[42] Perhaps it was this movement of resignification – or *reinscription* – that made the continuation of capitalism even possible. What Fraser in this article and in her most recent writings following the 2016 election singles out is a new level of commodification in the relentless extraction of surplus value, i.e. the commodification of what Kant called 'the good will' as the essence of morality in the service of a curious 'differential logic'. Such a logic is endlessly churning out both victims and victimisers, or the offenders and the offended, in a new hyperpartisan politics for which there can only be one true 'sovereign' left standing – the completely virtualised and financialised neoliberal *cosmopolis* whose reigning 'Caesar' is the nihilistic ego itself. According to Fraser, and in keeping with the diagnosis offered by Streeck, this neoliberal species of *haute commodification* can be traced to the mandate of *de-sociation* which neoliberalism dictates.

Fraser argues that globalisation has given rise to a post-Fordist and *post-disciplinary* world where both the *coercive* and the *cohesive* power of the nation-state fails to foster any kind of meaningful solidarity. Neoliberalism has taken Foucault's question of 'governmentality' to a whole new level. Fraser notes that 'we should recall that discipline was Foucault's answer to the following question: how does power operate in the absence of the king?' However, Foucault's answer, she says, 'is no longer persuasive and needs to be reformulated'. One reformulation might be as follows: 'how does power operate after the decentring of the national frame?'[43]

Power operates, as we have already discussed in terms of the 'symbolic economy', through the conveyances of what might be termed *intensive signification*. In the early stages of consumer capitalism such intensive signification was largely *erotic* in the broad meaning of the term, even though it could also be codified through the counterpoise of symbolic violence as part of what Guy Debord called the 'society of the spectacle', offering a cathartic encounter with the death drive through violent action films, snuff pornography, bone-crushing sports such as professional football or roller derby, and of course the emergent politics of demonisation and vilification. Intensity – or what some social commentators have termed 'reactivity' – is the only motivating force that keeps the *oikonomia* going. The more recent vicious polarisation of media to reinforce the vicious polarisation of political rhetoric is only the latest exemplification of this tendency. But power as the intens-ification of political passion in the absence of effective political constraint points to the fact that the 'political' itself has been eviscerated of all substance. Despite Schmitt's representation of the political, the antagonistic nature of politics has always betrayed historically a dialectical trajectory towards new types of solidarity.

The absence of such a trajectory within the neoliberal topography rests on the fact that present-day politics turns out to be a gigantic sham whereby 'dialectics' is nothing more than a fig leaf for the infinitisation of difference itself without any possibility of resolution, or reconciliation. Cognizance of such a runaway 'difference engine' overshadowing not only our reasoning but our morality contributes to an intensification of the death drive and the immortalisation of the nihilistic proclivities that Nietzsche identified within democratic culture. The trend towards pure 'economisation' of human values and relationships under neoliberalism, which numerous critics who go way back prior even to Foucault have noted, constitutes the climax of these tendencies. The spurious *virtual solidarity* of Chouliaraki's 'ironic' spectator-ship is equivalent to a hyperreal social morality whose empty and desolate terrain is compensated only by the fanaticism of those who swear by it. How does the dominant paradigm of ironic spectatorship materialise under neoliberalism? As Baudrillard has stressed, the strictly virtual confused as real – the 'more real than real' – proves to be limitlessly generative as a 'precession of simulacra'.

At the same time, these 'simulacra' turn out to have significant political content. Indeed, the neoliberal order cannot survive without them. The intensification of these differential attributes, which simultaneously leads to the proliferation of reactive elements in the system, is vital to the mainte-nance of pastoral power. Pastoral power itself thrives on a kind of managed complexity of social, psychic and spiritual singularities that only preserve their unique valency within a biopolitical surveillance network. It is from this kind of pastoral power that the modern state is born. According to Ellen Samuels, what today we would dub 'identity politics' stemmed initially from a sudden realisation during the nineteenth century that the new industrial capitalism, and the concomitant de-pastoralisation of European society which it swept in its wake, was highly problematic. Familiar ontologies of political subjects could no longer be taken for granted. 'Rapid expansion and urbanisation taking place in the country during this period produced unprec-edented anxieties regarding the knowability of identity.'[44] Identity, therefore, was no longer something that could be construed as a given. It had to be fabricated. Samuels points to such inventions as fingerprinting and the fiction of the 'blood quantum', especially when it came to racial classification and domination, as illustrations of this process. The new style of biopolitics came to be founded on the profusion of methods of 'biocertification', which in turn made possible the new managerial rationality of the multi-ethnic and geographically sprawling industrial state. As an article in *The Economist* points out, identity is actually the reserve currency of neoliberal governmentality. Identity is what makes everything from marketing to political polling to comprehensive higher education achievable. Likewise, identity is what bestows power on the neoliberal state function. 'Identity, like tokens of monetary value, can be taken away by the state that issues it.'[45] If neoliberal 'political economy', providing such a thing exists, depends on the fiat creation and accentuated circulation of such hyperreal warrants of identification, then the production of difference at the symbolical level requires the intensification of partisan division in the context of everyday politics. However, in order to consider how this actually works from a theoretical standpoint we now need to enquire into the 'deep epistemology' of neoliberalism itself.

5   The Epistemic Crisis

> The real is not only what can be reproduced, but that which is always already reproduced.
>
> Jean Baudrillard

High Modernism

JUST AS THE nineteenth century was the age of industrialisation, the twentieth century can be summarised as the period of what political scientist and anthropologist James C. Scott dubs 'high modernism'. High modernism conspired to make all knowledge not merely 'scientific' but also to turn it into a universal, epistemic *map* that could be utilised not simply for charting and predicting the end points and outcomes of natural processes, but for masterfully explaining and regulating the whole of life, even that of the human species. Prior to the twentieth century, Descartes's *mathesis universalis* was but what the Spanish Romantic painter Francisco José de Goya by the late eighteenth century would term the 'dream of reason' that would inevitably breed monsters. Yet by the first few decades of the twentieth century the dream was well on its way towards becoming a reality.

'High modernism', a term that applies to far more than the aesthetic trends of the era, was the fruition of this effort to materialise what hitherto had been barely a fantasy. Turning its back on Immanuel Kant's claim that we can never know what something is 'in itself', high modernism sought to convert an increasingly complex and sophisticated mathematico-deductive schematic of the world, which had been evolving since the invention of the calculus by Newton and Leibniz simultaneously in the seventeenth century, into the very stuff of existence. It aimed to ensure that in the end *the map was indeed the territory*. The method of high modernism was, broadly speaking, to assign what Scott dubs a 'transformative power' to the twin transactions of abstraction and standardisation.

According to Scott,

> this transformative power resides not in the map, of course, but rather in the power possessed by those who deploy the perspective of that particular map. A private corporation aiming to maximise sustainable timber yields, profit, or production will map its world according to this logic and will use what power it has to ensure that the logic of its map prevails. The state has no monopoly on utilitarian simplifications. What the state does at least aspire to, though, is a monopoly on the legitimate use of force. That is surely why, from the seventeenth century until now, the most transformative maps have been those invented and applied by the most powerful institution in society: the state.[1]

Moreover, in Scott's penetrating analysis totalitarian politics and its glorification of the state, including its principal agents, was merely the administrative handmaiden of what at its core was *an epistemic transformation*.

This transformation did not rest on some dialectic between myth and enlightenment. Nor was it due to some kind of fetishising of techno-science, as for many who took mind-altering drugs and solemnly participated in the seductive candlelight liturgies of neo-romantic spirituality first favoured by the 'hippies' of the late 1960s and early 1970s. It was by and large the full flowering of tendencies which began with the ambitions of Baroque rulers to gather uncontested power through the rational and systematic control of populations, natural resources and of course the economy as a whole. Everything during that century – from the exercise of *raison d'état* by absolute monarchs to the invention of scientific forestry to mercantilist finance – was the first, callow gesture in a trend towards engineering entire societies and their livelihoods rather than simply armies and bridges. Foucault's models of both 'disciplinary' and 'biopolitical' ways of governing can be regarded, therefore, within this context not as divergent but rather as continuous markers along the same spectrum. 'Certain forms of knowledge and control require a narrowing of vision', Scott writes. 'Combined with similar observations, an overall, aggregate, synoptic view of a selective reality is achieved, making possible a high degree of schematic knowledge, control, and manipulation.'[2] The difference comes down, as Max Weber noted in his critique of both positivism and historicism, to what the enquirer considers relevant in drawing up the schematics of 'knowledge' and its application within a specific setting.

Only a narrow segment of such knowledge, so far as Weber was concerned, can be formalised by means of mathematical attributes, logical notations or 'covering theories' that purport to serve as omnicompetent explanations for everything, along with the experimental procedures and lawlike propositions employed in the natural sciences. The more expansive range of what we construe as 'knowledge' always remains contextual, or *site specific*. What we come to know depends invariably on some kind of 'judgement call' for which there is no general rule that can be deployed in every comparable situation, mainly because the number of relevant variables are often incalculable. In other words, the 'facts', as Nietzsche reminded us, are forever amenable to *interpretation*. Weber writes that 'every interpretation attempts to attain clarity and certainty, but no matter how clear an interpretation as such appears to be from the point of view of meaning, it cannot on this account alone claim to be the causally valid interpretation'. On this level it must remain only a peculiarly plausible hypothesis. Furthermore, context is everything. 'Even though the situations appear superficially to be very similar we must actually understand them or interpret them as very different; perhaps, in terms of meaning, directly opposed.'[3]

As Scott points out, it is contextualised understanding (what the Greeks called *mētis*) as opposed to *epistêmê* (the type of rule-based, rigorously deductive knowledge) that has been the norm for millennia. *Mētis* is localised and situational, not categorical and all-determinative. 'Knowing how and when to apply the rules of thumb in a concrete situation is the essence of *mētis*. The subtleties of application are important precisely because *mētis* is most valuable in settings that are mutable, indeterminant (some facts are unknown), and particular.'[4] The history of 'high modernism' has been the irreversible replacement of *mētis* with *epistêmê*. In Scott's reading of history, the development of the modernist epistemology has gone hand in hand with the evolution of *techne*, a close affiliation that can be traced all the way back to the Greeks and constitutes the essence of what Heidegger dubs *Seinsvergessenheit*, the 'forgetting of Being'. 'Where *mētis* is contextual and particular, *techne* is universal.'[5]

Scientific universalism – what Kant referred to as 'pure reason' – cannot be separated from the quest for global dominion. As Barbara Aneil suggests, the impetus for recasting Medieval theological stipulations concerning 'natural law' in terms of the 'natural rights' of humanity (specifically, the proprietary right to land and natural resources that became the sacred principle of the Glorious Revolution of 1689 in England and eventually the so-called 'labour theory of value') was founded on the actual experience of colonial disposses-sion of America's indigenous peoples by British and Dutch merchants with their superior weaponry. By the late eighteenth century, it had also become the scaffolding for international law.[6] The intimate connection between 'reason', 'liberty', 'industry' and the 'law of nations' was delineated in terms of the success of early colonial trading companies in both subduing refractory populations and streamlining the market for both raw materials and finished goods. Liberalism, like neoliberalism centuries later, became the new 'image of thought' for an unprecedented system of fostering national wealth and commercial efficiencies through the exploitation by ideological as well as military means of certain forms of humanity. The legendary eighteenth-century figure of the 'enlightened despot', who combines advanced 'military science' with the carefully computative administration of the well-being of the citizenry, serves as the apotheosis of both Foucault's regime of biopolitics and the high modernist ethos.

The goal of an all-encompassing *mathesis universalis*, however, was not so much the glory of the sovereign as the creation of a new form of human solidarity that would replace, at least in the West, the organismic with a smooth-running Baconian *orbis terrarum machina* ('world machine'), the *corpus Christianorum* with something like Hobbes's Leviathan. The intrinsic rationality of the natural world no longer emanates from divine design, but from the technological genius of human beings themselves, who bring the *mathesis* to bear on political life itself, as we have in the famous opening lines of Hobbes's great classic.

Nature (the art whereby God hath made and governes the world) is by the art of man, as in many other things, so in this also imitated, that it can make an Artificial Animal. For seeing life is but a motion of Limbs, the begining whereof is in some principall part within; why may we not say, that all Automata (Engines that move themselves by springs and wheeles as doth a watch) have an artificiall life? For what is the Heart, but a Spring; and the Nerves, but so many Strings; and the Joynts, but so many Wheeles, giving motion to the whole Body, such as was intended by the Artificer? Art goes yet further, imitating that Rationall and most excellent worke of Nature, Man. For by Art is created that great LEVIATHAN called a COMMON-WEALTH, or STATE, (in latine CIVITAS) which is but an Artificiall Man; though of greater stature and strength than the Naturall, for whose protection and defence it was intended; and in which, the

> Soveraignty is an Artificiall Soul, as giving life and motion to the whole body . . .[7]

The 'Leviathan', as opposed to the polis, is created by 'art' (*techne*). Such an 'artificial' solidarity which conjures up Golem-like the 'life and motion' of the 'whole body' derives from what Kant would later come to characterise as 'pure practical reason' (*reine praktische Vernunft*). Pure practical reason is *mētis* stripped of its contextual (or what Kant calls 'sensible') elements. It is 'categorical' because as a 'command' (*Befehl*) of pure reason one has no choice, or discretion, whether to follow along with it. As the only true 'moral' order of society, it cannot be justified in terms of custom, precedent or even the habitual and instinctual bonds of human solidarity we associate with parenting, family, cultural heritage and of course ethnic commonality. The social is no longer a predicament, but a project.

Kant, Hayek and the Genesis of Neoliberal Thinking

Kant is the progenitor of liberalism and neoliberalism alike because, in contrast with the tradition of English utilitarianism, he was the first to understand within the ambience of Frederick the Great's Prussia that the 'freedom' esteemed by the eighteenth-century philosophes was impossible without the internal conviction of being obliged towards an abstract universal totality. Such a totality came to be expressed in Kant's so-called 'kingdom of ends' or 'moral commonwealth' for which garden variety nationalism must ultimately give way to the 'supreme good' to which the 'good will' without any desire for private satisfaction must dedicate itself in every ethical situation. Thus, in his *Groundwork for the Metaphysics of Morals*, Kant hazily anticipates Brown's entrepreneurialism of the self. Brown's self-entrepreneur is the polar opposite of the self-seeker, the virtueless paragon of the Enlightenment consumed by self-love, or *amor propre*. The self-entrepreneur is constantly improving and refurbishing oneself, always striving to conform to a bloodless and asymptotic ideal of the 'good' that can never be filled, as Kant would say, with 'empirical content'. In the same way that Kantian personal agency can never have a specific end in view for acting morally, but must, as his first formulation of the categorical imperative conveys it, *act only according to that maxim whereby one can at the same time will that it should become a universal law*, so the demands of entrepreneurial selfhood rigorously contend for the same 'ascetic' sacrifice of one's immediate goals for the sake of a cosmopolitan harmony of both private and public incentives, one which may in fact by achieved optimally by market forces.

It is no accident that Hayek's 'big idea' of market self-regulation – what we might call *pure transactional reason* – could in the long run become the occasion for a postmodern, stateless, global commonwealth for educated elites. As Stephen Metcalf in an insightful article in *The Guardian* about the origins of neoliberalism has put it, Hayek 'thought he was solving the problem of modernity: the problem of objective knowledge. For Hayek, the market didn't just facilitate trade in goods and services; it revealed truth.'[8] Neoliberalism's 'truth' of the market, as it turned out, was also inseparable from the truth of what it means to be human. In his insightful account of the rise and fall of neoliberalism, Daniel Stedman Jones stresses how its early exponents such as Hayek, Karl Popper and Ludwig von Mises were mainly motivated by a recoil against the revealed horrors of Nazi Germany, followed forthwith by the mushrooming spectre of totalitarian Stalinism during the decade after World War II.[9] Neoliberalism was initially, according to Jones, less an economic than a political theory.

Given the way in which the state had in response to the Great Depression increasingly seized control not only of the economic but also the political apparatus, even in the Western democracies, Hayek in particular was bent on reasserting the values and virtues of the classical liberal ideal of individual freedom. Like advocates of so-called 'democratic capitalism' throughout the 1980s and 1990s, Hayek was convinced that *laissez-faire* economics was but the handmaiden to the centuries-old commitment among the Anglo-Saxon peoples, in particular, to personal liberty. Whenever a regime abandoned the former, they inevitably sacrificed the latter. Nazism was but the nightmare liberal democracies might expect if they took the principle of state interventionism to its logical conclusion. In order to mobilise against the Nazi war machine, the democracies, Hayek wrote in 1944, were compelled to take the first steps in a march down the very same road as Germany in the early 1930s.

It was not coincidental that economic fruits of the mobilisation had been the unexpected remedy for over a decade of economic stagnation, because the goal of postwar prosperity now required the acceptance of a permanent measure of full-blown state superintendence for social and political affairs, a drip-by-drip inoculation against the ever-present danger of chaos through the kind of top-down regimentation of all spheres of cultural life the National Socialists had named *Gleichschaltung* (loosely translated as 'forced co-ordination'). According to Hayek, 'at least nine out of every ten of the lessons which our most vociferous reformers are so anxious we should learn from this war are precisely the lessons which the Germans did learn from the last war and which have done much to produce the Nazi system.'[10] *Gleichschaltung* rested on control of thought through both subtle and overt manipulation of available ideas within the educational system and a mastery of mass media messaging. Ironically, Hayek had almost exactly the same insight as the Frankfurt School, which early on recognised that the Marxist aim of 'expropriating the expropriators' by commandeering the 'means of production' necessitated going after the captains of 'the culture industry' as well. 'To make a totalitarian system function efficiently', Hayek argued, 'it is not enough that everybody should be forced to work for the same ends. It is essential that the people should come to regard them as their own ends.'[11] Hayek wanted to restore personal freedom as the most consequential 'end' which the people should view as their own.

Market 'truth', therefore, in the early days of neoliberal cloud-gazing functioned simply as the practical correlate to the liberal bromide and its attendant politics of sanctifying personal freedom, which Hayek believed had been pushed aside with the new fashion for centralised economic planning and the articulation of what came later to be known as 'industrial policy'. In an essay that subsequently came to serve as one of the foundational texts for second-wave neoliberalism during the 1970s and 1980s, Hayek took much the same tack as Scott does, insisting that 'rational' analysis, prediction and decision-making in economic theory is restricted by the finitude of what any actor knows at any moment in any given situation. It is impossible for either anyone with even maximal expertise to 'know' the entire scope of things, or even the lion's share of all the interlocking causal factors from which one might improvise a 'stable' solution to economic problems, or systemic dysfunctions. Economic savvy must be adduced from local knowledge. It amounts to *metis.*

> The shipper who earns his living from using otherwise empty or half-filled journeys of tramp-steamers, or the estate agent whose whole knowledge is almost exclusively one of temporary opportunities, or the *arbitrageur* who gains from local differences of commodity prices, are all performing eminently useful functions based on special knowledge of circumstances of the fleeting moment not known to others.[12]

What Scott describes as the 'high modernist' enterprise of rationalising society as far as possible, Hayek was convinced, can be considered the real impetus for the kind of massive social engineering that attained its grim apotheosis in totalitarian experiments. On this score Hayek's position was not much different from that of Horkheimer and Adorno in *The Dialectic of Enlightenment*, authored roughly around the same time. But what distinguished the prophets of neoliberalism from the critical theorists was their respective strategies for doing battle with the behemoth of both an actual and latent 'fascism' stalking the Western democracies. The critical theorists, with Herbert Marcuse later as its arch advocate, relied on fleshing out the 'revolutionary' capacity of reason itself. Hayek, in contrast, took what might be somewhat metaphorically characterised as a 'fideistic' approach. If we cannot control the economy – and we do so only at the peril of writing the script for a dystopian horror movie along the lines of Orwell's *1984* – we must fall back on the mysterious power that makes all things work for good, despite our failures at social engineering.

For Adam Smith it was the 'invisible hand' of the market. For Hayek, it was something even more subtle – the price mechanism as the behind-the-scenes arbiter of unfettered economic competition. The measure of price is the measure of liberty in any set of circumstances. Furthermore, it is truly the 'God particle' that can in the long run explain why liberal democracy must remain inseparable from economic freedom. 'Any attempt to control prices or quantities of particular commodities deprives competition of its power of bringing about an effective co-ordination of individual efforts, because price changes then cease to register all the relevant changes in circumstances and no longer provide a reliable guide for the individual's actions.'[13]

Hayek, like Kant, was caught up in what might be called the paradox of rational free agency. For Kant, one can only be 'free' if one conforms one's motivating maxim to a 'necessary law' of pure moral reason. In other words, one only has liberty if one submits oneself totally to the 'majesty' of the moral law itself. In Hayek's *Weltanschauung* both economic and political freedom demand that people subjugate themselves completely to the workings of the market and the pricing mechanism. The only alternative is tyranny, or 'serfdom'. Early on in *The Road to Serfdom* Hayek talks about 'the common hostility [on both the left and right] to competition' because the outcomes are always uncertain. The tendency is always to give the state an important, if not a final, say in order to ensure a modicum of justice in the balance between those favored and those who are not so favored in the competitive struggle. In other words, 'mixed economies' are invariably the preferred model insofar as they seem to strike a reasonable compromise between liberty and autocracy.

But this 'moderate' stance, according to Hayek, gives the edge to cartels and monopolies, and monopoly is inevitably a malignant force that consumes everything in its path. Once the stage of monopoly is attained, 'the only alternative to a return to competition is the control of the monopolies by the state, a control which, if it is to be made effective, must become progressively more complete and more detailed'.[14]

Kant makes a comparable argument in *The Groundwork for the Metaphysics of Morals*, where utilitarian forms of moral reasoning designed to secure either personal or collective 'happiness' perform the same role as state intervention does for Hayek in the economic sphere.

> To secure one's own happiness is a duty (at least indirectly), because discontent with one's condition – bundled along by many cares and unmet needs – could easily become a great temptation to transgress against duties. But quite apart from duty, all men have the strongest and deepest desire [*Neigung*] for happiness, because in the idea of happiness all our desires are brought together in a single sum-total. But the injunction 'Be happy!' often takes a form in which it thwarts some desires, so that a person can't get a clear and secure concept of the sum-total of satisfactions that goes under the name 'happiness'.[15]

Contra Aristotle, the goal of happiness is impossible because it necessitates that we surrender our 'autonomy' as free and rational agents to the attainment of certain enjoyments over which we have absolutely no control. We thus lose our freedom, while our actions are what Kant terms 'heteronomous', subject to a 'law' other than ourselves – in this case, an increasingly tangled calculus on how to achieve happiness. Morality can never have as its aim anything besides what is right in its own right regardless of the incentives or consequences. A 'mixed' morality, like a mixed economy, unfailingly ensues in the loss of personal freedom.

Both Kant and Hayek opt in their own ways for a *mathesis universalis* that paradoxically delivers 'freedom' in a form that lacks all contingency or ambiguity. Both Kant and Hayek, therefore, serve as exemplars of a 'high modernism' that its critics have derided as 'formalistic'. But, for them, such a formalism becomes a hedge against the triumph of its opposite. Better a utopia that can never be realised than one that seeks to impose perfection on refractory human projects and desires! In certain key respects neoliberalism has evolved along these formalistic lines, and that is why it is always somewhat inchoate and elusive. Neoliberalism is the formal epistemic operating system of our times that fobs off on us a rigid logicism of multiplicity, dissolving the tacit tendons of social solidarity in the sulphurous acid of differentialism, all in the name of 'emancipation'. It is the casual assent of the mind to this unobtrusive, yet invidious and all-pervasive, formalism that has made the neoliberal moment possible in the first place.

Both Kant and Hayek sought in their own respective milieus to recapture the ancient Athenian idea of ελευθερία, or 'freedom'. But each in their own way came to the conviction that freedom was not an ontological but a moral postulate. For Hayek, the price mechanism was not some impersonal force of nature like gravity, or centrifugal momentum. It was the sovereign moral arbiter of conflicting human longings and aspirations. It was similar to Kant's 'good will', which in the end sorts out every competing inclination towards whatever we think will make us 'happy', while in fact making these arbitrary inclinations our end-all and be-all merely turns us into *unhappy* 'slaves of the passions', as David Hume phrased it.

What joins both Kant and Hayek at the hip is their disdain for naturalism and their recognition, which few social scientists even today share, that relational transactions among human subjects cannot be reduced to the kinds of interactions observed among molecules. It is this realisation that ironically explains how the ethical 'de-ontology' of Kant and the 'free market' dogmatism of a Hayek could engender the 'progressive' politics of contemporary global neoliberalism. It is highly significant that the term 'progressive neoliberalism' was first coined by obscure authors of an article on teacher education. Randall Lahann and Emilie Mitescu Reagan in a 2011 article in *Teacher Education Quarterly* sought to show how the 'progressive' political objectives of the programme Teach for America, designed to offer a quality education for marginalised social groups, were crucial to the formation of a new corporatist national consensus about the intimate relationship between economic power, egalitarianism and class. The authors make the case that the key to economic performance in today's 'knowledge society' is education, and that education from the early twentieth century onwards has transitioned from a form of life preparation to a crucial international commodity like silicon or petroleum. Furthermore, the critical importance of education in the global economy means that it can no longer be considered simply an elite privilege.

The authors write that 'the "commodities" of education are not just test scores and knowledge, but equity and justice'.[16] Thus 'equity and justice' in the sense of the elimination of discrimination and disadvantage in every conceivable location come to replace Hayek's 'spontaneous order of the market'. Both correspond to an abstract principle of freedom. However, as even the neo-classical economists demurred, the rationality of the market may underpin the value of freedom, but not equity. For Lahann and Reagan equity becomes the formal regulative principle of neoliberalism in the same way autonomy was for nineteenth-century liberalism. Under neoliberalism 'the market cannot be trusted to rectify inequity by itself, and instead positive action is required to offset historical disparities'.[17] This 'positive action' comes in the guise of 'affirmative action', if we can expand the significance of the term beyond its narrower legal implications. As Julie Wilson argues, 'left neoliberalism' simply ups the ante in reinforcing the liberal precepts of 'justice for all' with the pure formalism of offering a calibrated edge for those handicapped in the competitive struggle. However, she notes, progressive neoliberalism does not really in any sense of the word support an equity of outcomes, only an equilibration of starting positions that cancel out historical or biological discrepancies. Both conservatives and neoliberalism

> want a more perfect competition, where the cream of the crop can rise to the top regardless of their station in life. Simply put, left neoliberalism seeks to actively construct a more competitive market for historically marginalised groups . . . What distinguishes left neoliberalism, then, is its emphasis on social justice and remediating the hurts of the past. However, the goal is not a truly egalitarian society, but just a 'fairer' meritocracy.[18]

The Advent of Progressive Neoliberalism

Whereas theories of classical liberalism in the nineteenth and twentieth centuries were regularly ingrained with incipient convictions concerning the superiority of democratic government, even if the historical reality was altogether different, the often-*unself-conscious* forms of advocacy for twenty-first century neoliberalism speak less and less of egalitarianism and more often than not about the intractability of historic forms of 'injustice'. The language of neoliberalism is at an accelerating pace couched in terms also of the inevitability of preformed identities and the way in which these 'rainbow' spectra of group self-representations need to be both differentiated and administrated by certain people with expertise to promote the greater good of society. At the same time, the greater good towards which neoliberal 'governmentality' holds out before the populace is almost always cast in regard to making extensive recompense for past injustices rather than general reconciliation and the manifestation of real equity in the present tense.

In the same way that the prestige of the 'pastorate' in both imperial and feudal society, in accordance with Foucault's research, was moored within a penitential system that relentlessly redefined both sin and grace while scrupulously distilling the kinds of expertise indispensable to administering it effectively, so the role of the neoliberal elites at a global level is to constantly craft and re-craft the means of identifying how 'inequity' is stifling the deployment of capital and labour in its most productive allocation. The meritocracy of neoliberal governance replaces the type of democratic order once extolled by Theodore Roosevelt in the salad days of the Progressive Era as a 'fair deal'. Although it claims to be perfecting democracy by making it more 'inclusive', progressive neoliberalism undermines the very fabric of democracy by unravelling the threads of mutual accountability that make democratic participation possible in the first place.

But progressive neoliberalism, like the Catholic penitential system, could not succeed without contriving its own internal and psychological control devices that keep it intact. For Catholicism it was the fear of hell and the sacral aura such a psychology invested in the personae of those theological 'experts', who might somehow know the mysterious ways of God and how he might mete out proper portions of divine punishment and prevenient grace. For progressive neoliberalism it is anxiety about one's place in a vast, economically integrated yet infinitely diverse *cosmopolis* of humankind itself with proper regard for the authority of the secular world's elites as today's 'priests'. These 'priests' manage the technics of human well-being in every imaginable situation and concoct appropriate remedies for all the incalculable horrors of human history that predate the present generation. In Wilson's terminology the stranglehold of neoliberalism on the minds of the Western intelligentsia nowadays derives from its unique 'cultural power' rather than any subterfuge of political persuasion, or social coercion. The 'fear of hell' in the present day comes down to a consummate existential dread that the world might just blow up – or burn up – any day if each one of us does not do our utmost to join in a mass effort to exorcise those ubiquitous demons that are constantly threatening, whether it be the burning of fossil fuels, the mistreatment of minorities and immigrants, or the activation within oppressed populations of their age-old resentments against those who have done them wrong and never been requited for it.

Foucault's genealogy of neoliberalism, of course, rests on what might be termed *an historical process of composition and division* whereby the classical ideal of the 'care of the self' (*epimelesthai sautou*), which finds its most fertile expression in Stoicism, gradually mutates into the Christian, ascetic ideal that Nietzsche so famously castigated. Then, it is through what we may loosely term an effect of 'secularisation' that the ascetic ethic commutes the politics of sovereign rule into Foucault's 'governmentality', wherein 'neoliberalism' was birthed. Foucault admitted, as his Collège de France lectures unfolded, that he had previously focused too much on structures of power and the means of institutional surveillance at the expense of exploring those collective psychological formations that should be characterised as *technologies of self-domination*.[19] These technologies had their origin in the elaboration of the complex moral and confessional economies of post-Constantinian Christianity, Foucault's 'pastorate'. The pastorate came to the fore during the transmutation of the ancient *polis*, or city-state, just before the beginning of the first millennium into the *cosmopolitan* imaginary that legitimated the brutal hegemony of imperial Rome.

Shepherd Power

As Foucault notes in *Security, Territory, Population*, 'pastoring' or 'shepherding' as the regnant paradigm of authority emerges whenever divinity has been separated from spatiality, when the 'political' in its etymological sense has been thoroughly de-localised and disembedded. 'The shepherd's power is essentially exercised over a multiplicity in movement.'[20] The shepherd is the archetype for 'leadership', broadly conceived, when indigenous forms of authority have been either trivialised, or liquidated. Only in what Augustine named the *civitas Dei*, which is both intangible and transmundane, can the true, constitutive identity of the new de-territorialised persona – i.e. 'the soul' in classical terminology – be properly detected. The 'care of the self', i.e. the ethics of self-discipline, morphs into the 'cure of souls', requiring both an omniscient God and a panoptical *curia* to oversee a pedagogy for the upbringing and training 'citizens' to be admitted eventually into God's own *polis*. Whereas the *politician* is concerned only with those territorial 'constituents' for whom he speaks, and whom he represents within the classic Greek framework of an incommensurability between *politeia* and the exercise of *logos*, the 'pastor' is charged with a universal calling. He has his eye 'on the whole of humanity'.[21] Whereas government of the *polis* derives from an abstract method of reconciling concrete differences (which is why Aristotle's *zoon politikon* was by definition a *zoon logikon*), the job of the shepherd is to ignore such differences for the sake of a higher 'cosmopolitan' aim in view.

Thus, in classical thought the 'politician' is invariably a *mediator*, which is why Hegel, more than two millennia after Socrates, could identify the perfection of *Staatsrecht* as the outcome of dialectical reason. The Prussian despot was lionised de facto as the stand-in for the Platonic philosopher king. But the Christian cleric, the prototype of the shepherd, has always had little interest in the 'political' in this sense. Even the Jesuits throughout the Age of Absolutism, who were technically 'politicians', did not assume such a role. Their objective was by and large to uphold the universal authority of the Pope, the grand shepherd or 'vicar of Christ on earth', through various schemes and intrigues serving the undivided sovereignty and supreme majesty of the monarch.

Hannah Arendt insightfully characterises the political as a unique expedient for ciphering the natural heterogeneity that counts as the human condition. Human beings 'organise themselves', Arendt argues, 'politically according to certain essential commonalities found within or abstracted from an absolute chaos of differences'.[22] Shepherding, or pastoral administration, takes what might be considered a 'univocal' approach to this welter of differences. Although politics in the final analysis amounts to an arithmetical consignment within a regulated gridwork of harmonised diversity, pastoral 'rationality' is strictly instrumental. It can be considered 'humanitarian' insofar as it constitutes a technology for mobilising all with even the most minimal human status (i.e. those who are defined merely by what Agamben terms 'bare life') to achieve some transcendental purpose, one that remains *soteriological* rather than political. This contest between the political and the pastoral has been the hallmark of the modern era, if we go along with Foucault's argument. We can see the same challenge raising its great, grisly head today in the struggle between populism and cosmopolitanism, between ethno-nationalism and the kind of transnationalist humanitarianism that places demands on the Western democracies to accept and absorb the burgeoning flows of refugees from all over the world because of the collapse of civil society and the proliferation of 'failed states'. Foucault writes that 'the great battle of the pastorate traversed the West from the thirteenth to the eighteenth century and ultimately without ever getting rid of the pastorate'. He adds that 'the Reformation was undoubtedly much more a great pastoral battle than a doctrinal battle'.[23] It was a battle over who truly sustained the supreme authority to shepherd a flock. The pastoral system, according to Foucault, is one of command and subordination. It is 'a generalised field of obedience that is typical of the space in which pastoral relationships are deployed'.[24]

For Foucault, pastoral governance is invariably authoritarian. The Protestant version of the pastoral system simply replaced the mandate of the Pontiff with the unconditional authority of scripture (or in the case of the Radical Reformation with the illumination of the Holy Spirit), clearing a space for what we might term a 'democratic' zone of reciprocal accountability in accordance with the interpretation of God's Word. But it was not until the mid-seventeenth century that the Reformation principle of *sola Scriptura* would yield to demands for rational validation. Interestingly, it was the Westphalian accord of 1648, ending the horrendous Wars of Religion and forging an uneasy entente between the key claimants to pastoral primacy, which allowed for a resurgence of the idea of the 'political' in both its ancient and modern connotations, that during the following two centuries of republican revolution relentlessly pushed the demands of the pastorate towards the margins. Ironically, it was the Kantian critical philosophy that revived the fortunes of the pastorate, transforming the Anglo-Gallic ideal of liberty into the strange and paradoxical notion that one could only be 'free' if one's formulary thus altered the republican political calculus of the nineteenth and twentieth centuries in ways we are still struggling to unravel today. Bismarck's image of the *Bürger* ('citizen') as one who is educated or 'constantly formed' (*ausbildet*) to serve the state in order to realise, as we would say nowadays, their authentic human potential slowly supplanted throughout Western society the Jeffersonian idyll of the self-made, self-disciplined and self-reliant individual exercising an intuition of what it means to live both freely and virtuously. Such an image became the baseline rationale for public education, both in Prussia and America, laying the wider, cultural framework for the rise of neoliberalism with its secularised 'pastorate' and the kind of neurotic psychology of endless self-invention that Brown describes.

The New Paradigm of 'Political Theology'

But something else was also afoot in the preservation of the pastorate over the centuries. It is only recently that this peculiar factor, which the ancient Greeks understood as an inherent tension between the realm of the political and that of the household (*oikos*), has come to the fore. The publication of Dotan Leshem's massive, detailed historical study, which may be described as an 'economic' genealogy of neoliberalism, has brought this factor into focus (even though it should be also noted that his erudition is not always matched by his theoretical sophistication).[25] Leshem essentially updates and revises with dramatic flourishes what Hannah Arendt observed in the late 1950s about the relationship between *to politkon* and *to oikonimikon*.[26] In addition, he aims to go beyond Foucault's own genealogy of the pastorate by criticising and refurbishing Agamben's paradigm of the political that we find in *The Kingdom and the Glory*. In that provocative but controversial work Agamben argues that Schmitt's model of a 'theopolitics' proves to be inadequate to explain how politics has evolved from a religious standpoint since the Middle Ages.

We return once again, then, to Schmitt's dictum that

> all significant concepts of the modern theory of the state are secularised theological concepts not only because of their historical development – in which they were transferred from theology to the theory of the state, whereby, for example, the omnipotent god became the omnipotent lawgiver – but also because of their systematic structure, the recognition of which is necessary for a sociological consideration of these concepts.[27]

Although Schmitt's quote is often taken as a kind of *Ur-text* for political theology for all time, he was merely reinterpreting Jean Bodin's formulation of the problem of sovereignty in the 1500s, which in turn must be viewed against the horrific aftermath of the Thirty Years' War. Bodin contended that political and religious unity within a state are necessary to each other (a position that had been entertained by all theorists since Roman times), and that the only visible token of this unity could be *executive power*. Political cohesion is of necessity grounded in some kind of consensus concerning the singular, 'ultimate reality' that anchors all representations of how people should live together in community.

But, as Agamben has shown, there have always been two 'paradigms' operating across the spectrum of political thought – the one founded in the singularity of sovereign will and decisions and the other in what he terms a divine 'economy', which can be traced all the way back to the Trinitarian specifications of the Church Fathers. Agamben wants to 'supplement' Schmitt's formulation with what he terms a second 'paradigm' advancing

the thesis according to which the economy could be a secularised theological paradigm acts retroactively on theology itself, since it implies that
from the beginning theology conceives divine life and the history of
humanity as an oikonomia, that is, that theology is itself 'economic' and did
not simply become so at a later time through secularisation.[28]

Agamben's rundown is exceedingly complex and does not often encapsulate
the arcane textual sources on which he often relies. But the gist can be
summarised as follows. If we go back to Aristotle, we cannot avoid his
dictum in Book I of the *Politics* that the life of the *polis* is constitutively
founded on the 'law' (*nomos*) of the 'household' (*oikos*), from which we derive
the principle of *oikonomia*, or 'economy'.[29] For Agamben, any political theology therefore must be twinned with a discernible *political economy*. However,
the tradition of political economy cannot be viewed strictly as a modern,
'secular' convention. It is foundational to the organisation of the state, even as
Aristotle understood it. Whereas Aristotle's *Politics* is primarily concerned
with the 'natural' power relationships that constitute the household,
Agamben focuses on what might be considered the magnification and diffusion of the domestic order of *oikonomia* throughout the much larger sphere of
'political' administration that have defined both the modern state as well as
post-Hellenistic empires. For Agamben, economy is no less important than
sovereignty. If, as Aristotle asserts, 'justice' (*dike*) is 'the bond of men in
states',[30] any concept of 'social justice', for Agamben, must appear to be the
relational analogue of all those who are normatively and reciprocally
connected with each other both within and outside of the global order of
nation-states.

   We can locate the source of this double paradigm of sovereignty and
economy in Jesus's proclamation of the 'kingdom of God' (*basileia tou theou*).
On the one hand, *basileia* signifies unconditioned divine sovereignty, but as
we can easily adduce from both the Great Commandment and Jesus's own
radically relational interpretation of what it means to be a participant in the
'kingdom', it equally implies limitless mutual obligations that we have to each
other. Christianity thus acquires a form of a *familialism* reaching beyond
blood, kinship and the makeup of any particular concrete 'household'. It was
under the influence of Saint Paul that the classical notion of *dike* morphed
into the broader 'cosmopolitan' ideal of what nowadays we term *social justice*.
Politics within the modern context of 'representative democracy' follows the
trajectory of economy rather than sovereignty. The democratic imaginary of a

'people' invested with sovereignty was always viewed as a conceptual sleight of hand by Schmitt. He would have also regarded Stephen A. Douglas's maxim of *vox populi vox Dei* as unworthy of serious consideration.

Yet Agamben is correct that the divine 'force' of any would-be 'political theology' does not necessarily have to be infused with overtones of monarchical supremacy. Its axis can be horizontal as well as vertical. What any serious political philosophy can, and must, do is to maintain plausibly and consistently the balance between the vertical and horizontal axes in demonstrating an integral affiliation between the divine and the human when it comes to any 'reasonable' legitimation of governments. That is where Leshem's approach becomes so timely and instructive. Leshem makes the case that it is not only within the internal dynamics of the heavenly Trinity that *oikonomia* is disclosed. Leshem takes pains to show how the theology of the Church Fathers was not merely some kind of speculative wool-gathering, but was designed to bring heaven down to earth, to activate and regulate human life so that it might reflect the *communio sanctorum*. Thus, the Church Fathers altered irrevocably the relationship between *oikos* and *polis*, fashioning an ecclesiastical 'economy' for the curation of all human souls that expresses at both a theological and practical level the goal of 'pastoral' administration. Especially in the post-Constantinian subsumption of this economy under the reign of the Emperor, then the Pope, did the template for what eventually became a secularised neoliberal analogue to the pastorate begin to emerge. The theological innovations of the fourth and fifth centuries were basically a metaphysical doubling of the metamorphosis of the pagan, Roman *cosmopolis* into an already profoundly theorised, and sanctified, *oikonomia*. As Leshem points out,

> the greatest transformation occurred in the nature of the thing economised. Whereas in the classical moment the needs of the life process itself, common to humans and all other living beings, are economized, in the Christian moment the divine within humans – that which humans and God hold in common – is economized.[31]

Leshem, of course, is referring here to the kind of argument Arendt made sixty years ago, which he believes falls short in depicting the genesis of modern political economy. Leshem maintains that Arendt's argument does not work because it traces the *economisation* of politics to the Age of Discovery, starting in the sixteenth century, and assumes an almost

2,000-year lacuna between Plato and Columbus. He insists that Arendt was more intent on chronicling the 'defeat of the political' than on attempting to tell the story of the evident 'victory of the economy'.[32] The reorganisation of human life under the magisterium of Roman Catholicism, therefore, serves as the 'missing link' between the notion of the political as found in the ancient Greek city-states and what comes into play with the appearance of mercantile capitalism. 'While in the classical moment the economy was seen as originating in and subsequently corresponding to the human condition of necessity, in the Christian moment it was seen as corresponding to the condition of freedom.'[33]

In *The Human Condition*, Arendt presumes as a legitimate reading of Aristotle that the political, or the realm of freedom, must be wrested from the economic as the sphere of necessity. The *oikos*, the private sphere of family (including slaves), is in Aristotle's rendering the foundation stone upon which the *oikodespotés*, or 'master of the house', could achieve the kind of self-sufficiency necessary for political freedom. Arendt insists that the decline of the political can be attributed in many respects to the historical fusion of the public with the private, i.e. of the political with the economic. This amalgam is what we mean by 'society', according to Arendt. Society amounts to 'the public organisation of the life process', which in classical times was a private matter. 'The victory of equality in the modern world', Arendt writes, 'is only the political and legal recognition of the fact that society has conquered the public realm, and that the distinction and difference have become private matters of the individual'.[34]

But what Christianity did, according to Leshem, was not to economise the political so much as to 'politicise' the economic through the Pauline principle that 'in Christ' there is neither male nor female, slave nor free. The *ekklesia* became the genuine radius of freedom under the guidance of the church, insofar as the Christ-principle serves to provide 'political' status for even the most *unfree* members of the *oikos*, which was its overwhelming appeal to those excluded from Roman patriarchal governance. It is in the *ekklesia* that 'political economy' is nurtured for the first time.

> The difference between the Christian economists and their predecessors lies in the radical change of the nature of the economic activity they are entrusted with and the master they serve, so that instead of being charged with the management of the earthliest of all things in the service of their despots, the Christian economist is entrusted with the

management of divine matters and with the mission of divinisation for the sake of their subordinates. Another crucial difference between the two is that the Christian economist labours to include all spheres of life in the economy instead of generating political and philosophical spheres that are 'economicless'.[35]

This evolution of the content of the 'political' in Patristic times not only illuminates Foucault's theory of the pastorate with a different lens but aids us in understanding the rise of 'identity politics', a locution that would have been an oxymoron for Arendt. And, as we have seen, identity politics – mistakenly construed as some mongrel offspring of the 'culture wars' during the past quarter-century – functions as the symbolic currency that entrenches through its rhetorical strength the 'stealth' regime of neoliberalism. But this symbolic currency has its own kind of 'high modernist' genealogy, one that like so many innovations of the last two centuries can be traced to the writings of Hegel. So-called 'identity politics', according to Fraser, is in many respects the vulgarisation of an aspect of Hegel that was for the most part ignored until about a half-century ago. Identity politics is but a form of pseudo-politics that replaces both the Hegelian dialectical and the Marxist historico-materialist categories of analysis with the 'soft' cultural hermeneutics of what in German is called *Anerkennung*, or 'recognition'. It is to this framework for genealogical investigation that we now turn.

6   Globalism, Multiculturalism and
     the 'Politics of Recognition'

> A spectre is haunting Western academia . . . the spectre of the
> Cartesian subject.
>
> Slavoj Žižek, *The Ticklish Subject*

The Political Theology of Neoliberalism

WITHIN THE GROWING body of academic literature and broader social
commentary regarding the growth of neoliberalism, one obvious, but often
unspoken, observation stands out. That is to say, there is a *deep structure* to
neoliberalism that is neither exclusively economic, nor political, nor even
social or culture, but *theological*. Agamben's, Leshem's and Singh's forays
into the topic draw attention to this fact. But, as we have seen, the kind of
governmentality which characterises the planetary, neoliberal *spectral
state* serves as the mimetic double of the 'pastorate' that begins to unfold as
a unique configuration of *biopower* in the nineteenth century. Moreover, it
unfolds alongside the liberation and gradual enfranchisement of once politically ineffective components of the *demos*, and therefore cannot be so
easily dismissed as, at best, a mere theoretical construct or, at worst, a
rhetorical trope. Historically speaking, the lines between the ecclesial and
the political have been far more blurred than we care to admit. That was
true even in ancient Athens, when the very notion of the *politeia* as it has
been handed down to us first came to be recognised. It was because of this
shadow 'ecclesial' state in the fourth century BC that Socrates was
condemned and executed.[1]

Philosophy itself began as a critique not merely of the sophists' preoccupation with rhetoric, converting *logos* into a purely utilitarian type of rationality
and thus reducing politics to the art of persuasion. But philosophy also took

aim in its critique at the 'priestly' defence of social convention and the ritual legitimation of state functions that service to the gods exemplified. Socratic 'dialectic' hence played a primitive but vital political role for philosophy in the same manner that Marx's critique of political economy performed centuries later (which is why it was so threatening to authorities). As we see in the ground plan of Plato's *Republic*, for which the Greek title is πολιτεία, which can very loosely be translated as 'political economy', the aim of the dialectic was not merely to 'interpret' the world, but to change it. The ultimate question for political economy is 'justice' (*dikaiosyne*), which only a true philosopher, as opposed to a rhetorician, can competently address. And the demand of justice is at the same time for something more than immanent critique. It requires political purification as well as transformation.

It is for this reason that in the evolving discourses of political economy 'priestcraft' and the tendency towards state bureaucracy and clerical hegemony have been viewed with suspicion throughout the modern era. These familiar features of the social landscape have been singled out as targets by so-called 'free thinkers' as impediments to both political liberty and intellectual emancipation for humanity. Voltaire's *ecrasez l'infame* was motivated by this two-sided hostility to institutional religion. But, as Foucault makes evident, modernity has also spawned a certain penchant for 'pastoral' forms of social organisation that turn out to be secular rather than religious as a direct result of the diffusion of sovereignty within emerging democratic polities. How might we begin to trace a genealogy of these secular forms?

Foucault's notion of the pastorate debuts in a demonstrable fashion with his lectures of 1977–8, one year before *The Birth of Biopolitics*. It is in these lectures that Foucault ostensibly discovers the historical *mise en scène* for the attenuation and gradual dissolution of the principle of monarchical rule, the passage from sovereignty to 'governmentality'. In his lecture of 8 February 1978 (chapter five in the compiled and translated version of his addresses), Foucault begins by apologising for his use of the term 'governmentality', an 'ugly word' that is deployed strategically to distinguish 'reigning' or 'commanding' from the new 'way of governing' that he associates directly with the rise of so-called 'enlightened despotism' in the eighteenth century and the adoption of mercantilist economic practices. Such a new means of administration is what the physiocrats termed 'economic government', Foucault writes. It depends no longer on the strength of 'institutions', such as the royal court and its ministers, or even the national church, but 'on trying to discover in a wider and more overall perspective what we can broadly call a technology of power'.[2] Such a shift entails a 'de-centreing' of previously institutionalised power, which in practice means its diffusion throughout the body politic, not necessarily in the form of a new kind of sovereignty assigned to the *demos* (something feared by Enlightenment theorists as much as the ancient Greek philosophers), but as mere 'functions' that paradoxically engender 'a global, totalizing institution that is, precisely, the state'.[3]

For Foucault, modern state power functions by enforcing a 'regimen'. This regimen is *disciplinary* in Foucault's sense, yet its disciplinarity depends on the exertion of a kind of 'moral' rather than physical force. The regimen itself is undertaken for the 'good' of the populace. Prisoners are not incarcerated so much because they have violated some exalted standard of law, but because they pose a 'threat to society'. Governmentality always has built into it a copious *teleology* of the public good. The monarch is no longer concerned for his own personal *gloire*, but for the sundry general accomplishments and the well-being of his subjects. His kingdom is a 'commonwealth'.

As a result of this transition from sovereignty to governmentality, Foucault thereby stumbles upon the root metaphor of the pastorate. Later in the very same lecture Foucault notes that the idea of governmentality cannot apply to the ancient world, even to the Roman Empire. The ancient 'ruler' merely oversees the state. The welfare of the people under the jurisdiction of the state is not important. The origin of what Foucault dubs the 'government of men', contrasted with the government of the state, is Hebraic, not Graeco-Roman. It is found nowhere in the Mediterranean Basin, but is found in the 'pre-Christian East' and later the 'Christian East' in 'the idea and organisation of a pastoral type of power' as well as 'in the practice of spiritual direction, the direction of souls'.[4] Foucault's figure of the 'pastor', therefore, manifests a unique modality of power that contrasts fundamentally with the classical, territorial state. Unlike classical political authority, pastoral power is what Deleuze and Guattari call 'de-territorializing'. Furthermore, it is essentially 'beneficent'. However, at the same time it is not technically sacral, or 'religious'. 'Its only *raison d'être* is doing good, and in order to do good.'[5]

Nevertheless, its 'goodness' comes at a price. Whereas the raw power of sovereignty is in principle value-neutral and tends to be maintained through the wielding of *raison d'état*, pastoral power depends on the mutuality of moral obligation along with a general social credulity concerning the symbolic matrices within which it is legitimated. It can be taken as a variation on the *ars salubris*, whence we derive the notion of 'soteriology'. Such power is what today we in politics as a whole term 'soft power'. At the same time, the act of 'shepherding' requires persistent attention on the part of rulers not only to the exterior behaviour of the 'flock', but also their interior disposition to be compliant and obedient. Hence, the distinctive pastoral practice of 'confession'. The pastor's power is radically dissimilar from that of the sovereign, whose visibility in the splendour of the court as well as in public representation and ceremonial rigour keeps his, or her, subjects bowed and dazzled at a distance. The pastor's power is both impersonal and immanent, insofar as it manifests through *making all things visible*. 'The shepherd is someone who keeps watch.'[6]

Pastoral power, therefore, rests on what Foucault describes as an 'economy of salvation'. But, starting with the seventeenth century and the ascendancy of mathematics and natural science, a significant transformation takes place, according to Foucault. Pastorality with its religious convictions and supernatural sensibility slowly morphs into *governmentality*. The economy of salvation becomes the *principia naturae*. 'There is a sovereignty over men that is required to take upon itself something specific that is not directly contained in it, which conforms to another model and another type of rationality, and this something extra is government.'[7] The modern state turns out to be the secular phenotype of the pastoral ideal, a worldly *community of saints*. In fact, Foucault suggests, that is how modern 'economic' theory comes into play. Both liberalism and neoliberalism serve as inherent corollaries to the providential economy of the cosmos that was once religiously superintended, and its mysteries harboured, by the pastorate. Smith's 'invisible hand' as the secret of a *laissez-faire* economy is the most obvious example of this sort of conceptual symmetry. During the following year, in the lectures that have been transmitted to us on the general topic of 'biopolitics', Foucault undertakes to explore how the 'cure of souls' and the 'economy of salvation' converged in the seventeenth century, particularly with the new emphasis among the mercantilists on the accumulation of national wealth. Building on Weber's famous account of the impact of Calvinist theology in *The Protestant Ethic and the Spirit of Capitalism*, Foucault claims that 'wealth was a sign that God had gained his protection to that individual and that he showed by this certainty of salvation which could not be guaranteed in by anything in the individual's real and concrete works.' Overall, at a collective level, the 'economy produces political signs that enable the structures, mechanisms, and justifications of power to function'.[8]

The Necessity of State Power

The source of the liberal and neoliberal valorisation of political freedom, Foucault insists, has always been state power. This is precisely the theme advanced by Harvard historian Quinn Slobodian in his ground-breaking history of neoliberal thinking.[9] Freedom requires laws and regulations, especially a complex juridical system, to maintain it as well as prevent it from sliding into tyranny. But the state can more readily stand aside and not be compelled to introduce coercive measures if its subjects are accorded the right to enrich themselves, all the while adding to the treasury through taxation the wherewithal to do what the state naturally does – fight wars and 'promote the general welfare', as the preamble to the United States Constitution states. 'The answer given by the eighteenth century', Foucault writes, 'was ultimately simple and consisted in saying that what will give a place to market freedom and allow its insertion within raison d'État and the police state is quite simply that left to itself and governed by laissez faire the market will be a source of the state's enrichment, growth, and therefore power.' Foucault sums up this strategy quite succinctly. For the age of Enlightenment 'the answer' was 'that you will move toward more state by less government'.[10]

But what kind of 'enlarged' state does one obtain through the solution of classic liberalism, which increasingly substitutes the economic for the political? One does not necessarily derive the early modern *juridical* model of such an entity, which was founded on the unity of the national state through the self-communication of the sovereign and his or her laws. It does not matter whether both *ius* and *lex* are compressed into the person of the monarch or apportioned according to what Jefferson in the American Declaration of Independence labelled 'the Laws of Nature and of Nature's God'. Indeed, contra Agamben, there is no 'double model' of sovereignty at all after the eighteenth century. *Oikonomia* does not sustain itself as an alternative to the distinct, 'decisionist' paradigm of sovereignty constituting the essence of the type of 'political theology' advanced by Schmitt. As Foucault crisply puts it, 'there is no sovereign in economics'.[11] There is only administration, or *governmentality*.

It is on this note that Foucault begins to construct the nascent theory of the new economy which Marxists such as Harvey miss, and which such new critical theorists as Brown and Fraser factor out. As Foucault remarks, classical liberalism was not as 'fundamentalist' about untethered markets as many assume.[12] Neoliberalism, especially in its *American* denomination, simply acknowledged the previously unacknowledged hypocrisy of classical liberalism in regard to markets, and carried things one step further. According to Foucault, the American neoliberals realised that the 'rationality' of economic performance, always fragile at any given historical moment, relies on numerous factors that are more than 'economic'. American neoliberalism sought at the outset to streamline the rationality of the market by extending 'schemas of analysis' and 'decision-making criteria' to 'domains which are not exclusively or not primarily economic: the family and the birth-rate, for example, or delinquency and penal policy'.[13] They invoked a whole new conception of political power as *social power* – strictly speaking, as *biopower* – and transposed it into a different key. Although Foucault does not really talk the same language as Nietzsche, he is implying that neoliberalism undertook to leverage the theory of valuation as a strategy for revisioning political economy. Moreover, these 'values' were not the same as Marx's 'use values' or 'exchange values'. They were *moral values*.

Therefore, we must ask: does such a theory of moral valuation actually postdate the advent of a value-independent and 'scientific' approach to political economy, which putatively originated with Adam Smith and found its most strenuous disciples in Marx, Ricardo and later Keynes? Casting a broader eye, we must not confuse Smith, the progenitor of modern political economy, with his successors. As intellectual historians are fond of reminding us, Smith held the chair of 'moral philosophy' at the University of Glasgow throughout his later career, and it was against this backdrop that he developed the outline for *The Wealth of Nations*. Political theorists often shrink from connecting his earlier book *The Theory of Moral Sentiments* with that of his *magnum opus*. But while *The Wealth of Nations* often strikes us as something of a dry, but brilliant, treatise on human customs and behaviour in the staunch tradition of British empiricism, a more careful reading suggests how it follows directly from the ground plan of *The Theory of Moral Sentiments*. *The Theory of Moral Sentiments* was a somewhat convoluted effort at mapping the kinds of conditions under which people within a select society can be expected to look out only for themselves and in what circumstances they might behave altruistically. The book was as much *moral ethnography* as moral philosophy.

During the conclusion of the sixth section of *The Theory of Moral Sentiments*, Smith offers one of his signature generalisations:

Concern for our own happiness recommends to us the virtue of prudence: concern for that of other people, the virtues of justice and beneficence; of which, the one restrains us from hurting, the other prompts us to promote that happiness. Independent of any regard either to what are, or to what ought to be, or to what upon a certain condition would be, the sentiments of other people, the first of those three virtues is originally recommended to us by our selfish, the other two by our benevolent affections. Regard to the sentiments of other people, however, comes afterwards both to enforce and to direct the practice of all those virtues; and no man during, either the whole of his life, or that of any considerable part of it, ever trod steadily and uniformly in the paths of prudence, of justice, or of proper beneficence, whose conduct was not principally directed by a regard to the sentiments of the supposed impartial spectator, of the great inmate of the breast, the great judge and arbiter of conduct.[14]

In short, 'conscience' lurks without fail behind acting on self-interest. But considered from a moral standpoint, self-interest and self-aggrandisement are not necessarily commensurate with each other. Here Smith is going in a different direction than Kant, piecing together the conceptual latticework for later iterations of what would come to be seen as *utilitarianism*. Whereas the sage of Königsberg would have regarded any 'maxim' of prudence, an ancient virtue, as merely 'teleological' and therefore not decisively moral, Smith suggests that if such self-regard is 'enlightened' (insofar as it takes into account its wider range of effects on others), the sentiments of 'prudence' 'justice' and 'beneficence' are all cut from the very same cloth. Thus, the similitude of the 'invisible hand', the mainstay of an *evaluative* economy, is birthed. What we call capitalism itself derives from such an evaluative economy. 'Every individual', Smith avers in *The Wealth of Nations*,

is continually exerting himself to find out the most advantageous employment for whatever capital he can command. It is his own advantage, indeed, and not that of the society, which he has in view. But the study of his own advantage naturally, or rather necessarily, leads him to prefer that employment which is most advantageous to the society.[15]

In *The Wealth of Nations* Smith was *not* making the minimalist sort of claim associated with libertarianism that the general economy flourishes whenever the constraints of state regulation are lifted from it. Nor is Smith offering a defence of 'capitalism' per se, since the meaning that Marx would later assign to the word did not apply to the 'relations of production' prevalent in the

British Isles during the late eighteenth century. Good Calvinist that he was, Smith had simply zeroed in on the kind of felicitous paradox concerning God's providential economy that Weber subsequently dissected from a sociological standpoint. The historical tendency that Hegel would later baptise the 'cunning of reason' (*List der Vernunft*) had already been identified by Kant in his political essays during the period of chaotic, revolutionary upheavals that both he and Smith witnessed.[16] The paradox was founded on the perception that the redemptive advancement of the human race through the cultivation of private virtue – or what the Reformation would have termed 'works righteousness' – more often than not turned out to be a cul-de-sac.

The *philosophes* of the Enlightenment had believed passionately and sincerely that if a new social order free of religious superstition and toadying fealty to clerical elites could be forged, virtue would flourish and the progress of society ensure almost automatically. The horrific rending of the social fabric wrought by the French Revolution, and the widespread devastation of the Napoleonic Wars, gave the lie to that innocent presumption. However, the age-old Christian conviction, as old as Job, that God works mysteriously for the ultimate good of all things despite appearances was always a ready-made option for the more secular minded. In England, especially during the early phases of the Industrial Revolution, which can be dated to the opening of the first textile factory in 1771, Smith could easily observe the paradox. Social conditions were growing worse, yet materially people were becoming more advantaged, which was of course the providential 'sign' of election for English Protestants, broadly speaking. If people were behaving badly *and* the social and economic order was collapsing, Smith could not have dared to go out on a limb the way he did.

The 'Politics of Recognition'

Ironically, we might compare Smith to Fukuyama, who celebrated the dawn of neoliberalism as a global phenomenon in much the same manner as the eccentric Glasgow professor of moral philosophy glorified the infancy of industrial capitalism. Just as Smith had argued that it is in the 'liberal' and 'progressive' state 'that the condition of the labouring poor, of the great body of the people, seems to be the happiest and the most comfortable',[17] so Fukuyama argued that humanity has with the victory of democratic capitalism over totalitarian Communism 'achieved a form of society that satisfied its deepest and most fundamental longings'.[18]

But what exactly was this achievement? Again, Fukuyama did not wax rhapsodically as did many Reagan conservatives about the immense economic benefits of limited government. Fukuyama asserted out of the gate that his objective in writing *The End of History and the Last Man* was 'to recover the whole of man and not just his economic side'.[19] What he really wanted to talk about, Fukuyama insisted, was 'the struggle for recognition'. According to Fukuyama, human beings 'seek not just material comfort, but respect or recognition, and they believe that they are worthy of respect because they possess a certain value or dignity'.[20] The concept of 'recognition' in the manner Fukuyama uses it comes from the brief portion of Hegel's *Phenomenology of Spirit* which is known to scholars as the section on the 'master-slave dialectic'. The section was a critical text for Alexandre Kojève's famous lectures on Hegel during the 1930s, which influenced an entire generation of French post-structuralists as well as the New Left revolutionaries in American during the 1960s, who claimed to be 'humanistic Marxists'.

But the term 'recognition' has also performed a significant function in the maturation of discourse on identity politics. It was Fraser herself who first applied the Hegelian category to the transition among radical anti-capitalist theorists in the transition during the 1960s and 1970s from historical materialism to what its conservative critics contemptuously termed 'cultural Marxism'. Unlike most of her contemporaries, who did not yet have the vocabulary for the critique of neoliberalism, Fraser prophetically discerned a trend, as she did almost two decades later with the 2016 election, that activist politics had had fatefully shifted. The language of activist politics had retained its form while emptied of its original content. The question of the total structural transformation of society, so eloquently voiced by the critical theorists a half-century earlier, had faded into oblivion. Fraser wryly termed this condition 'postsocialism'. 'Many actors appear to be moving away from a socialist political imaginary', she wrote, 'in which the central problem of justice is redistribution, to a "postsocialist" political imaginary, in which the central problem of justice is recognition'.[21]

The new *politics of recognition*, however, was far removed from the Marxist vision – and by extension its 'New Left' counterpart previously championed by Herbert Marcuse. Marx had seen Hegel's master-slave dialectic as the cipher for world revolution among the proletariat. But, as Fraser observes, the politics of recognition was thoroughly *anti-dialectical*. It became at its core a 'communicative' mobilisation towards the 'recognition of difference'. The French post-structuralists, who in their disdain for both dialectics and orthodox European Marxism helped shape the matrix for the dominant critical discourse of the 1970s, 1980s and 1990s, had a good deal to do with this conceptual realignment. But, as we have already stressed, the *recognition of difference* was also part and parcel of the *differentialist* logic of post-industrial markets that had been an impelling force behind the growth of consumer capitalism. Fraser herself made the following observation: 'as the centre of political gravity seems to shift from redistribution to recognition, and egalitarian commitments appear to recede, a globalizing wall-to-wall capitalism is increasingly marketizing social relations, eroding social protections, and worsening the life-chances of billions'.[22]

At the time, Fraser aptly construed the new mood of 'postsocialism' as mainly a loss of energy, if not a failure of nerve, on the part of political activists at the end of the Cold War era. She did not ascertain that there was a more intimate conjuncture between the politics of recognition and the entrenchment of neoliberal hegemony. Fraser, who remains to this day a feminist philosopher more than any kind of 'intersectionalist', has never seen millennial politics itself as an unrestricted forum for the assertion of various and sundry 'identitarian' interests. It is gender difference that historically has always been both the sparkplug and the circuit-breaker for the politicisation of difference. Writing almost two decades after her early book *Justus Interruptus*, Fraser laments the way in which feminism itself has entered into a 'dangerous liaison with neoliberalism'. The fault, Fraser argues, lies not with feminism per se, nor with any enunciation of political rights based on social identity for that matter. The problem resides profoundly in the fact that any politics of identity based primarily on cultural rather than class signification inevitably enables a co-optation of the former by the power of capital. Fraser asks:

> are we the victims of an unfortunate coincidence, who happened to be in the wrong place at the wrong time and so fell prey to the most opportunistic of seducers, a capitalism so indiscriminately promiscuous that it would instrumentalise any perspective whatever, even one inherently foreign to it? Or is there some subterranean elective affinity between feminism and neoliberalism?[23]

The affinity, she argues, can be found in the critique of traditional authority (which, of course, has been the grist for all radical politics down through the age). Traditional authority constitutes 'an obstacle to capitalist expansion, part of the surrounding social substance in which markets have historically been embedded and which has served to confine economic rationality within a limited sphere. In the current moment, these two critiques of traditional authority, the one feminist, the other neoliberal, appear to converge.'[24]

Hegel and Honneth

In any case, Fraser is only clutching the big toe of the entire, unseen elephant in this specific context. While it is true that neoliberalism, following Marx's prediction of the limitless malleability of capitalism over time, is able easily to 'resignify' for its own exploitative aims what were initially catalytic agents for emancipatory political causes, the reasons for this expropriation have little to do with resistance to traditional authority. They lie instead in the nature of the symbolisation mechanisms of the new global capital. Returning to Fraser's earlier diagnosis of the 'postsocialist' split between a politics of distribution and a politics of recognition, we confront the paradox that it is the very grammar of 'oppression' baked into identity politics that has enabled neoliberalism's hostile takeover of emancipatory discourse. The grammar of oppression has developed as integral to the articulation of social theory over the last fifty years or so. It can be regarded in large part as a decanting of the familiar Marxist rhetoric of class struggle and domination into the politics behind the culture wars.

Classical liberal theory from Locke to Mill had always looked upon 'oppression' as an exclusively political category, as the violence of the state abridging the indisputable rights of individuals. Such a notion suffused social contract theory, as epitomised in Rousseau's well-known line about human beings as 'born free' but finding themselves everywhere 'in chains'. It was Hegel, of course, who in his *Philosophy of Right* made the crucial distinction between 'negative' and 'positive' freedom, which in retrospect can be seen as the very conceptual innovation that birthed the postmodern notion of social, as opposed to political, oppression.[25] It is what philosopher Axel Honneth, one of Germany's most distinguished heirs to the legacy of the Frankfurt School, has termed 'reflexive freedom'. In this instance 'freedom' is cast 'solely on the subject's relationship-to-self'. In accordance with this notion, 'individuals are free if their actions are solely guided by their own intentions'.[26] Furthermore, acting on one's intentions demands both respect and reciprocity within the fretwork of social values. It is not so much a matter of having 'rights' as deserving recognition. That is why Honneth construes the ideal of justice through which intentions are validated as 'reflexive' rather than simply 'positive'. Freedom for Hegel, insists Honneth, is inescapably social as well as political.

At the same time, Honneth shows, in thinking through the unprecedented impact of the emerging market economy on political relations of his day, Hegel had to account for the authentic emancipatory potential that the principle of commodified exchange had on traditional configurations of hierarchy, authority and social status. 'As a consequence of having included the market in his conception of social freedom, Hegel learns to grasp the society of his day as a layered arrangement of recognitional relationships.'[27] These 'layered arrangements' constitute the embryo of a later neoliberal rationality that almost invisibly incorporates a burgeoning social dynamic of egalitarian cultural aspirations into a system of covert economic codings, which in turn function in the opposite manner of how they purport to operate. Such a sinister alchemy only becomes possible once the kinds of concrete social linkages comparable with the networks of status recognition out of which the Prussian state of the early nineteenth century evolved – and which comprised the scaffolding for the amassing of industrial capital through the 'sacred' liberal guarantee of historic property rights – have been completely *virtualised*, i.e. only when capital itself *tout ensemble* has been converted into its *semiotic double*.

The turn in the late twentieth century, therefore, from the dialectics of class struggle and the relentless distributional claims of the labour movement to the multi-positional politics of recognition has its own interior logic, which even those identitarians who still retain a minimalist language of Marxist theory routinely miss. The central theme of Hegel's master-slave dialectic, as laid out as a highly compressed unit within the earlier chapters of Hegel's *Phenomenology of Spirit*, is that the 'slave' (the German word is *Knecht*, which implies more an indentured servant or 'bondsman') only achieves his or her identity through an emerging self-consciousness out of fear of the master and through the performance of 'labour', or 'formative activity' (*Bilden*). As Hegel writes: 'For this reflection of self into self the two moments, fear and service in general, as also that of formative activity, are necessary: and at the same time both must exist in a universal manner. Without the discipline of service and obedience . . . consciousness does not become objective for itself.'[28] In other words, per Marxist theory itself there is no identity without a *struggle for recognition*, a process of 'consciousness raising' that arises from a concrete engagement between oppressed and oppressor. That was the point of Fanon's famous anecdote regarding the white child who encounters the black child trembling from the cold,[29] and it is very Hegelian. The black child achieves a certain self-recognition in this moment of humiliation. It is the 'white gaze' that incubates his new-found, black self-consciousness. For the white man, however, there is no recognition of the rich, if not the unfathomable, humanity of the other. He does not see the black man looking back, although if he did, it would be revelatory and transformative.

Recolonising Subjectivity

But neoliberalism does not in any way allow for such a struggle. It assumes the struggle is over, and through a warped, *non-dialectical*, faux Hegelian rationale it *recolonises* the subjectivity of the 'other' under the gaze of the identity theorist as 'master' through the formal authorisation of the method of signification by which both the oppressed and the oppressor are permitted to express themselves. The colloquial phrase is 'political correctness', but such *rectification* of discourse results straightaway from the prohibition of the very linguistic and intersubjective dynamic inherent in the struggle for recognition. In that respect neoliberalism truncates the struggle for self-realisation that reverberates throughout the post-colonial intermezzo and thereby scripts a whole sort of *neo-colonial* masquerade in which all are obliged to participate. The actual cultural forms out of which authentic personal identities are forged are over-processed into standardised *cultural personae* carefully sectioned off from each other through the formal logic of 'diversity'. There is no recognition, only name-calling.

The cultural logic of neoliberalism summarised here remains isomorphic with Foucault's continuous spectrum of 'managerial' rationality that runs from the late Roman and Medieval 'pastorate' to the biopolitical regimen of modern liberal institutions. The neoliberal model is but its most recent instantiation. Like its predecessors, neoliberalism poses a *soteriological* innovation, one that does not stop even at insuring some baseline measure of the 'good life' (*bios*) beyond 'bare life' (*zōē*) to shore up social well-being, but aims to offer a benevolent, if not quasi-authoritarian, *curam animarum*. Christianity gave birth to the politics of 'pure reason' associated with the European *Aufklärung*, which in turn gave us a double portion of ideological motivation for the 'civilising mission' of the colonial epoch. There have of course been 'revolutionary' *interregna*, when the false mask of the kindly master was ripped off and the subjective self-recognition of the 'bondsman' suddenly crystallised amid historical strife, leading to a defiant 'here I stand'.

The first moment was the Protestant Reformation of the sixteenth century. The second was the colonial independence movement of the second half of the twentieth century. The third was of course the uprising of socially and culturally marginalised demographies throughout the industrial West during the postwar era. Early on, the public rhetoric marking these last two moments was derived from both the language of classical liberalism and the neo-Marxism of the period. Each one of these nascent insurgencies on their own styles themselves specifically and characteristically as a 'liberation' movement. Each one viewed itself in some manner as unacknowledged discrete instances of a familiar and universalisable common cause (e.g. equal pay for women as an extension of the rights of workers, abortion and sodomy laws as violations of the broader principle of individual liberty, anti-colonialism as the championing of human dignity and collective self-determination on a global scale).

As the legal system gradually recognised the justice of these claims and grievances at a formal level and began to reaffirm the more abstract liberal principle of immanent rights recognised by the state in order to enforce 'anti-discrimination' statutes, the original calculus for the 'politics of recognition' could no longer contain the idea of political exclusion within a standard *civic* or *juridical* framework. The conservative critique was that in an age of identity politics *rights* had perversely morphed into *entitlements*. But that was always beside the point. Entitlements, as opposed to rights, ultimately have only a spurious legal status. They are inevitably the outcome of the formation of a common value consensus, which may or may not be imbricated in the details of the law. The law can guarantee access for any previously excluded minority to public housing, but it cannot force one to act respectfully towards one's neighbour. The conservative critique was essentially that the law cannot force a person to assume a moral stance towards another member of society. It mimicked the time-honoured classic liberal 'minimalist' position that laws were intended to prevent injury, not promote virtue.

It was this sort of argument that was notoriously adapted by the segregationist resistance during the Civil Rights era in America with its slogan that 'you can't legislate morality'. Of course, the argument of the segregationists was completely fulsome, since it was designed to deny African Americans even formal legal protection. But the dilemma of what the law prescribes versus what the 'heart' persuades is as old as Jesus and the prophets who preceded him.

The Commodification of Critique

The politics of recognition was fraught from the start with the anomaly that the moment of the intersubjective, 'eye-to-eye' encounter that Hegel crudely described in the *Phenomenology* could not be turned easily into a touchstone of critical theory. What Fanon would stipulate as the starting point for racial emancipation could never be codified or delineated as any kind of principle of political *right*, no matter how hard one tried. Even Hegel did not make the attempt, although he certainly could have done so when he sketched out his *Grundlinien der Philosophie des Rechts*.

Marx, to be sure, tried to carry it through in his critique of Hegel's concept of 'right'. Formal rights are merely 'bourgeois' rights, according to Marx, because they are vitiated by what Alfred North Whitehead dubbed the 'fallacy of misplaced concreteness'. One reifies what yet remains an abstract entity. For abstract rights to become 'concrete', for Marx, in the way that Hegel's own dialectic demanded, there must be a space of recognition that instantly throws up an ethical barrier to the 'expropriation' (*Enteignung*) by one party of what is 'appropriate' to the other party, what is the other party's 'own' (*eigen*). Capitalism, which valorises the right of 'ownership', clandestinely and hypocritically expropriates what is most 'essentially' (*wesentlich*) human, that is 'labour power'. Capital formation relies on this action of expropriation and thus totally exploits the value of another's labour in the service of a *pseudo-value*, which may be called 'property'.

Marx's youthful critique of political economy, therefore, came to serve as one large overture to Book I of *Capital* in which he analyses the 'commodity form' as it emerges from concrete human interactions. It is the market as the mechanism of exchange where all intersubjective dealings become transactional – and ultimately commercial – that serves as the crucible for the transformation of persons into things, of 'essences' into mere objects, of relationships into commodities. It was Georg Lukács who skilfully captured this version of Marx's thought in his theory of 'reification'. For Lukács, it is the commodity form of capitalist production that alters all modes of *cultural production*, alchemising the organic sinews of society into an autonomous apparatus of computative rationality. Capitalism is the sorcerer's apprentice of history that casts a fateful spell over the process of human generativity, an enchantment that can neither be reversed nor controlled, a massive and world-consuming 'auto-affection' (as Derrida would call it) of the species' own will to power. 'Commodification', which is the technical term for the ubiquitous *modus operandi* within modern society best described as 'reification', penetrates not only the labour process but consciousness itself. It becomes, according to Lukács, 'increasingly difficult and rare to find anyone penetrating the veil of reification'.[30] Lukács understand reification fundamentally as the confusion of content with form. In that respect it is the 'formalisation' of experience as a whole (which according to Lukács begins with the Greeks) that is the central agency of the reification process as it infects the entirety of society. Thus, the concept of reification is cognate in key respects with Stiegler's notion of 'grammatisation', which we explored earlier.

Lukács also makes the point that it is the separation of politics from economics that marks what we might term the 'catatonic' phase of social reification.[31] The catatonic phase is when the real, that is, the *relational*, character of social activity – which from the perspective of both Marx and the classical sociologists such as Weber and Simmel was always shaped by one's role in the system of both cultural and economic production – becomes completely abstruse, ideologically overdetermined and well-nigh unrecognisable. 'Class', which for Marx and his heirs was always a word connoting such a relational dynamic, is converted into a mere *matheme*. It is this kind of pseudo-Marxism which gave birth half a century ago to the politics of identification (which perhaps is a better phrase for our purposes than 'identity politics') that happens at the same time to be a *politics of commodification*.

As feminist theorists such as Lisa Duggan[32] and Ange-Marie Hancock[33] have stressed, the politics of identification was initially an act of feminist blowback against classical Marxism – even in its 'humanistic' innovations starting in France in the 1950s and reaching America in the 1960s. The gendering of capitalist instruments of exploitation could no longer be overlooked nor dismissed as irrelevant. While traditional Marxists, including many sympathetic to feminist grievances, were apt to criticise the new politics of recognition as separating the 'political' and the 'cultural' from economics in the way that Lukács had admonished throughout the 1920s, they merely, Duggan argues in a somewhat sly poke at Fraser, perpetrated 'a ruse that obscures the intricate imbrications of relations of race, gender, sexuality, and class in the institutions of capitalist modernity'.[34] In truth, the politics of recognition, impelled then as well as now by the perception of *en-gendered* consciousness as heterogeneous with class consciousness, was aimed at reversing the commodification of both female bodies and female labour under the false flag of socialist 'emancipation'. It was a project of making Marx real again by a return to the dialectic of reciprocal recognition that Hegel had described in the master-slave dialectic.

But, as Fraser herself implies, there was always a tendency for the neoliberal machinery to 'reify' à la Lukács the relational dynamics of the politics of recognition, and with a certain black wizardry to perform an almost imperceptible act of political thaumaturgy. Žižek's 'indivisible remainder', when it comes to class consciousness, turns out to be the face of woman. But the turning of such a face (or the faces of all those heretofore disrespected, brutalised or marginalised) towards the collective gaze whereby it appears within such a social field as the *face of the other* paradoxically also gives rise to the occasion whereby it can be absorbed into the neoliberal logic of *commodification through differentiation*. In this moment of absorption what was initially the face that has been overlooked and its demand for recognition is reified and fetishised simply as the 'excluded'. The pure *matheme* of difference is transmuted into the bare notion of *identity* – a class that exists not by virtue of its rich potential for new social interactions, but by merely singling it out for its *lack* of whatever has previously defined the political. The excluded, therefore, operates as a *null set* that drives the differential logic of neoliberal capitalism further and further in its mastery of the political *and* the economic. It is the proverbial wolf in sheep's clothing. It is a bald abstraction which can now be marketed with supreme effectiveness, especially in that no man's land where politics and the 'hidden persuaders' of intrusive advertising, who rely on ever more sophisticated data crunching and customised 'message crafting', are no longer distinguishable from each other.

The 'We' of the World

Neoliberalism's globalised economy of symbol fabrication and 'value-added' provision, reaching even down into the deep well of religious passion (as Olivier Roy has astutely analysed[35]), can mass-produce and proliferate these empty signifiers, which have all the appearance of 'real' human assemblages. The kind of 'identity politics' which has fed upon these algorithms of exclusion now reorganises itself into the politics of 'inclusion' (the so-called 'big tent' or 'rainbow' paradigm). A new threshold has now been crossed.

A brilliant analysis of how the politics of inclusion has been used for over a generation to promote neoliberal hegemony in both the economic and cultural spheres is Jaap Koojman's *Fabricating the Absolute Fake: America in Contemporary Pop Culture*. Koojman, a professor of media studies at the

University of Amsterdam, has scrupulously analysed how the giant global soft drink corporations Coca-Cola and Pepsi both scripted and engineered through their commercials and market messaging during the 1970s and 1980s the genesis of the 'one world' ideology that now underpins the present neoliberal hegemony.

In a section of the book entitled 'We Are the World' Koojman describes how Atlanta-based Coca-Cola and Purchase, New York-based PepsiCo leveraged the mystique of pop music celebrities, international humanitarian causes such as famine aid to Africa and Haiti, and the yearning of youth during this period for the end of the Cold War both to incubate and inculcate an emergent conviction that globalism in some vague, 'multicultural' sense was the powerful wave of the future.[36] In the very same year (1971) in which John Lennon released his smash hit single 'Imagine' envisioning a peaceful planetary utopia without nations, wars or religion, advertising executive Bill Backer, who managed the Coca-Cola account, came up with the idea of taking a variety of young people from different ethnic backgrounds and having them sing on a hilltop 'I'd like to buy the world a coke.' The so-called 'Hilltop' commercial ended with the following words from Coca-Cola:

> On a hilltop in Italy,
> We assembled young people
> From all over the world . . .
> To bring you this message
> From Coca-Cola Bottlers
> All over the world.
> It's the real thing. Coke.[37]

The pseudo-philosophical pitch that Coke was the 'real thing' combined subliminally with its implicit appeal to a loving and strife-free world. The commercial opens with a blue-eyed, blonde woman lip-syncing the following line: 'I'd like to buy the world a home and furnish it with love.' The entire group then starts lip-syncing as well the basic meme for an avalanche of subsequent globalist or 'cosmopolitan' messages: 'I'd like to teach the world to sing in perfect harmony.'

As Jeff Chang points out, the 'Hilltop' ad served the beleaguered Vietnam and Watergate generation as something like a spiritual epiphany, a miraculous and transformative promise of a new earth, if not a new heaven, for young Americans who had been tragically and rudely disabused in recent years of their childhood faith in democratic nationalism. He concludes with a paean to the looming neoliberal future that does not sound ironic. 'As the American Century roared to a close, capitalism's destiny would belong to identity', Chang proclaims. 'Buy the World', which was the name of the Coca-Cola marketing campaign crafted by the agency McCann Erickson, 'had stumbled upon a key to unlocking not just for Coca-Cola, but all of American business, the young world of the coming Global Century. From capital's dream of one America, a New World Order might be born. But it would be decades before many realised that such a world was even possible.'[38]

But, as Koojman stresses, the fantastic success of 'Buy the World' did not stop with its impact on commercial advertisers, who now began to 'imagine' not just a gargantuan transnational Woodstock festival but endless riches to be had by 'going global' and embracing the 'multi-cultural' tomorrow. It was like the Scramble for Africa on the part of the European colonial powers in the three decades leading up to World War I, except that this time the sentiment of the 'white man's burden' was flipped on its head. With white America and its European confrères edging for the first time into what would become a long, seemingly irreversible demographic decline, the focus was now on the inconsequence of 'whiteness' in what detractors would sardonically portray as the 'coca colonisation' of peoples across the globe. At the same time, the music group who had made the commercial, were instantly vaulted into the empyrean of pop culture. They became known as the Hillside Singers and were gradually disconnected in the public mind with Madison Avenue. Within a year the song entitled 'I'd Like to Teach the World to Sing in Perfect Harmony', which had already been re-recorded by a different group, had sold well over a million copies in both the United States and the United Kingdom.[39]

A decade later, former Hollywood actor and conservative California governor Ronald Reagan was unexpectedly elected president, and with his telegenic charm and down-home political bromides immediately announced that it was 'morning in America'. Concurrently, an even more telling and effective, albeit rather disingenuous, new venture was launched that came to be associated with Coke's rival Pepsi-Cola. The campaign was known as 'We Are the World', which was the name of a soundtrack written by superstars Michael Jackson and Lionel Richie and recorded by United Support of Artists for Africa in 1985. The song was ostensibly a celebrity-driven charity venture to call attention to, and raise money to feed the victims of, persistent famines in Africa. Quickly it became a hit single with 20 million copies eventually sold. It was reissued in 2010 as 'We Are the World 25 for Haiti' as another charity blitz in the aftermath of the devastating earthquake in that country. But, as Koojman points out, Jackson and Richie were simultaneously starring in their own Pepsi commercials, which resembled the supposedly 'non-profit' African initiative. Furthermore, 'We Are the World', he writes, 'does sound like a Pepsi commercial', inasmuch as it contains the frequently reiterated line 'there's a choice we're making'.[40] That line also came across as strikingly similar to Pepsi's own trademarked motto 'The Choice of a New Generation'. As Koojman remarks, 'The choice that USA for Africa makes may not be a commitment to fight famine in Africa, but rather a preference for Pepsi over its main competitor Coca-Cola.'[41]

Around the same time that the 'We Are the World' initiative was in the making, a little-known futurist and social science researcher named John Naisbitt, who had worked also as Assistant Secretary of Education during the administration of John F. Kennedy and as a special assistant to President Lyndon Johnson, was writing what quickly became an all-time best-seller under the title of *Megatrends: Ten New Directions Transforming Our Lives.* *Megatrends* with its target audience of not just business executives but virtually the whole of the emerging, educated elites of the world in mind, was written in a snappy, almost hypnotising style with an almost overbearing authoritative tone of 'the future is now, so you'd better get with it'. Even at the height of the Cold War with the Soviet Union ravaging with its massive military might the ragtag *mujahideen* of Afghanistan and newly elected President Reagan vowing to face down once and for all the 'evil empire' of world Communism, Naisbitt was lyrically picturing the gauzy, corporate but 'democratic' neoliberal future that lay just over the horizon. The social and economic landscape we now take for granted was not yet evident, but Naisbitt had it down almost to its most mundane, present-day minutia – the decline of unionised labour and the ascendancy of the so-called 'knowledge worker', the ubiquitous influence of digital technology on everything and everybody, the swift transition from a nation-based to a global economy, the new alliance between commercial interests and environmentalists, the preoccupation with 'diversity' in corporate planning and management, the shift in business management methods from 'top-down' control to horizontal networks along the lines that the infant Silicon Valley firms were just pioneering, an explosion of 'consumer choices' in both the workplace and the marketplace, along with the rising importance and leverage of women in both sectors.[42]

Many suspected at the time, and one can even wonder now, whether Naisbitt's breathtaking vision was really his own uniquely personal one or whether shadow and influential opinion-makers with a very special, global agenda were not somehow whispering in his ear. In 2007 Naisbitt started his own 'institute' in China to work closely with its government and major businesses to promote development. In a book entitled *China Megatrends*, published in 2010, authored along with his German wife Doris, Naisbitt came out as a full-throated and enthusiastic apologist for China's unique author-itarian form of neo-Communist/neoliberal governmentality.[43] Despite the Chinese Communist Party's notorious, ever-present and at times ruthless methods of surveillance, censorship and the suppression of dissent, the Naisbitts were glowing in their assessment of what was going on in China and how that former 'sleeping giant' was perhaps the social, economic and politi-cal archetype for all the world's peoples. The book was even filled with quotes from China's leader Deng Xiaoping.

In an interview concerning the book with Germany's *Spiegel Online*, the Naisbitts made the astonishing claim that China was a 'country without an ideology' and that its system was far superior to Western democracy because it did not have to worry about governing through elections, only by getting 'results'. Now that democracy has been virtually eliminated in even token form for the Chinese people with the elevation of the current Communist Party chief Xi Jinping to 'leader for life', John Naisbitt's comments in the interview about the future of democracy under what might be perhaps a China-dominated global neoliberal regime are telling:

> What does democracy mean? Rule of the people. In China, they respond to the people's wishes. You may not believe that, but a study done by the Pew Research Centre found that the Chinese government has an 89 percent approval rating. There is a lot of openness and freedom. The entrepreneurs and the artists, they love it. The energy it releases is palpable in China.[44]

The 'We' of 'We Are The World' has increasingly taken on a neo-Communist, neo-Confucian hue.

If the vision of the 'soft totalitarianism' of the current Chinese variety, akin more to Huxley's *Brave New World* than Orwell's *1984*, may always somehow have been in the genetic makeup of the neoliberal outlook from the outset, what were the mutations that gave rise to it in the first place? To answer that question, we must now in the final chapter take a close look at what exactly the quasi-religious nature of neoliberalism itself is. We must plumb its 'deep' political theology, of which Foucault in the 1970s had prescient glimpses but did not yet have the full panorama.

7   The Deep Political Theology of Neoliberalism

The crisis consists precisely in the fact that the old is dying and the new cannot be born.

Antonio Gramsci

Beyond the Market

IN HIS LECTURES of 21 March 1979 Foucault characterised the uniquely American variety of neoliberalism as 'the generalisation of the economic form of the market beyond monetary exchanges'. The hypertrophy of the economic market principle transfigures it into 'a principle of intelligibility and a principle of decipherment of social relationships'. Moreover, such a shift makes it possible now 'to reveal in non-economic processes, relations, and behaviour a number of intelligible relations which otherwise would not have appeared as such – a sort of economic analysis of the non-economic'.[1] Foucault goes on in the same paragraph to talk about how child-rearing and the educational processes in a neoliberal society – i.e. the process of personal 'formation' – 'can be analysed in terms of investment, capital costs, and profit – both economic and psychological profit – on the capital invested'.[2] This insight, of course, is precisely the one on which Brown successfully builds her analysis of neoliberalism as the general practice of entrepreneurial selfhood. But we must remember that in *The Birth of Biopolitics* Foucault uncharacteristically is far more *hermeneutical* than genealogical, striving mainly to unlock the distinctive *episteme* for what is slowly coming to be known as 'postmodern' society rather than exposing the underlying values and forces that give rise to it. The majority of Foucault's contemporary heirs and imitators do much the same thing. Hence, the kind of latter-day 'great transformation' (to use the language of Karl Polanyi) Foucault uncovered *in ovo* during the late 1970s still nowadays remains enigmatic as to its origins.

We can trace the full flowering of Fraser's 'progressive neoliberalism' to the late Bush and Obama eras. George W. Bush, who in regard to foreign policy was a decided neo-conservative, was for the most part a neoliberal when it came to domestic policy. The 'No Child Left Behind' programme, which he regarded perhaps as his signature domestic accomplishment, was a dyed-in-the-wool neoliberal project along the lines Foucault characterised as 'formative'. It was a pure exercise in generalised 'governmentality' that banked on the already highly rationalised educational system to create a calculus and an industrial apparatus for the production of 'human capital', starting with the 'non-economic' building block of society and culture that is the family. At the same time, it was Bush's accelerated 'financialisation' policies with such exotic investment vehicles as subprime mortgages and trading in derivatives that precipitated the economic crisis of 2018, which his successor Barack Obama promised to solve. The year 2008 was to neoliberalism what 1929 was to industrial capitalism, which had expanded with global overreach from the second half of the nineteenth century onwards. But Obama, as Fraser emphasises, was no Franklin Roosevelt.

> Barack Obama might have seized the opportunity to mobilise mass support for a major shift away from neoliberalism, even in the face of congressional opposition. Instead, he entrusted the economy to the very Wall Street forces that had nearly wrecked it. Defining the goal as 'recovery' as opposed to structural reform, Obama lavished enormous cash bailouts on banks that were 'too big to fail', but he failed to do anything remotely comparable for their victims: the ten million Americans who lost their homes to foreclosure during the crisis.[3]

Why was Obama unwilling to act? What Fraser and many of his political critics on the left often let slide is that Obama's political *modus vivendi* was indisputably 'neoliberal' from start to finish. His signature political slogans of 'hope' and 'change', already clichéd and vaporous tropes that were instrumental in vaulting him to presidency, were never designed to be substantive concepts of political critique and renewal, let alone militant calls to action. They were nothing more than *differential signifiers* with the kind of rhetorical and emotional impingement that Levitt had singled out in the 1960s as a kind of secret sauce for marketing products in the purely symbolic register. 'Change' of course meant nothing more than things might be 'different'. But its extraordinary combination of banality and inspiration amid a broad-based fatigue with the kind of cultural conservatism that had overshadowed politics since the election of Reagan created a strange sort of 'messianic' fervour (as many journalists named it during the 2008 election) surrounding Obama. It was Franz Kafka who quipped that the messiah would come when he was no longer needed. That sentiment could have been slightly revised to characterise the Obama phenomenon in its germinal stages; namely, that the messiah had come but he was nothing more than a pipe dream.

The fantasy had been building up since Reagan the actor was elected in 1980 and had governed with the kind of down-home, boy-next-door charm that enchanted so much of grass-roots America. It was the fantasy that 'politics', if we adopt Aristotle's definition of it as the 'practical science' of making people happy, was really all about fostering fictional worlds.[4] Of course, Aristotle – along with Jefferson – assumed that happiness was unattainable without something called 'virtue'. The Greek word in Aristotle's writings for 'virtue' was *arête*, which can also be translated as 'excellence'. The so-called 'Reagan revolution' was more about America feeling good about itself than it was about serious policy. Reagan's famous anti-government stance, which lined up with both the inveterate American myth of the self-made individual and the monetarism as well as market libertarianism of the Chicago School to which the label 'neoliberalism' was first applied, did not accomplish much economically throughout the 1980s.

The first two years of Reagan's tenure saw the worst economic downturn in America since the Great Depression, unmatched until the Great Recession of 2008–16. Despite Reagan's boast that less government intervention would mean more entrepreneurialism and individual prosperity, it was rapidly rising military spending during that decade aimed at countering the global influence of the Soviet Union that fuelled the economic recovery in the late 1980s. Reagan overturned so-called 'industrial policy' – centralised support or the subsidisation of major national manufacturers on the part of the federal government – as plied by his predecessors. When combined with mounting economic competition from countries in Europe and East Asia, such as Germany, Japan and South Korea, the result was the rapid de-industrialisation of America along with the loss of high-paying jobs for blue-collar workers. Today's neoliberal economy with its massive income inequalities was the indirect, even if it was not the immediate, outcome.

At the same time, the American electorate seemed to love what came to be called by his supporters the 'Reagan revolution'. Whether Reagan's rhetoric of 'morning in America' with its implication that national pride and purpose was returned corresponded in any way to what was happening on the ground is debatable. Drug use and abuse mushroomed.[5] Economic scams from the Savings and Loan disaster to Wall Street insider scandals to revelations about the pervasiveness of organised crime in not just traditional 'black markets' but legitimate business abounded. Decadence and hedonism, once considered the lifestyle of bohemian outliers, now became socially respectable – indeed, it belonged to the new canon of 'common sense' – under the ideological banner of 'unfettered capitalism'.[6] The presidential personalities of both Bill Clinton and Donald Trump were moulded during this era. What were the leading causes of this second 'great transformation' that empowered the eventual hegemony of neoliberalism?

The 'Deep Theology'

It is here, in contrast with the vast preponderance of the theoretical literature that occupies a broad interdisciplinary spectrum dominated by political philosophy and the social sciences, that we must begin to unearth what we will term the *deep political theology of neoliberalism*. What do we mean by such a 'political theology' in the first place? Such a 'theology' has gone by a wide assortment of names over the past century, but it is probably best to designate it as a kind of *secular theology*. For the lay person as well as secular pundits and adherents to established disciplines who do not start with any kind of religious assumptions, the phrase 'secular theology' would seem to come across as an oxymoron. But ever since the 1960s the term has acquired both currency and respectability among many religious thinkers, both clerics and those with non-confessional academic training.

The initial manifesto for such a new *mentalité*, as the French would call it, was theologian Harvey Cox's best-selling book *The Secular City*, published in 1965. In the book Cox offered a long and extended riff on Dietrich Bonhoeffer's cryptic prediction in his *Letters and Papers from Prison*, scribbled during his incarceration in a Nazi prison towards the end of World War II for his involvement in the plot to assassinate Hitler, about the coming of a 'religionless Christianity'. Cox believed that such a Christianity had arrived by the mid-1960s. The book, published right after the death of John F. Kennedy and just before the escalation of the American military presence in Vietnam, celebrated the new spirit of secular optimism which had been captured oratorically in the young president's inauguration speech about a 'new frontier' to be tamed by Americans. Indeed, it was 'secularisation' as the historical corollary to urbanisation that challenged the world view of Christianity as a whole. It was no longer a question of Biblical literalism versus scientific cosmology and historicist renderings of traditional narratives. Cox proclaimed:

> The rise of urban civilisation and the collapse of traditional religion are the two main hallmarks of our era and are closely related movements. Urbanisation constitutes a massive change in the way men live together, and became possible in its contemporary form only with the scientific and technological advances which sprang from the wreckage of religious world-views. Secularisation, an equally epochal movement, marks a change in the way men grasp and understand their life together, and it occurred only when the cosmopolitan confrontations of city living exposed the relativity of the myths and traditions men once thought were unquestionable.[7]

In plucking the harp strings of what had come to be called the 'secularisation hypothesis' that gained tremendous prestige during this period, Cox was simply imbibing the intellectual atmosphere of his own 'secular' academic colleagues. The leading exponents of the hypothesis during that decade were Dutch social scientists such as C. A. van Peursen and Arend van Leeuwen. American sociologist Peter Berger and his German colleague Thomas Luckmann were also highly influential in shaping the argument. These theorists built in various ways upon Max Weber's characterisation of modernity as the 'disenchantment of the world'.[8]

Yet while these theorists saw secularisation as the inevitable result of Christianity itself, especially the long-term impact of the Protestant Reformation, Cox celebrated it with a triumphalist ebullience. 'Secularisation rolls on', he crowed, 'and if we are to understand and communicate with our present age we must learn to love it in its unremitting secularity'.[9] And he noted: 'the age of the secular city, the epoch whose ethos is quickly spreading into every corner of the globe, is an age of "no religion at all."'[10] A decade later, especially with the advent of the American counterculture and its fascination with the 'mystic, crystal revelations' – as a song from the musical *Hair* called it – of various forms of Eastern spirituality and esotericism, Cox would do a certain about-face. But the core premise of *The Secular City* would spread rapidly, especially among the 'disenchanted' Protestant clergy and intelligentsia, and eventually by the late 1970s it had become almost an article of faith. German luminaries such as Jürgen Moltmann and Wolfhardt Pannenburg along with University of Chicago professor Langdon Gilkey and

Thomas J. J. Altizer, Gabriel Vahinian and William Hamilton, the so-called 'death of God theologians', all imbibed and incorporated in their own distinctive style and outlook the secularisation hypothesis. By and large these figures all regarded themselves as 'secular theologians', or in the case of the 'death of God' movement as 'radical theologians'.[11] While writers such as Mark C. Taylor in the 1980s added a certain post-structuralist, or 'postmodernist', savour to the soufflé – and Catholic philosopher John D. Caputo from the late 1990s onwards would revive the agenda of earlier 'radical theologians' with his own idiosyncratic interpretation of the work of the famous French philosopher Jacques Derrida – the same consistent themes endured for almost five decades and are still very much with us today.

What exactly have been these themes? One might summarise them as *a secular sacramentalism* that revels in a certain sacral celebration of worldliness, Caputo's 'religion without religion'. As Ingolf Dalferth observes, radical theologians in general are keen on

> converting theology to a description of the undemanding variety of gods that human beings create out of their own desires or their boredom with life . . . [or] replacing what was once known as religion with the variety of spiritualities, which everyone is free to explore or not, according to their own needs and preferences.[12]

Or as Jeffrey Robbins, one of the leading spokespersons with Caputo for the project of 'radical theology', puts it, such a theology signifies an 'ecumenical theology that speaks to and from the multiple faiths and contesting values that constitute our all-too-human identities as selves in community and communities in conflict'.[13] With the increasing popularity and influence over the last thirty years of the French philosopher Deleuze, his signature notion of 'pure immanence' has become something of a watchword among the latest generation of 'secular', or 'radical', theologians.

The 'New Materialism' and the Immanence Movement

That is not to say that the motif of immanence has been appropriated by these theologians in exactly the manner that Deleuze, a very erudite, encyclopedic and highly nuanced thinker, intended. The bifold fashions of what we might term the *immanence movement* have been the writings of the so-called 'speculative realists', centred on the writings of the philosophers Ray Brassier,

Graham Harman and Quentin Meillassoux as well as the proponents of what has been named 'the new materialism', an interdisciplinary hodgepodge of different thinkers and methods of critical engagement that draws on everything from quantum theory to the ecological sciences to feminist politics. While claiming Deleuze as their precursor (not to mention some of Deleuze's own historical 'mentors' such as Spinoza and Bergson), the new materialists often misread him as a latter-day metaphysician who has somehow reinvented what was once popularly called 'secular humanism'. In contrast with those thinkers such as Diana Coole and Samantha Frost who were instrumental in coining the expression 'new materialism' and have sought to identify 'the productivity and resilience of matter' as the latest Archimedean point for the enunciation of theory,[14] Clayton Crockett and Jeffrey Robbins propound a breathtaking new 'radical theological vision' of material reality that 'stretches what is usually understood by theology almost beyond recognition'.[15] It is a theology of matter as constant 'energy transformations' and the mobilisation of intensities at the ground level of collective being and action. At the same time, it does not 'repudiate, but radicalizes religion'.[16]

But Crockett and Robbins do not view the new materialism as the latest iteration of a secular, albeit a 'postsecular', theology. The latter term has become something of a buzzword.

we can identify a shift in the classical materialist critique of religion to a new materialism, so too can we identify a shift from a secular to a postsecular political mindset. To put the argument in schematic form: the historical transition and the cultural and political transformation from the modern to the postmodern, from the national to the postnational, and from the secular to the postsecular, while not yet complete, represents a dramatic change that consequently requires a grappling toward a new language and a new conceptual framework. With this transition, the modern separation of powers has been weakened by the generalized erasure of borders and hybridisation of identities characteristic of globalisation.[17]

Basically, Crockett and Robbins have simply updated Cox more than half a century later in casting a vision of a new, global, 'postsecular' city, a *cosmopolis* of infinite spiritual potentials and human, if not *posthuman*, agencies. We might call it a 'neo-Stoic' as well as a non-dialectical, post-Hegelian, Deleuzean differentiated *world spirit*. They extol it as a 'radical theological sketch for a potential postcapitalist world'.[18] But is it?

144 | NEOLIBERALISM AND POLITICAL THEOLOGY

We come back to the problem which critics of neoliberalism have implicitly raised repeatedly – that is, the real meaning of the 'cosmopolitan' ethos. As Costas Douzinas reminds us, there is only a hair's difference between cosmopolitanism and imperialism, and the argument for the latter throughout the nineteenth and early twentieth centuries was always to enforce a supposedly self-evident global ethical regime. Hence, Western Europe's 'civilizing mission' as it ravaged and plundered the less militarily advanced segments of the planetary population. Douzinas makes the obvious point that in order to propagate such an order a military hegemon must arise, and that the inevitable outcome is the stabilisation of the dominant, transnational commercial interests.[19]

A good example would be George H. W. Bush's description of a 'new world order' following the collapse of Communism as a subterfuge for launching the Gulf War in 1991. Any vision of a global egalitarian community expressing an unbounded pluralism of religious normativities, political allegiances, social values and identities (which is what the concept of a 'pure' planetary democracy would entail anyway) turns out to be more a utopian fantasy than a strategic agenda. Any kind of normativity – even the normativity of endlessly proliferating value options – demands some kind of 'imperial' oversight that more often than not necessitates military intervention. Empires are never established merely by brute force, and the ones that seek to do so, like Hitler's Germany, tend to disappear very quickly. At the same time, for righteousness to become effective requires a good army, as illustrated in Stalin's famous quip about how many divisions the Pope had at his disposal. Every church universal must indefatigably mutate into a church militant and triumphant.

Douzinas notes, as an illustration, that the ancient Stoic notion of the *cosmopolis*, especially as evoked by the Cynic Diogenes, was originally *antinomian*. The break-up of the numerous warring *poleis* following the decline of Alexander's empire spurred the belief that a retreat from life in the *polis* and a return to *physis*, or 'nature', was the sole pathway to lasting virtue. But as Roman domination throughout the Mediterranean accelerated, 'the idea of a law common to all imperial subjects, of a *jus gentium*, started to take hold'.[20] Romantic primitivism morphed into a new *Roman* 'cosmopolitan' rationality that demanded a source of absolute valuation – *the majesty of law*. We often forget that the notorious cruelty of military governors and magistrates as the means to establishing a *pax Romana* was always legitimated by an appeal to an infinitely differentiable pluralism of life options as well as an autonomy of local values and customs, so long as they could be rationalised as reflexively self-limiting manifestations of the one true law of empire. The Christian – or for that matter the Jewish – belief in a 'one true God' was abhorrent to Roman officials because it implied a higher, insuperable source of value other than the *lex Romana*, which in turn was always at its core a *lex multitudinis*. Foucault's argument in *The Birth of Biopolitics* that the juridical principle of *raison d'état*, derived from Roman law, diffuses during the eighteenth century into a 'policy of society' based on a more subtle managerialism of markets through the emancipation and regulation of private desires – and that this transition is in every important respect the inaugural instance for the development of neoliberalism – thus elucidates also the beginnings of an implicit theology of *immanent spirituality* to buttress the emerging neoliberal hegemony.[21]

The New Age Movement

One of the most significant, yet still largely unanalysed, interfaces between the neoliberal economy and neoliberal culture – Gramsci's 'hegemonic' ideology – is the so-called New Age movement, whose historical inception coincides with the growth in the influence throughout Europe and America, starting in the 1970s, of libertarian economic theory. The term 'New Age movement' has never been a real social or political movement, but through the osmosis of mass communications was adopted as a loose descriptor – often consciously as a marketing label – for the plethora of 'alternative' cultural and spiritual practices that burgeoned during and after the Vietnam era.

There have been attempts of course to define it as something real as well as to envision it as an actual social movement with a certain inner logic, or intentionality. Marilyn Ferguson's *The Aquarian Conspiracy*, which exploded on to the publishing scene in 1980, characterised the phenomenon as a 'movement that has no name' and throughout her career until her death in 2008 she refrained from actually using the term New Age.[22] The language of *The Aquarian Conspiracy* superficially resembles the New Left political rhetoric of the period, but Ferguson was self-consciously more a spiritualist than a materialist – even while she constantly cited in both the book and her highly popular newsletter *Brain-Mind Bulletin* the latest discoveries in neuropsychiatry – suggesting perhaps a covert scientific warrant for her 'revolutionary' world picture. At the same time, it was indeed the ubiquitous interest among New Agers in a new globally inclusive, metaphysical paradigm of reality that allowed for a kind of religious reframing of what were at bottom material – one might even say 'consumer' – preoccupations with everything from physical fitness to pleasurable sexuality to healthy eating to successful business entrepreneurship – that made it what it now appears very much in retrospect to have been (and still is), i.e. an interculturally compelling ideology for the open-ended *entrepreneurialism of the self.*

Such a project had a distinct political and ethical advantage over libertarianism, insofar as it was packaged as embracing a vague, universalistic commitment to the welfare of the human race as a whole. 'Saving the planet', while a watchword specifically of the ecology movement, was simultaneously a rallying cry of the New Age movement. A basic transcendentalist catechism for Fraser's 'progressive neoliberalism' would, therefore, be inscribed from among snippets of the extraordinary volume of New Age pamphlets and publications flooding society throughout the 1980s and 1990s.[23] The New Age sensibility was what Naisbitt in his celebratory prophecy of the coming of New Age neoliberalism characterised as the transition from a binary cultural logic of 'either/or' to 'multiple option'.[24] Only the logic of multiple option could square with a metaphysics of pure immanence. But the logic of multiple option has a more profound genealogy perhaps, if we are to mine the genuine implications of Foucault's original account of the genesis of neoliberalism; if, as Foucault reminded us persistently after 1970, the symmetry between the Christian pastorate and the emergence of the biopolitical versions of modern governmentality is not in any sense accidental.

The incarnate one true God who can only be deciphered as an 'economic' species of sovereignty along the lines Agamben has outlined for us progressively undermines the monarchical cast of the theological doctrine of divine transcendence. The 'death of God' – portrayed as something of a cosmic horror show by Nietzsche's madman yet curiously embraced by the clueless habitués of the 'marketplace', who take delight in taunting him – becomes the sentimental valediction for two centuries of Christianity as well as a smug ovation for the onset of the neoliberal epoch. God is dead, but it is not the 'overman' who shall live, as Nietzsche anticipated. We are witnessing instead a staid sort of *entr'acte* for the entrepreneur of the self, an impresario serving not so much the feckless Mammon but the veiled and nameless divinity whose actual name is 'legion'.

For Foucault, we may call the 'naming' of this unknown God the *veridiction* of the market itself – a resolute ontological affirmation of a ceaseless self-propagating emporium of symbol-saturated desires and inexhaustible value-choices. The 'univocity' of Being – a concept which Ramey attributes to Deleuze's often unspoken 'hermetic' commitments[25] – now stands forth less as the sign of pure immanence but rather as a symptom of the exhaustion of the energies of history itself, which the trope of 'God' insinuates. The war on transcendence has finally run its course. Let us call it the 'new polytheism', as cultural faddists in the late 1960s were wont to do. But it cannot be disentangled from the 'new materialism', which when all is said and done amounts to the 'new' (that is, 'neo-') liberalism with a *posthuman* face.

The War on Transcendence

At the same time, the war on transcendence conceals a war on human solidarities of all kinds. It is the fierce maintenance of these solidarities – whether they be traditional ones or those that belong to the eschatological imaginary – that has proven to be the engine of resistance throughout human history. Transcendence *is* resistance whenever history is projected forwards rather than backwards, as a variety of scholars of both messianic and 'political' religions have theorised.[26] But what exactly is behind the war on transcendence, which in many respects constitutes an effort to pacify all and everything for the sake of a new totalising regime that allows not even the 'irrational' any longer? It seeks not to exclude or *extrude*, as 'totalitarian' systems have done historically, but to uncover new logical operators for *inclusion*. The only thing that is 'excluded' is the personality that demands not to be 'included'. The example of early Christianity is instructive here. The early Christians held fervently, as Paul articulated in the thirteenth chapter of his Epistle to the Romans, that everyone should 'be subject to the governing authorities, for there is no authority except that which God has established, authorities', and 'the authorities that exist have been established by God'.[27] But the rule was suspended when it came to demands by the authorities to compromise divinely inspired conscience, as the refusal of the early Christians to throw incense before the statue of the emperor exemplified. Christians were condemned and persecuted because they would not sanctify the pluralistic legal order by worshipping its presumed apotheosis in the person of Caesar.

It was for this reason that Christians were regularly singled out over several centuries, not just as enemies of the state, but as 'enemies of humanity'. Roman state polytheism divinised what it had come to believe was a concurrence of the cosmic and humanistic order in the new imperial *cosmopolis*.

Caesar must be revered as a 'god' because in his very manifestation, his *substantia*, he incarnated that very order. Thus, the Romans fabricated their own distinctive *theopolitics of pure immanence*, which neoliberalism has revived in the twenty-first century. The logic of pure immanence, as even Agamben has insinuated, impels us towards a latter-day secular Caesar-worship under the guise of forcing us to bow before the *mathesis universalis* that defines and suffuses neoliberal rationality. Even today there can be no compromise between Christ and Caesar, between a politics of *immanent transcendence* and one of *transcendent immanence*. What Paul in Romans 13:5 called 'conscience' (*synedeise*) is that spark of revelation that discerns the seemingly indistinguishable difference.[28] Although a number of Biblical scholars will surely disagree on this interpretation of Paul, it can be found implicitly in Agamben's presentation of *oikonomia*, and it is in close accord with Badiou's take on Paul himself as laying the 'foundation of universalism'.

It is this discernment that Foucault takes up with his typically broad historical brush in his lectures of 1982–3 entitled *The Government of Self and Others*. Although Foucault does not connect these lectures with his explorations of biopolitics and the neoliberal norm of governmentality, they undoubtedly inscribe one more thread of discourse to amplify the themes he had introduced a decade before. The lectures are not as coherent as those from the 1970s, but they add a significant twist to the articulation of his general position. Foucault centres the lectures on 'veridiction' (*vrai-dire*), or 'truth-telling', in politics. Foucault's thesis ostensibly is that 'the obligation and possibility of telling the truth in procedures of government can show how the individual is constituted as subject in the relationship to self and the relationship to others',[29] a topic he examines extensively throughout the literature of ancient Greece. These lectures constitute Foucault's most detailed and protracted enquiry into the meaning of the rhetorical term *parresia*, which can be translated as 'telling the truth' or even 'speaking freely'. It is another term we find in the New Testament, often in connection with the early apostles' mode of language used during witnessing and evangelism. It can also connote 'public' speech and is contrasted with private or guarded conversation.

The importance of the word *parresia* when it comes to politics, for Foucault, comes down to how it characterises democracy. 'For there to be democracy there must be parresia; for there to be parresia there must be democracy.'[30] *Parresia* is associated with the 'strength', or *dynamis*, of citizens, who are capable of self-motivated decisions and actions. Yet neither can autonomous agency be divorced from the exercise of conscience, the rational spark within all of us that empowers us to think for ourselves and behave as 'free' beings. That is why Foucault spends the first several weeks of his 1982–3 lectures dissecting Kant's 1784 essay *Was ist Aufklärung?* ('What is Enlightenment?'). Kant, of course, answered his own question with the famous formulary that Enlightenment is 'release of human beings from their self-incurred tutelage'.[31] However, this familiar translation of the opening statement of the essay is often misleading, because the German word rendered as 'tutelage' (*Unmündigkeit*) has the literal meaning of 'immaturity', 'minority' or 'nonage'. It connotes a child who cannot make responsible decisions for himself or herself. In addition, the German expression *selbstverschuldet* ('self-incurred') suggests one who is heavily laden with debt. Debt and the incapacity for decision-making are the condition of servitude. Enlightenment, Kant suggests, is the opposite of what Brown in her anatomy of the neoliberal subject terms 'responsibilism', a nebulous and blind obedience to 'demands emanating from an invisible elsewhere'.[32] It is 'responsibility' without being responsible to others, a spurious obsession with self-entrepreneurship masquerading as moral concern. Kant does not regard 'tutelage' as ignorance or lack of critical awareness, but as a 'laziness and cowardice'(*Faulheit und Feigheit)* when it comes to deploying one's rational faculties. *Unmündigkeit* amounts to a forfeiture of the God-given potential in 'every rational being' both to recognise oneself in another person and to act in such a way that the other is acknowledged, dignified and treated for what they uniquely represent.

The Autonomy of the Self

Activation of this potential, as opposed to its default, is quintessentially conveyed, for Kant, in decisions that, according to Foucault's commentary, are eminently *political*. They are not calculations, nor are they gestures to the 'invisible elsewhere'. As Foucault aptly and elegantly summarises the lessons of Kant's *Critique of Practical Reason*, 'we must use our own conscience to determine our conduct'.[33] Submitting to 'authorities' must be *authorised* by our own autonomous reason, as Paul emphasised. Therefore, 'the condition of tutelage is characterised by this relationship, this vitiated relationship between government of self and government of others'. Yet 'to what is this superimposition of the direction by others and the use we can and must make of our own *Verstand* or *Gewissen* due? It is not due to the violence of an authority but simply to ourselves, to a certain relationship to ourselves'.[34]

Neoliberalism as a form of self-imposed collective, psychic dissociation is the reimposition of this 'tutelage' that both Kant and Foucault describe for the post-Enlightenment era. 'Resistance' to neoliberalism rests on a radical recovery of the force of 'conscience' (*synedeisis, Gewissen*) that has been the linchpin of all forms of 'critical theory' not only in the ancient world but ever since the eighteenth century. Nevertheless, matters of 'conscience' have been ruthlessly exploited by the neoliberal cognitive machinery. The machinery – enforced through the shock-and-awe communicative ordnance of the cognitive elites themselves that seeks to account for every episode of human misfortune as supposedly weighing (and preying) on the 'conscience' of the masses of which they have in their own minds cleansed themselves – reinforces not only their sense of economic entitlement but their distinctive *moral* privilege.

This subterfuge is most patently illustrated in the case of the global immigration. Ida Danewid in a powerful and polemical article on the 'sentimental' politics of welcoming immigrants unconditionally among American and European progressive neoliberals makes the case that their implicit policy of open borders turns out to be not some grand ethical gesture for the evident good of humanity but a cynical ploy to deflect attention from their own 'neo-colonialism' at the expense of the domestic working class.

> By focusing on abstract – as opposed to historical – humanity, they contribute to an ideological formation that erases history and undoes the 'umbilical cord' that links Europe and the migrants who are trying to enter the continent. This replaces questions of responsibility, guilt, restitution, repentance, and structural reform with matters of empathy, generosity, and hospitality – a move that transforms the responsible colonial agent into an innocent bystander, confirming its status as 'ethical', 'good', and 'humane'.[35]

In other words, the profound, historico-political and economic issue of Western exploitation of its former colonial subjects, both then and now, is etherised into the pseudo-Kantian – and we will throw Jesus in there for good measure – mantra of an obligatory cosmopolitan hospitality that does not challenge the existing world order in the slightest. In fact, it is intended to keep the populist 'peasants' from revolting through the practice of selling 'indulgences', not so that their souls can go to heaven, but so that they can be 'forgiven' for whatever collective sins of omission in contributing to the elite-defined misery of the human race they have somehow committed. The cosmopolitan elites, as Foucault's lectures on neoliberalism imply, see them-selves in such a priestly or 'pastoral' role. Good 'global citizenship' and the righteous self-satisfaction that goes with it is the new, secular 'kingdom of heaven', as far as neoliberalism is concerned. Hell is the psychic equivalent of having failed to do one's part in relieving the world's billions of their misery, mourning and suffering, however that might be defined. Naturally, as is the case with all priestly caste systems, the 'pastors' themselves do not have to have served as paragons of self-sacrifice. Because of their high rank and status, they are exempt from the moral strictures they lay upon others. Someone else – the 'deplorables', so to speak – must play the exculpatory role for the dysfunctionality of the indecipherable world system (i.e. Brown's 'else-where') they are daily exhorted to support.

At the same time, the fact of exploitation does not necessarily invalidate the universalistic assumptions behind the cosmopolitan ethic itself, as contrasted with the leveraging of the ethic to uphold the privileges of the elites themselves. As Alex Sager suggests, the dilemma of 'hospitality' to the foreigner is often framed principally as a political challenge, presupposing as a procedural starting point the problem of how nation-states should include, or exclude, outsiders. He terms this bias 'methodological nationalism', which conventionally has dominated academic discourse in light of the ascendancy of the social sciences. In contrast, Sager calls for what he terms a 'critical cosmopolitanism'. A critical cosmopolitanism adopts as its *point d'appui* the universalistic ethical imperative inlaid within the foundation of so much international law, which postulates 'the equal moral worth of all people'. Such a postulate remains 'skeptical of any justifications for institutions that provide people with sharply different opportunities'.[36]

But Sager also distinguishes between his own 'critical' version of cosmo-politanism and the kind of categorical ethics that can be found, for example, in *Kant's Religion within the Limits of Reason Alone*. The very Kantian notion of 'critical' contains certain provisos concerning the necessary limitations of any unconditional claim, and Sager does the same with any attempt to assert a cosmopolitan ethic without qualification.

Critical Cosmopolitanism

The boundaries of the cosmopolitan ethic are decidedly political, and one can cite what, for instance, is the right of national self-determination incorpo-rated since the 1940s into international law (although the principle, known as *ius cogens*, goes all the way back to the mid-nineteenth century and has been historically advocated by both those on the left as well as those on the right). Article 1.2 of the United Nations Charter enshrines this right in stating that the essential purpose of the organisation is 'to develop friendly relations among nations based on respect for the principle of equal rights and self-determination of peoples, and to take other appropriate measures to strengthen universal peace.'[37] The right of national self-determination has been afforded even more clout in recent decades with the movement to affirm indigenous rights and their claim to political autonomy and a certain measure of their own sovereignty within historically constituted nation-states. Sager's 'critical cosmopolitanism' does not question national sovereignty *carte blanche*, which (as in the case of indigenous rights) actually protects certain peoples against persecution and exploitation. What it does do is invoke international 'human rights' and the goal of human thriving as the ultimate litmus test of any declaration of sovereignty.

One might stress that the not infrequent resort of neoliberals (in contrast with classic liberals) to cosmopolitan rhetoric, while de facto demanding proprietary considerations in terms of social advantage and economic privilege, has been one of the chief and more insidious reasons for its growing ideological stranglehold over the Western political imagination. It preserves the form of cosmopolitan moral directives while concealing its substance as old-fashioned predatory economic behaviour. Moral pretence increasingly is more vital to commercial success than competitive advantage.

The oxymoronic nature, as well as the irony in the nomenclature, of what has come to be known as 'ethical' corporatism, favoured within neoliberal discourse, can be identified in a recent US Supreme Court decision that settled after many years the issue of whether individual states can compel online retailers to collect and remit sales taxes on all transactions, reversing earlier precedents which the justices themselves had set forth in 1967 and 1992.[38] A narrow court majority cited the ubiquity of online commerce and the sudden transformation of the retail landscape in the previous two decades as the guiding rationale for their decision. The minority dissent focused on the impact on small online businesses, which would be obliged now to collect and transmit sales taxes for over 10,000 different entities. Most economic analysts immediately surmised that the decision would mostly benefit major online retailers such as Amazon, Inc., which could then force smaller operators to become subservient to the former because of their existing command of the distribution and tax collection system. At the same time, the decision would also level the increasingly unequal playing field between brick-and-mortar shops and online vendors, which have benefited from not having to collect sales tax. The majority opined that allowing remote sellers *not* to collect taxes was 'unfair and unjust', but it was also clear that previous practice had helped to curb the monopolisation of e-commerce by online predators such as Amazon.

The use of high-minded moral justifications for predatory conduct, of course, is nothing new. As we have pointed out previously, it was one of the prevalent instruments in the nineteenth and twentieth centuries for the defence of colonialism and imperialism, and frequently has permeated the discursive practices of democratic states in their interventions in conflicts abroad. But what we experience for the most part nowadays is not so much a recourse to *rationalisation* of occasional violent or predatory acts on the part of sovereign states (an after-the-fact attempt at self-vindication), or certain corporate actors, but the saturation of the field of self-aggrandising patterns of deportment with unself-conscious attestations of moral rectitude. The prevalence of private virtue signalling, internet shaming and the viral propagation of moral and political outrage through social media constitute only a portion of the symptomatology of this toxic trend. If these phenomena were merely the evident outcome of some kind of new 'puritanism', as a number of commentators have surmised, that would be one thing. But recent psychological research is beginning to show that social media such as Facebook is beginning to have powerful negative effects not only on personal well-being but on the cohesion of society as a whole. Competition to make oneself appear favourable to others, together with a compulsive fixation on negative facts and news and the easy option of reacting to them immediately, gestates its own logic of mutually assured psychological destruction.[39]

The multiplier effect of such tendencies, when combined with the real-world passivity and lack of interpersonal engagement that the dominant digital culture necessarily fosters, solidifies the hegemony of neoliberal 'responsibilism' and the guilt/debt syndrome which analysts such as Lazzarato have so incisively diagnosed. The shibboleth that 'there is no alternative' becomes more than a closure of economic policy choices. It takes on the semblance of a collective psychological life sentence. The 'politics of recognition' thus has morphed into a metastasising pseudo-polity of ever accelerating, narcissistic self-aggrandisement behind the screen of an overstimulated moral fervour for righting all the world's wrongs, while identifying for the sake of 'punishment' and exclusion an ever more proliferating menagerie of virtual malefactors. If there is a way out of this epistemic and neuropathological cul-de-sac, it cannot simply be charted through heightened criticism. It must be traced through a radical revisioning of the way in which we look at the world and at others.

8   Endings

> Politics is opposed to morality, as philosophy to naïveté.
>
> Emmanuel Levinas

The 'Eschatology' of Neoliberalism

IF HEGEL SOUGHT to resolve the problem of recognition in his *Philosophy of Right* by subsuming it under the ethical ideal of citizenship emblematic of the bourgeois state, neoliberalism has defined away the issue entirely through a variety of highly subtle, sociological sophisms. It has rendered the question of recognition largely irrelevant by replacing it with concrete social analysis, which invariably depends on models of effective *intersubjectivity*, with a *subjectless* denominator of socio-political set theory. Its covert method has been to explain away the bonds of relationality and reciprocity that constitute both *Gemeinschaft* and *Gesellschaft* by postulating a purely *agonistic* – not to mention an *antagonistic* – system of constantly shifting contrarieties between all the multiplying 'identities', or identity-positions (one is reminded here of the development of social theories of 'intersectionality'), which go into the making of a global covering law of *inclusivity*. Inclusivity is like integral calculus. It is all about calculating a fictional totality of infinite differential segments which remain 'atomised' and abstract. It is a pure economy of difference that mathematises, and thereby falsifies, the real sociality, affectivity, affiliation and interrelationality of human beings. It pits all these segments against others, both designating and dissolving with the abstruse logic of differentiated identity-postulates.

As Yale Professor of Law Amy Chua wryly comments, '"inclusivity" has long been a progressive watchword, but today's anti-oppression movements are often proudly exclusionary'.[1] If *communitas* under the regime of neoliberal rationality has lost all its meaning while strangely morphing into an interminable diffusion of pseudo-collective taxonomies designed to amplify competitive frictions and animosities, is there a way back to the centre of sustainable forms of 'communitarian' solidarity that has not yet been charted, or even discerned? Is it even possible any longer to envision something of what Derrida in *Spectres of Marx* dreamily called a 'new internationale'?

If old-style global capitalism destroyed all historic forms of social and communal solidarities and, as Marx and Engels wrote in *The Communist Manifesto*, 'left remaining no other nexus between man and man than naked self-interest' with the result that it 'resolved personal worth into exchange value',[2] then the new-style global capitalism we call neoliberalism has taken this process to an ever higher level. Derrida's hope for a new 'internationale', pronounced at the very end of the Cold War, was premised on a rallying call to multifarious democratic constituencies around the world to the 'impossible' hope of an empowering new universalism fired by countless commitments to the futuristic spectre of 'undeconstructible' justice. But such an ideal itself has been captured by the cynical neoliberal computation that pits these constituencies against each other in the 'intersectionalist' *circus maximus* of social justice warriorship. Only a universalism that radically takes into account the demand for recognition and respect at a level that is far deeper and more foundational than the politics of identity can truly save us.

What might such a universalism look like, and how exactly can be begin in our own stuttering singularity to frame envision, and articulate it? The politico-ethical solidarism of the bourgeois state à la Hegelian *Rechtsphilosophie* – a venerable and ever beguiling modern concept from which even such contemporary institutions as the European Union have been adduced – is quickly sinking into disrepute. If it reached its heyday in the early 1990s when the Hegelian eschatology of the 'end of history' seemed finally to have arrived, we have discovered in the meantime that it was really little more than a coruscating mirage enabled by the false promise of 'democratic capitalism'. Just as the Maoist revolution in China in the 1940s turned out to be nothing resembling the humble peasant uprising it was romantically portrayed to be throughout the early postwar years, so the fall of Communism from 1989–91 proved to be something far more epochal and indecipherable than it was ideologically tagged by 'free market' enthusiasts in the immediate aftermath.

As Slobodian points out, the project itself 'focused on designing institutions – not to liberate markets but to encase them, to inoculate capitalism against the threat of democracy, to create a framework to contain often-irrational human behavior, and to reorder the world after empire as a space of competing states in which borders fulfill a necessary function'.[3] Neoliberalism has, in effect, been a perpetual *war on solidarities*, as its numerous critics that we have surveyed show forth from countless angles and with sundry methodological flourishes. It has been a war that marshals all the advanced and 'weaponised' technology of certain semiotic *praxes* that serve to empty of any meaningful content both self and the engagement of the self in the material and reciprocal processes of the world. The neoliberal is the authentic signature of the 'posthuman' wherein it is not a nuclear Armageddon but the *apocalypse of the sign* itself (expressed in the ubiquity of digital codings of the 'real', the transformation of learning into a robotised professionalism, and the financialisation of all human transactivity that desiccates the landscape of global civilisation). In that respect, it has truly proven to be 'the end of history', but not at all in the sense that Hegel, Kojève or Fukuyama intended.

Towards a New Universalism

It is here, then, that the so-called 'religious question', along with the issue of what might be called a *new solidarism*, leaps to the fore. Is it possible to imagine a new universalistic solidarism which incorporates an authentic politics of recognition, yet in the same breath does not mummify it, as neoliberalism has done, into the strategic *bellum omnium contra omnes* that we know as the politics of identitarianism? We are confronted with a number of outmoded 'grand narratives' with a soteriological flavour which have dominated universal history in the past century – and for a time prevailed within the discourse of fledgling globalism during the so-called 'postcolonial era'. These overshadowing *grand récits* have been, of course, Christianity, Islam, the Enlightenment 'religion of reason', Marxism and to a certain extent Mignolo's 'decolonial option', which seeks to foreground indigenous and non-European narrativity as commensurate with the Western fable of its 'civilizing mission'. We are loathe, yet compelled, to admit that neoliberalism has its own distinctive universalised narrative, founded on but aggrandised well beyond the modern liberal construct of the atomic, reflexive self as pursuing its own existential teleology in the quest to fulfil the sum of all private desires and the unlimited expansion of its own self-valuation. It is perhaps the 'immanent' kingdom of God on earth as a timeless shopping mall where buyers and sellers revise and register the centuries-old protocols of human life as an emporium of exchange, as a cradle-to-grave amphitheatre of production and consumption and investment wagering with the collective aim of achieving advantage for a fleeing moment over others. Such a grim optics of neoliberalism is all the while founded on a curious but inescapable morality of 'responsibilism', where '"social responsibility", which must itself be entrepreneurialised, is part of what attracts consumers and investors'.[4] It is the diametric opposite of Kant's proverbial 'unsocial sociability'. It amounts to a worldwide *social unsociability*, the great, rough beast slouching towards the new Jerusalem of secular ethics in the disguise of identity politics in order to be born.

Any kind of global civilisation, no matter how fervently fancied *sub coelum*, remains hallucinatory if deprived of the leaven of a *universal solidarism* integral to it. Such a solidarism must be strongest at its very marrow, that is at the rudimentary level of human relationality and reciprocity. Most often the kinds of grass-roots convictions which motivate people over time to dedicate their lives to realising such a universal solidarism are not the result so much of philosophical arguments, or strategies of political persuasion, as the outgrowth of an 'event'. This event somehow finds its own experiential confirmation, or reduplication, among its followers. That is certainly the case with the great religious narratives of Western monotheism, whether we have in mind the story of Moses's confrontation with Yahweh on the mountain in Midian and his subsequent supernatural contest with Pharaoh over the status of the *habiru* slaves in Egypt, Mohammed's encounter with the angel Gabriel in the cave outside Mecca, or the eyewitness testimonies of Jesus's disciples after that fateful Sunday morning when they claimed to have come face to face with 'the risen Lord'. As Alain Badiou makes clear in his important and highly influential interpretation of Saint Paul's theology as the 'foundation of universalism', it is only the 'fidelity' of the emergent historical subject to the unprecedented and disruptive truth of *l'eventement* that can genuinely ground the meaning of the solidaristic narrative in the first place. Badiou writes that 'either one participates in it, declaring the founding event and drawing its consequences, or one remains foreign to it'.[5] The solidarism of the 'Christian' event of resurrection, so far as Paul is concerned, not only entails the declaration that all who have accepted the saving power of Christ Jesus now share, or 'participate', in the universal aspects of the *communion sanctorum*, but that the end of history itself is to realise this solidarity when at the *eschaton* 'there is no Gentile or Jew, circumcised or uncircumcised, barbarian, Scythian, slave or free, but Christ is all, and is in all'.[6] For Badiou, such an eschatology can be as secular as it is 'religious' (even though its origin depends on what he calls the 'fable' of the Resurrection), inasmuch as 'evental' principles follow upon their own *mathesis universalis* which he claims to have discovered in set theory.

Badiou, of course, maintains that the implicit 'theory of the subject' as correlated with the genesis of the event, a reading which is supposed to elucidate Paul's interpretation of the Road to Damascus experience, applies not only to religion but to 'godless' accounts of human emancipation and solidaristic apologues for the glorious future, especially revolutionary Marxism. Such apologues draw their inspiration from a certain rendering of the past as well as the hereafter – and the *hereinafter*. In any case, they constitute a radical critique, if merely an implicit one, of the present order. The problem with these apologues under neoliberalism is that they have been relegated to the realm of either the antiquarian or the inconsequential. To confess that today we are now freed from the 'wages of sin' because Christ triumphally overcame death on the Cross, although repeated liturgically by Christians the world over, means very little these days to the debt slaves of neo-colonial hegemony in the Global South and among the affluent bohemian bourgeoise of the urban mega-centres for the neoliberal economy.

Paul's formula was always predicated on a certain cosmicisation of the imperial political and military power that held his world in seemingly irreversible thrall. The 'principalities and powers' of his day could be visualised as earthly as well as celestial mirror representations of one another. The same applies to the now fading secular *mythologem* of the 'withering away of the state' and the coming of the worker's paradise, especially when workers are no longer the 'universal class'. If there is a universal class these days, it is the machine.

What summons us now on the historical threshold of what is often called the 'transhuman' is the epochal – dare we even use the expression 'eschatological' – manifestation of what human history has always been about in the first place; namely, the culmination of the Anthropocene in a portentous, truly 'damascene' flash of recognition. That is perhaps what Nietzsche himself – the fierce critic *avant la lettre* of the neoliberal condition – had in mind with his parable of the *Übermensch*. Neoliberalism with its ever more finely granularised political 'inclusivity' mimics and mocks the transformative power of this new kind of universal community, and perhaps even 'apocalyptic' solidarity.

Levinas and 'Responsible' Solidarism

To envision what lies beyond neoliberalism we must reach across the conventions of academic and religious thought to that most seemingly *unpolitical* thinker, the Jewish philosopher Emmanuel Levinas. For, after all, it is an epochal re-enactment of the original call by God to Abraham, the sometimes-imperceptible summons among the storied *habiru* by the infinite god out of the timeless tribalism of the *multitudo hominem*, that defines what we mean by this 'eschatological' event at which we find ourselves today gathered along its thin perimeter. This event has little to do with the crisis over the occupation of land in the Middle East. It has everything to do with how we are finally going to comprehend and attest to what has been dormant within the Anthropocene all along, what it means truly to be human. A radical new solidarism, an increasing densification of *communitas*, must rest on a radical revision of the very ontology that has blinded the political mind since the Greeks. The neoliberal theory of computational inclusivity can be traced all the way back to Plato's own paradigm of the *politeia*, which he describes in Book II of *The Republic*.[7] For Plato, 'politics' is always founded on the growth and diversification of the 'city' (*polis*), whose 'health' demands that it must 'always be gorged with a bulky mass of things'.[8] That rule is even more applicable for the neoliberal *cosmopolis*. The computational model, which Plato as the patriarch of the Western *episteme* inscribed two and a half millennia ago, has reached its outer limits in a world that is beginning to look more (spiritually, if not physically) like the Los Angeles of *Bladerunner* than Augustine's *De Civitate Dei*. It is founded ultimately on the Hellenic epistemology of *ta onta*, the 'mass of things'.

Yet, as Levinas argues throughout his many writings, the dialectic of being and non-being that constitutes the logical connectivity involved in the act of predication is wholly inadequate for the encounter between mutually facing subjectivities. There is what Levinas calls a 'diachrony' in such encounters, and if one tries to cognise it the language of ontology falters decisively. This diachrony is 'more than a term of negative theology'. It has nothing to do with 'being' but is 'otherwise than being'. It is not a moment of *l'autre*, but of *l'autrement*. In a word, it amounts to 'my responsibility for others'.[9] Levinasian responsibility, therefore, radically outstrips any kind of neoliberal 'responsibilism'. Furthermore, it can only be a 'politics of recognition' to the extent that there is a radical, intersubjective *re-cognising* that goes on in the moment of *responsivity*. What would all this mean for the challenge of community in the present age?

It is not our business to carefully explore Levinas's phenomenology of the other to drive home our objective. The particulars of Levinas's 'ethics' of the other are quite familiar to many philosophers. But what is not so evident is a possible 'eschatological solution', a veritable *parousia* of politics, that emanates from this well-known Levinasian approach to the enigma of alterity. Levinas characterises this solution – indeed, he employs the term *eschatology* itself – in the preface to *Totality and Infinity*. For Levinas, the history of Being is a history of 'war', what Heraclitus termed πόλεμος as 'common to all'. All 'thought' in that sense is the upshot of the clash among dialectical opposites. 'The visage of being that shows itself in war is fixed in the concept of totality, which dominates Western philosophy.'[10]

Philosophical thought, in particular (what Heidegger dubs the *Gestell*, or 'frame' of 'calculative' or 'representational' rationality that dominates the schematics of the Western mindscape), puts us on such a constant 'war' footing. It projects itself as a 'politics' that reaches far beyond the regional *logos* that indigenises the commonality of the community, the speech of the immediate *polis*. Such an expansive – dare we say 'imperial' – politics is inherent in the metaphysics of the Western world itself. It comes down to the insatiable thirst to 'know' all (what Nietzsche ironically characterised as the 'will to truth') and to control all (after all, did not Francis Bacon say 'knowledge is power') that encompasses the boundless battlefield on which the warring contrarieties within the field of being itself, fragments that we identify as *ta onta*, are in interminable play against each other. This expansion designates the 'end' of all theology and philosophy, and it all comes to be 'gathered', as Heidegger might say, in a *cosmopolitics* constituting the horizon of neoliberalism per se, one that solidifies a hegemony not only of the production of things but also of the production of how we *think through the meaning of things*, including ourselves.

At the same time, the metaphysics of Being as the true 'state of nature', as the war of all against all, and its concomitant neoliberal logic of proliferation, differentiation and totalisation under the name of 'inclusion', opens up a possibility of thinking beyond such a cosmopolitics. This way of thinking can be conceived to the extent that community itself can be re-envisioned as an aggregation of *interpenetrating mutual subjectivities*. Here we have, as Levinas calls it, an 'eschatological vision' that 'breaks with the totality of wars and empires in which one does not speak'.[11] It is an *eschatology of the totally responsible other*, which can never amount to an intelligible politics, but which grounds the very communitarian ethos that makes any sustainable global politics possible in the first place. If politics by Levinas's reckoning boils down to a play of 'existents' (*étants*) across the combat zone of history, then 'eschatology' itself has to do with the emergence of the 'human' existent 'that can speak rather than lending their lips to an anonymous utterance of history'.[12] For, as Levinas declares, 'the eschatological vision breaks with the totality of wars and empires in which one does not speak. It does not envisage the end of history within being understood as a totality, but institutes a relation with the infinity of being which exceeds the totality.'[13] The end of history is the beginning of the divine kingdom. Such an excess of history is the resolution of politics overall as a universal community of reciprocal recognition, a *re-cognition* of the infinite claim on us and a call to responsibility in the face of the other, one which utterly confounds our inclination to persist as 'entrepreneurs of the self'. Rather, we are summoned to become *entrée points* for the revelation of the other as the fullness of history as a whole.

Rethinking the 'End of History'

One might easily object that this vision of an 'end of history', once scrutinised for its consequences and constituent factors, is as utopian as the neoliberal imaginary concocted by Fukuyama. But it is also incumbent on us to consider what this means in a much larger sense. Fukuyama's proclamation was utopian because it advocated for an 'eschatology' (i.e. a panorama of the 'end times') that idealised present conditions and made disastrous inferences about what might be in store down the road. It mistakenly supposed that democracy and capitalism are somehow intimately entwined with each other with a naïve nod, scanting the long-established historical record, to the 'moral' priorities of the latter. It did not anticipate how the new hegemony of a global 'communicative capitalism' would undo the demos, rather than nurturing it. When we come to the Levinasian 'responsibility to the other', in contrast with neoliberal *responsibilism* as a veiled ethic of peonage and exploitation, we are not projecting a new political order per se, nor are we sanctifying in any way the present one. We are calling for a new ethical frame of perception and reasoning that undergirds any theory of politics as a whole.

We may, therefore, hark back to the ancient formulations of Aristotle that ethics and politics cannot be separated from each other, insofar as they are both forms of 'practical wisdom' (φρόνησῐς). They are immanent reflections on how one can, and does, achieve 'happiness' (ευδαιμονία) as the goal of human existence. Aristotle, as is well known, stressed 'virtue' (αρετή) as the key to both ethics and politics, though he did assume that a certain mastery of the technology of power over other human beings was instrumental in achieving political aims. The persistence of the Aristotelean connection between ethics and politics has continued into the modern era. One often underemphasised feature in both Aristotle's *Politics* and the *Nichomachean*

Ethics is the role of *logos*, or speech. For Aristotle, the human being is a *zoon politikon*, but one is only 'political' because they are primarily a *zoon logistikon*. It is the question of how one deploys the feature of *logos* that, at least from the classical perspective, constitutes the 'political'.

In ancient Athens *logos* among its public practitioners was distinguished by the art of political persuasion. In Socrates's time the Sophists tended to construe such an art, or *techne*, as the manipulation of language and its extensions for the sake of what Foucault would later term 'power/knowledge'. Socrates and his disciple Plato sought to reconstitute language as the 'science' (*dianoia*) of 'entities' (*ta onta*) rather than as the play of 'signs' (*ta semeia*). Out of this early 'ontological turn', which was in fact an effort to anchor politics for the first time in a theory of 'the good' (*to kalon*), philosophy was birthed. Aristotelean philosophy emends Platonic thought by redesigning ontology as *teleology*, distinguishing between a theoretical and a practical application of *logos* that identifies the 'end' of human existence as what Thomas Jefferson would later dub the 'pursuit of happiness'.

But what if *logos* were in fact understood essentially as *interpersonal*, which both anthropologically and neurologically has always been its genetic function? What if *logos* were quintessentially 'dialogical', and what if its semantic variability and peculiarities were for the most part derived from these initial conditions of human speech itself? What if the human being at bottom turned out to be *zoon dialogistikon*? How would that impact the political, especially in a post-neoliberal world order?

Both utopian and insurrectionary political movements have historically been fired by a sense of what Derrida terms a 'justice to come', a still inchoate possibility of a fullness to human flourishing that cannot be captured in the representational order of the present. That is why Derrida calls such justice 'undeconstructible'.[14] But its 'undeconstructibility' implies that by its very nature it must remain what Hegel called an 'abstract universal'. Its concretion requires the passage of time and the indeterminability of historical events. The structure of political representation for justice to be instantiated in any given order of the day demands a limiting of its infinite and open potentiality for the sake of day-to-day 'governmentality'. Thus, to the degree that such a representation of justice remains abstract rather than concrete, as Hegel points out in *The Phenomenology of Spirit*, it is always on the brink of transmittal as an agency of terror. Totalitarianism is not the raw product of confused minds, but the finished commodity of those who have before them what is clearly and distinctly a political *mathesis universalis*, which only with

Procrustean ingenuity can they adjust to the roiling contingencies of human history. No representational system for any concrete *politeia* can long withstand the ravages of social 'climate change'. Political representational systems themselves, henceforth, are at the mercy of what Lacan refers to as the 'desire of the other'. For political desire is forever predicated on the alterity of any such a *desideratum*. In consequence, there is no real politics – let alone any authentic *communitas* – without this 'regard', which prefigures responsibility according to Levinas, for the 'other'.

Beyond the Neoliberal Imperium

Neoliberalism has been to the postmodern world what the *imperium Romanum* was to the classical one. It has nominally fostered what might be designated as the first true world civilisation, albeit through a flood of finance capital rather than force of arms. Like the very idea of *Romanitas*, its new system of transnational order has been both welcomed and reviled on different occasions. Especially through digital communications and cross-cultural marketing, encapsulated in what Derrida in the early 1990s called its 'tele-technic' reach across borders, the 'globo-latinised' neoliberal *imperium* has raised standards of living in previously economic backwaters of the world. But, even more conspicuously, it succeeded in hollowing out long-enduring architectures of social solidarity and mutual assistance and the mass destruction of entire political regimes from what too often pretended to be 'humanitarian' military interventions to establish or restore 'democracy'.[15] We know from history that when Roman hegemony unravelled after the early fifth century, few actually celebrated its demise. No longer resentful of its brutality, they yearned for some kind of restoration of the *pax Romana* in the wake of the prolonged social and political chaos, and the bloody struggle for dominion among regional and tribal warlords that lasted for the next half-millennium.

A similar ambivalence today leaves its stamp on those whose economic status or 'moral compass' have been impacted by neoliberalism. Increasingly, both free trade and unrestricted capital flows are 'wired into' a seamless worldwide economic system that simultaneously supports extremes of wealth inequality while keeping a jackboot on the market for labour. That is why repeated attempts to 'disrupt' the system through what in the past were strategies of worker protection (the imposing of tariffs and laws protecting unionisation) often fail, as do 'socialist' policies of improving the 'safety net' or expanding economic entitlements. The openness of global networks of production, exchange and labour mobility favour oligarchy rather than democracy. Effective democracies, at least of the economic kind that seriously consider the rights of the proverbial '99 per cent', depend on closed systems with not entirely heterogeneous populations. The rise and fall of European 'welfare states' is a strong case in point. Democracy and a modicum of autarky are inseparable from each other.

Strangely, however, the key to any kind of effective 'resistance' to neoliberalism in a global setting depends on what on the surface seems like the embrace of contradictory political ends – the preservation of the sovereign nation-state with its capacity to enforce more egalitarian patterns of distributive justice and a rejection of the kind of identity politics that have been exploited both for neoliberal 'responsibilist' agendas and ethno-nationalist forms of populism that favour the subjugation and exclusion of cultural and racial minorities. If one studies carefully the social history of the late Roman Empire and its demographic makeup after its collapse, one discerns that the centrifugal momentum of ethnic heterogeneity, in which the religious heterogeneity, or *polyarchy* (as Eusebius called it), of imperial paganism was profoundly embedded, was in the long run overcome by the centripetal and unifying forces of the kind of religious universalism emblazoned in triumphalist Christianity. It is a cliché that European civilisation could not have arisen without the idea of 'Christendom', but what made Christianity so powerful was not any inherent pretence to political pre-eminence, but the opposite – i.e. what Jesus called a 'kingdom not of this world'. Medieval Christendom did, of course, function as a worldly kingdom, but it was its *transpolitical* and 'personalistic' spirituality of the dignity and uniqueness before God of every human being that propelled it beyond a barbarian backwater, particularly from the Reformation of the sixteenth century onwards.

The spiritual principle of radical responsibility to the other, which a figure such as Levinas draws out of the Hebraic tradition harking back millennia, means in reality that any 'political' solution to global challenges must bend back upon itself to the historic 'deep theology', or a *deep ethics*, of the West itself that ultimately contravenes and overrides the ethnic identity and history of the West as a whole. That amounts to the realisation that 'God' is, and *can be seen, at all times in the face of the other*, no matter how 'other' to myself the other may appear, relatively speaking, that we are all 'Christs to each other', as Luther put it, which transcends anything we yet know or understand by 'Christianity'. Etymologically, 'Christ' simply means the divine incarnate, ὁ λόγος σὰρξ ἐγένετο. That is where politics must start, defying all 'political solutions' based on abstract, moralistic mandates that recognise true 'identity in difference', which is the same as the revelation of the divine as Wholly Other in every other.

Let us call it the *Great Personalistic Insurrection* of every human tribe and tongue against neoliberalism. It is the revolution that does not 'represent' but *presents* the 'holiest of holies' at every turn in what we once knew merely as the 'marketplace'. It is the revolution *soon to come*.

Notes

Introduction

1. For a comprehensive history of the evolution of neoliberal economic thinking, see Philip Mirowski and Dieter Plehwe, *The Road from Mont Pelerin: The Making of Neoliberal Thought* (Cambridge, MA: Harvard University Press, 2015).

2. Wendy Brown, *Undoing the Demos: Neoliberalism's Stealth Revolution* (New York: Zone Books, 2015).

3. For a careful examination of how Foucault has deployed the words in his own writings and the difficulties with precise translation, see Jeffrey Bussolini, 'What is a Dispositive', *Foucault Studies* (November 2010): 85–107. See also Gregg Lambert, 'What is a Dispositif', *Religious Theory* (11 July 2016), http://jcrt.org/religioustheory/2016/07/11/what-is-a-dispositif-part-1/ (accessed 2 July 2018).

4. Carl Raschke, *Force of God: Political Theology and the Crisis of Liberal Democracy* (New York: Columbia University Press, 2015).

5. See Friedrich Nietzsche, *A Genealogy of Morals*, trans. John Gray (New York: The Macmillan Company, 1897). Original edition: *Zur Genealogie der Moral: Eine Streitschrift* (Leipzig: C. G. Naumann, 1887).

6. Karl Marx and Friedrich Engels, *The German Ideology* (New York: International Publishers, 1972), 64.

7. It should be noted that the classic Marxist concept of 'capitalism', although rhetorically deployed routinely on the left these days, is in the mind of certain forward-looking theorists becoming somewhat obsolete. A recent attempt to change the terms of the discussion comes from American sociologist Fred Block, who argues that the Mont Pelerin 'neoliberals' idealised the term

'capitalism' in an unprecedented manner and invented the term 'free markets' to resist totalitarian encroachments from both Stalinism and fascism. Much of the debate about capitalism in recent years, therefore, has been essentially a moral, not an economic, one. See his *Capitalism: The Future of an Illusion* (Berkeley: University of California Press, 2018). In an interview with the magazine *Dissent*, Block maintains that he prefers the word 'market fundamentalism' to 'capitalism' when talking about the equivalent to 'neoliberalism'. See Timothy Shenk, 'Booked: The End of an Illusion', *Dissent* (19 July 2018), https://www.dissentmagazine.org/online_articles/booked-interview-fred-block-capitalism-end-of-an-illusion (accessed 20 July 2018).

8. See Adam Kotsko, *Neoliberalism's Demons: On the Political Theology of Late Capital* (Stanford: Stanford University Press, 2018).

9. Mitchell Dean and Kaspar Villadsen, *State Phobia: The Political Legacy of Michel Foucault* (Stanford: Stanford University Press, 2016).

10. See Abdulaziz Sachedina, *The Islamic Roots of Democratic Pluralism* (New York: Oxford University Press, 2001).

11. See, for example, Sungmoon Kim, *Confucian Democracy in East Asia* (Cambridge: Cambridge University Press, 2014) as well as Lin Gang, *China's Long Quest for Democracy* (New York: Palgrave Macmillan, 2016).

12. Daniel Zamora and Michael Behrent, *Foucault and Neoliberalism* (Hoboken, NJ: John Wiley & Sons, 2016). Kindle Edition, loc. 4654–6.

Chapter 1

1. See Winfried Nöth, 'Crisis of Representation?', *Semiotica* 2003: 9–15.

2. Among many texts, see, for instance, Talal Asad, 'Redeeming the "Human" Through Human Rights', in *Formations of the Secular: Christianity, Islam, Modernity*, Cultural Memory in the Present series (Stanford: Stanford University Press, 2003); Saba Mahmood, *Religious Difference in a Secular Age: A Minority Report* (Princeton: Princeton University Press, 2016); and Edward W. Said, *Orientalism* (New York: Vintage Books, 1979).

3. Michel Foucault, *The Archaeology of Knowledge and the Discourse on Language* (New York: Vintage Books, 1982).

4. Michel Foucault, *Madness and Civilisation: A History of Insanity in the Age of Reason* (New York: Vintage Books, 1965, 1988).

5. See Joshua Ramos, 'Flashback—What is the Alt Right?', *Political Theology Today*, https://politicaltheology.com/flashback-what-is-the-alt-right-joshua-ramos/ (accessed 1 August 2017).

6. James Traub, 'It's Time for the Elites to Rise Up Against the Ignorant Masses', *Foreign Policy*, http://foreignpolicy.com/2016/06/28/its-time-for-the-elites-to-rise-up-against-ignorant-masses-trump-2016-brexit/ (accessed 8 July 2016).

7. See Michael Lerner, *The Politics of Meaning: Restoring Hope and Possibility in an Age of Cynicism* (Reading, MA: Addison-Wesley, 1996).

8. Michel Foucault, *History of Sexuality* I, trans. Robert Hurley (New York: Random House, 1980), 137.

9. See Georg Wilhelm Friedrich Hegel, *Phenomenology of Spirit*, trans. Arnold V. Miller and J. N. Findlay, Oxford Paperbacks (Oxford: Clarendon Press, 1977).

10. Michel Foucault, *Security, Territory, Population: Lectures at the Collège de France 1977–1978* (New York: Picador, 2009), 149.

11. See Richard Florida, *Rise of the Creative Class* (Topeka, KS: Tandem Library, 2003).

12. Maurizio Lazzarato, *Governing By Debt*, trans. Joshua D. Jordan (New York: Semiotext(e), 2015), 66.

13. David H. Freedman, 'The War on Stupid People', *The Atlantic*, https://www.theatlantic.com/magazine/archive/2016/07/the-war-on-stupid-people/485618/ (accessed 13 August 2016).

14. Maurizio Lazzarato, *The Making of Indebted Man*, trans. Joshua D. Jordan (New York: Semiotext(e), 2012), 38.

15. See Daniel Bell, *The Cultural Contradictions of Capitalism* (New York: Basic Books, 1976).

16. See David Harvey, *A Brief History of Neoliberalism* (New York: Oxford University Press, 2007).

17. Lazzarato, *The Making of Indebted Man*, op. cit., 158.

18. See '7000 B.C.: Apparatus of Capture', in Gilles Deleuze and Félix Guattari, *A Thousand Plateaus: Capitalism and Schizophrenia* (Minneapolis: University of Minnesota Press, 1987).

19. Harvey, op. cit., 40.

20. Op. cit., 41.

21. Lazzarato, *The Making of Indebted Man*, op. cit., 159.

22. Lazzarato, *Governing By Debt*, op. cit., 56–7.

23. Op. cit., 64.

24. Op. cit., 65.

25. Op. cit., 69.

26. See, for example, Narindar Singh's penetrating article 'Keynes and Hitler', *Economic and Political Weekly* 29(42) (15 October 1994), http://www.jstor.org/stable/4401913?seq=1#page_scan_tab_contents (accessed 12 September 2016).

27. Lazzarato, *Governing By Debt*, op. cit., 94.

28. Op. cit., 95. Neoliberalism from the outset wanted to govern as much as possible with the goal of making it appear that the minimalist facade of the liberal state remained somehow intact. Anti-statism, or what Dean and Villadsen have termed 'state phobia', was always more of a rhetoric than a policy. One could make the case that the fiction of *laissez-faire* liberalism in Britain throughout the nineteenth century contradicted the reality on the ground. Prior to around 1840 Britain's unprecedented industrial growth was due more to its favourable geography and its dominance over sea lanes, making it a formidable merchant power. Its traditions of common law and defence of popular freedoms, running all the way back to Anglo-Saxon days, together with its uncontested Protestant habits of enterprise, supported its competitive advantage in relation to other European powers. It was these advantages that inclined the British to resist throughout the seventeenth and eighteenth centuries the concentration of economic provision in the hands of monarchs and to inspire Adam Smith to launch his famous attack on mercantilism. Yet, as some scholars have shown, Britain's early nineteenth-century engine of economic productivity soon required overseas imperial expansion, which it did not necessarily undertake with enthusiasm. The acquisition of empire actually pushed the regime to abandon *laissez-faire* principles in favour of more interventionist methods, not only abroad but domestically. See, for example, E. H. H. Green, 'The Political Economy of Empire, 1880–1914', in Andrew Porter (ed.), *The Oxford History of the British Empire*, vol. 3 (Oxford: Oxford University Press, 1999).

29. Maurizio Lazzarato, *Signs and Machines*, trans. Joshua D. Jordan (New York: Semiotext(e), 2014), 38.

30. Lazzarato, *Governing By Debt*, op. cit., 95.

31. Carl Schmitt, *The Nomos of the Earth in the International Law of Jus Publicum Europaeum*, trans. G. L. Ulmen (Shortlands: Telos Publishing, 2006), 79.

32. Ibid. 354–5.

33. See Kurt Appel, *Preis der Sterblichkeit: Christentum und Neuer Humanismus* (Freiburg im Breisgau, Germany: Herder, 2015).

Chapter 2

1. Nancy Fraser, 'The End of Progressive Neoliberalism', *Dissent* (2 January 2017), https://www.dissentmagazine.org/online_articles/progressive-neoliberalism-reactionary-populism-nancy-fraser (accessed 10 March 2017). See also Nancy Fraser and Rachel Jaeggi, *Capitalism: A Conversation in Critical Theory* (Medford, MA: Polity, 2018).

2. Johanna Brenner, 'There Was No Such Thing As "Progressive Neoliberalism"', *Dissent* (14 January 2017), https://www.dissentmagazine.org/online_articles/nancy-fraser-progressive-neoliberalism-social-movements-response (accessed 10 March 2017).

3. See Antonio Gramsci, *Prison Notebooks*, ed. Joseph Buttigieg (New York: Columbia University Press, 1992), 7–10. For some good secondary studies, see Walter Adamson, *Hegemony and Revolution: A Study of Antonio Gramsci's Political and Cultural Theory* (Berkeley: University of California Press, 1983) and Peter D. Thomas, *The Gramscian Moment: Philosophy, Hegemony, and Marxism* (Leiden: Brill Publishers, 2009).

4. Nancy Fraser, 'Against Progressive Neoliberalism: A New Progressive Populism', *Dissent* (28 January 2017), https://www.dissentmagazine.org/online_articles/nancy-fraser-against-progressive-neoliberalism-progressive-populism (accessed 10 March 2017). See also David Graeber's observation more recently that 'to a large extent, our societies have come to be held together by envy and resentment: not envy of the rich, but in many cases, envy of those who are seen as in some ways morally superior, or resentment of those who claim moral superiority but who are seen as hypocritical.' See 'Bullshit Jobs and the Yoke of Managerial Feudalism', *The Economist* (29 June 2018), https://www.economist.com/open-future/2018/06/29/bullshit-jobs-and-the-yoke-of-managerial-feudalism (accessed 29 June 2018).

5. See Charles H. Smith, 'Dear Self-Proclaimed "Progressives": As Apologists for the Neocon-Neoliberal Empire, You Are as Evil as the Empire You've Enabled', *Of Two Minds* (9 January 2017), http://charleshughsmith.blogspot.com/2017/01/dear-self-proclaimed-progressives-as.html (accessed 10 March 2017).

6. For a particularly apt take on the relationship between Marcuse's New Left radicalism and the neoliberal control society that emerged from it, see Bernard Stiegler's 'Disbelief and Discredit' trilogy, especially Bernard Stiegler, *The Lost Spirit of Capitalism*, trans. Daniel Ross (Cambridge: Polity, 2014).

7. Joshua Ramey, *Politics of Divination: Neoliberal Endgame and the Religion of Contingency* (Lanham, MD: Rowman & Littlefield International, 2016). Kindle Edition, loc. 60–3.

8. See specifically Thomas Piketty, *Capital in the Twenty-First Century*, trans. Arthur Goldhammer (Cambridge, MA: Belknap Press, 2014).

9. Mark Lilla, *The Stillborn God: Religion, Politics, and the Modern West* (New York: Vintage Books, 2007), 7–8.

10. Friedrich Nietzsche, *The Will to Power*, trans. Walter Kaufmann (New York: Vintage Books, 1967), 3.

11. Ibid. 4.
12. Immanuel Kant, *Grounding for the Metaphysics of Morals*, trans. James W. Ellington, 3rd edn (Indianapolis: Hackett Publishing, 1993), 30.
13. Nietzsche, *The Will to Power*, 9.
14. Ibid. 11.
15. Friedrich Nietzsche, *Beyond Good and Evil: Prelude to a Philosophy of the Future*, trans. Walter Kaufmann (New York: Vintage Books, 1989), 2.
16. Nietzsche, *The Will to Power*, 13.
17. See Gilles Deleuze, *Difference and Repetition*, trans. Paul Patton (New York: Continuum, 2004).
18. This general argument can be found in chapter 5 of Aristotle's *Categories*. See Aristotle, *The Categories, On Interpretation, Prior Analytics*, trans. Harold P. Cook and Hugh Treddenick (Cambridge, MA: Harvard University Press, 1957).
19. See Benjamin Whorf, *Language, Thought, and Reality* (Cambridge, MA: The MIT Press, 1976). For a study of the so-called 'Sapir-Whorf hypothesis' and its status in current linguistics, see Renate Giesbrecht, *The Sapir-Whorf Hypothesis* (Munich: Grinn Publishing, 2009). See also Julia M. Penn, *Linguistic Relativity Versus Innate Ideas: The Origins of the Sapir-Whorf Hypothesis in German Thought* (Berlin: Walter de Gruyter, 2014).
20. Nietzsche, *The Will to Power*, 19.
21. Ibid. 27.
22. Ibid. 46.
23. Ibid. 75.
24. Ibid. 20.
25. Wendy Brown, *Undoing the Demos: Neoliberalism's Stealth Revolution* (New York: Zone Books, 2015), 95.
26. Francis Fukuyama, *The End of History and the Last Man* (New York: Free Press, 2006).
27. Brown, op. cit., 211.
28. Ibid. 215.
29. Ibid. 217.
30. See Karl Polanyi, *The Great Transformation: The Political and Economic Origins of Our Time* (Boston, MA: Beacon Press, 2001).
31. Kwame Appiah, *Cosmopolitanism: Ethics in a World of Strangers* (New York: Norton, 2010), xv. See also Appiah's definition of cosmopolitanism as 'universal concern plus difference'. Whitney Johnson, 'A Conversation with Kwame Appiah', http://mandala.uga.edu/cosmo/convo-kwame-cosmo.php (accessed 1 July 2018).

32. Lilie Chouliaraki, *The Ironic Spectator: Solidarity in the Age of Post-Humanitarianism* (Hoboken, NJ: Wiley, 2013), 213.

33. See Jodi Dean, 'Neoliberalism's Defeat of Democracy', *Critical Inquiry* (2015), https://criticalinquiry.uchicago.edu/neoliberalisms_defeat_of_democracy/ (accessed 17 June 2018). See also Joshua Ramey, 'Neoliberalism as a Political Theology of Chance: The Politics of Divination', *Palgrave Communications* (November 2015): 1–9, https://www.nature.com/articles/palcomms201539.pdf (accessed 5 June 2018).

34. Ernesto Laclau, *On Populist Reason* (New York: Verso, 2005), 83.

35. The distinction can be found in an essay by Claude Lefort. See his 'The Permanence of the Theo-Political?', in Hent de Vries (ed.), *Political Theologies: Public Religions in a Postsecular World* (New York: Fordham University Press, 2006), 148–87.

36. Laclau, op. cit., 97.

37. Ibid. 117.

38. Ibid. 153.

39. Ibid. 224.

40. Michael Kazin in his classic study of the history of populism contends that this sort of distinction is the only thing that marks populism in its various instantiations from the nineteenth century onwards. See *The Populist Persuasion: An American History* (New York: Basic Books, 1995). The slipperiness of the notion, combined with the recent transformation of its means of dissemination through digital communications, has led Benjamin Moffitt to claim more recently that populism is not at all a species of political movements, nor a strategy of political mobilisation, but a 'style of performance' that has ingeniously adapted itself to the age of social media. See *The Global Rise of Populism: Performance, Political Style, and Representation* (Stanford: Stanford University Press, 2016).

41. Jan-Werner Müller, *What is Populism?* (Philadelphia: University of Pennsylvania Press, 2016), 49.

42. Ibid. 48.

43. 'Cas Mudde and Cristóbal Rovira Kaltwasser', *Populism: A Very Short Introduction* (Oxford: Oxford University Press, 2017), 47.

44. Eduardo Bonilla-Silva, *Racism Without Racists: Colour-Blind Racism and the Persistence of Racial Inequality in America* (Lanham, MD: Rowman & Littlefield, 2014), 193.

45. Ibid. 192.

Chapter 3

1. Giorgio Agamben, *The Kingdom and the Glory: For a Theological Genealogy of Economy and Government*, trans. Lorenzo Chiesa and Matteo Mandarini (Stanford: Stanford University Press, 2011). Kindle Edition, loc. 113–19. See also my own article, 'Forget Schmitt! Political Theology Must Follow Agamben's "Double Paradigm" of Sovereignty', *Political Theology* 19(1): 1–3.
2. Plato, *Republic*, 331(e).
3. See Michel Foucault, *Power/Knowledge: Selected Interviews and Other Writings* (New York: Vintage, 1980).
4. Agamben, op. cit., 150–6.
5. See James B. Rives, *Religion in the Roman Empire* (Hoboken, NJ: Wiley-Blackwell, 2006), as well as Andrew Cain, *The Power of Religion in Late Antiquity* (New York: Routledge, 2009).
6. Jackson J. Lashier, however, in his close reading of Irenaeus's works suggests that Irenaeus was not the first to articulate an 'economic' model, but that he drew on various threads of commentary from an earlier generation of Christian apologists. See Lashier, 'The Trinitarian Theology of Irenaeus of Lyons', unpublished doctoral dissertation, Marquette University, May 2011.
7. Agamben, op. cit., 3917.
8. Ibid. 4316.
9. Ibid. 4385.
10. Karl Marx, *Capital*, Book 1, 6.
11. Ibid. 11.
12. Lazzarato writes: 'The "great transformation" that began at the start of the 1970s has changed the very terms in which the question is posed. Manual labour is increasingly coming to involve procedures that could be defined as "intellectual," and the new communications technologies increasingly require subjectivities that are rich in knowledge. It is not simply that intellectual labour has become subjected to the norms of capitalist production. What has happened is that a new "mass intellectuality" has come into being, created out of a combination of the demands of capitalist production and the forms of "self -valorisation" that the struggle against work has produced. The old dichotomy between "mental and manual labour," or between "material labour and immaterial labour," risks failing to grasp the new nature of productive activity, which takes this separation on board and transforms it. The split between conception and execution, between labour and creativity, between author and audience, is simultaneously transcended within the "labour process" and reimposed as

political command within the "process of valorization".' Maurizio Lazzarato, 'Immaterial Labour', in Paolo Virno and Michael Hardt (eds), *Radical Thought in Italy: A Potential Politics* (Minneapolis: University of Minnesota Press, 2006), 133.

13. Jean-Joseph Goux, *Symbolic Economies: After Marx and Freud* (Ithaca: Columbia University Press, 1990), 163.

14. Wendy Brown, *Undoing the Demos: Neoliberalism's Stealth Revolution* (New York: Zone Books, 2015), 36–7.

15. Jean-Jacques Rosseau, *The Works of Jean-Jacques Rousseau: The Social Contract, Confessions, Emile, and Other Essays* (Baltimore: Common Knowledge Publishers, 2004). Kindle Edition, loc. 1592–6.

16. Agamben, op. cit., 5288–98.

17. Jürgen Habermas, *Between Facts and Norms: Contributions to a Discourse Theory of Law and Democracy*, trans. William Rehg (Cambridge, MA: The MIT Press, 1996), 170. See also Jeffrey Flynn, 'Communicative Power in Habermas' Theory of Democracy', *European Journal of Political Theory* 3(4): 434.

18. Habermas, op. cit., 8.

19. Agamben, op. cit., 5332.

20. Ibid.

21. Bernard Stiegler, *For A New Critique of Political Economy*, trans. David Ross (New York: Polity, 2010), 46. See also Stiegler's *What Makes Life Worth Living: On Pharmacology*, trans. Daniel Ross (Cambridge, MA: Polity Press, 2013).

22. Ibid. 47.

23. Ibid. 4.

24. Plato, *Phaedrus*, 275a.

25. Stiegler, op. cit., 61–2.

26. Brown, op. cit., 69.

27. Ibid. 177.

28. Emmett Rensin, 'The Blathering Superego at the End of History', *Los Angeles Review of Books*, https://lareviewofbooks.org/article/the-blathering-superego-at-the-end-of-history/# (accessed 19 June 2017).

29. The French word *bêtise*, which Stiegler strategically employs, can also be translated as 'brutishness', 'senselessness' or even 'foolishness', depending on the context. Stiegler wants to drive home that is a condition of the late modern era that does not call in an obvious sense for moral opprobrium but is a kind of fatuousness that can precipitate ghastly results, as implied in Hannah Arendt's celebrated expression 'the banality of evil'. Stiegler draws to a certain extent on Derrida's critique of Agamben in his final lecture series around the question of

'what lives?', where the totalitarian politics of 'bare life' profiled by Agamben in *Homo Sacer* is reimagined as the transformation of the politics of experience (*savoir vivre*) into an automatism of the abstracted subject, where 'living' (*vivant*) substance becomes an empty 'set with no other unity'. See Jacques Derrida, *The Beast and the Sovereign*, trans. Geoffrey Bennington, vol. II (Chicago: University of Chicago Press, 2011), 8.

30. Max Horkheimer and Theodor W. Adorno, *Dialectic of Enlightenment, Philosophical Fragments*, trans. Edmund Jephcott (Stanford: Stanford University Press, 2002), xiv.

31. Bernard Stiegler, *States of Shock: Stupidity and Knowledge in the 21st Century* (Hoboken, NJ: Wiley Blackwell, 2015). Kindle Edition, loc. 817–20.

32. Antonio Gramsci, *Further Selections from The Prison Notebooks* (Minneapolis: University of Minnesota Press, 2015). Kindle Edition, loc. 3822–3.

33. Antonio Gramsci, *Selections from The Prison Notebooks* (New York: International Publishers, 1992). Kindle Edition, loc. 10500–1).

34. 'Bernard Stiegler and the Economy of Contribution', by Mariannetranslates, https://mariannetranslates.wordpress.com/2013/01/04/bernard-Stiegler-and -the-economy-of-contribution/. Translation from the French of interview, 'Bernard Stiegler: "Les gens consomment plus parce qu'ils idéalisent de moins en moins"', http://www.fondation-macif.org/bernard-stiegler-les-gens -consomment-plus-parce-quils-idealisent-de-moins-en-moins (accessed 20 June 2017).

35. Herbert Marcuse, *One-Dimensional Man* (London: Sphere Books, 1968), 75.

Chapter 4

1. Pierre Bourdieu, 'The Utopia of Exploitation – The Essence of Neoliberalism', *Le Monde Diplomatique* (December 1998), trans. Jeremy J. Shapiro, http://www. homme-moderne.org/societe/socio/bourdieu/varia/essneoUK.html (accessed 9 July 2017). For a critique of Bourdieu's argument, see Sean Phelan, *Neoliberalism, Media, and the Political* (New York: Springer, 2014).

2. Hannah Arendt, *The Origins of Totalitarianism* (New York: Harcourt, Brace, Jovanovich, 1973), 311.

3. See Thomas H. Eriksen, *Globalisation: The Key Concepts* (New York: Bloomsbury Academic, 2014), esp. ch. 1.

4. Bourdieu, op. cit.

5. Ibid.

6. *CDC Vital Signs*, 7 June 2018. Atlanta: Centre for Disease Control.

7. Alain Badiou, *Being and Event*, trans. Oliver Feltham (New York: Continuum, 2005), 2.

8. Ibid. 393.

9. Wolfgang Streeck, *How Will Capitalism End? Essays on a Failing System* (New York: Verso Books, 2016). Kindle Edition, loc. 3532–3. See also Streeck's earlier work, *Buying Time: The Delayed Crisis of Democratic Capitalism* (New York: Verso, 2014).

10. Liaquat Ahamed, *Lords of Finance: The Bankers Who Broke the World* (New York: Penguin Press, 2009).

11. Streeck, *How Will Capitalism End?*, 1732–40.

12. Ibid. 1764–6.

13. Ibid. 1774–81.

14. Ibid. 1806–9.

15. Ibid. 1825–6.

16. Wolfgang Streeck, 'The Return of the Repressed as the End of Neoliberal Capitalism', in Heinrich Geiselberger (ed.), *The Great Regression* (New York: Polity Press, 2017), 162.

17. Ibid. Other research backs up the transformation of neoliberalism over recent decades from a pure economism denying the importance of moral relations to the use of what Adam Smith termed 'moral sympathies' to advance its agenda. See, for example, Andrea Muehlebach, *The Moral Neoliberal: Welfare and Citizenship in Italy* (Chicago: University of Chicago Press, 2012).

18. Streeck, 'The Return of the Repressed', 169.

19. Karl Marx and Friedrich Engels, *The German Ideology*, ed. C. J. Arthur (New York: International Publishers, 1970), 64.

20. Streeck, 'The Return of the Repressed', 170.

21. Streeck, *How Will Capitalism End?*, loc. 1335.

22. Nancy Fraser, 'The End of Progressive Neoliberalism', *Dissent* (2 January 2017), https://www.dissentmagazine.org/online_articles/progressive-neoliberalism-reactionary-populism-nancy-fraser (accessed 10 March 2017).

23. Oliver Nachtwey, 'Decivilization: On Regressive Tendencies in Western Society', trans. Rodney Livingstone, in Geiselberger, op. cit., 141.

24. Joseph Conrad, *Heart of Darkness* (New York: W. W. Norton, 1988), 141.

25. Achille Mbembe, *On the Postcolony*, trans. A. M. Berrett, Janet Roitman, Murray Last and Steven Rendall (Berkeley: University of California Press, 2001), 31.

26. Nancy Fraser, 'Progressive Neoliberalism versus Reactionary Populism', in Geiselberger, op. cit., 44.

27. Ibid. 46.
28. John Atkinson Hobson, *Imperialism: A Study* (Dublin, Ireland: Albion Press, 2015). Kindle Edition, loc. 3122.
29. Ibid. 3264–5.
30. Jodi Melamed, 'The Spirit of Neoliberalism: From Racial Liberalism to Neoliberal Multiculturalism', *Social Text 89* (2006): 16.
31. See Ashis Nandy, *The Intimate Enemy: Loss and Recovery of Self Under Colonialism* (Delhi: Oxford University Press, 2009), xi.
32. Daniel Bell, *The Cultural Contradictions of Capitalism* (New York: Basic Books, 1976), 3.
33. Karl Marx and Friedrich Engels, 'Manifesto of the Communist Party', in *The Portable Karl Marx*, trans. Eugene Kamenka (New York: Penguin, 1983), 207–8.
34. Bell, op. cit., 295.
35. In section 3 of his *Phenomenology of Spirit* Hegel employs the Newtonian notion of 'force' to explain how the contradictions of sense-perception, which sceptics had documented since antiquity, are resolved into a 'concept' expressed as identity-in-difference. 'Difference' is the key to dialectical reasoning, insofar as it is that which stabilises the 'play of appearances'. But force is not something inherent in things but the result of the expansion of self-consciousness in its effort to make sense out of what it immediately perceives. 'Force is . . . this universal medium for the subsistence of the moments as differentiated elements; or, in other words, it *has* expressed or externalized itself, and what was to be something outside it attracting or inciting it is really force itself.' G. W. F. Hegel, *The Phenomenology of Mind*, trans. J. B. Baile (New York: Harper & Row, 1967), 185.
36. See Sigmund Freud, *Beyond the Pleasure Principle*, trans. James Strachey (New York: W. W. Norton, 1961), 38.
37. Freud wrote in *Civilization and its Discontents*: 'At one point in the course of this enquiry I was led to the idea that civilization was a special process which mankind undergoes, and I am still under the influence of that idea. I may now add that civilization is a process in the service of Eros, whose purpose is to combine single human individuals, and after that families, then races, peoples and nations, into one great unity, the unity of mankind. Why this has to happen, we do not know; the work of Eros is precisely this. These collections of men are to be libidinally bound to one another. Necessity alone, advantages of work in common, will not hold them together. But man's natural aggressive instinct, the hostility of each against all and of all against each, opposes this programme of civilization. This aggressive instinct is the derivative and, the main

representative of the death instinct which we have found alongside of Eros and which shares world-dominion with it.' Sigmund Freud, *Civilization and its Discontents*, trans. James Strachey (New York: W. W. Norton, 1989), 81–2.

38. See Erich Fromm, *Escape From Freedom* (New York: Henry Holt and Company, 1941).

39. Herbert Marcuse, *Eros and Civilization* (New York: Vintage Books, 1962), 105.

40. Herbert Marcuse, *One Dimensional Man* (New York: Routledge & Kegan Paul, 1964), 62.

41. Ibid. 75.

42. Nancy Fraser, 'Feminism, Capitalism, and the Cunning of History', *New Left Review* 56 (March–April 2009): 114.

43. Nancy Fraser, 'From Discipline to Flexibilization: Rereading Foucault in the Shadow of Globalization', *Constellations* 10(2003): 170.

44. Ellen Samuels, *Fantasies of Identification: Disability, Gender, Race* (New York: NYU Press, 2014). Kindle Edition, loc. 164–5.

45. Anonymous, 'Establishing Identity is a Vital, Risky, and Changing Business', *The Economist* (22 December 2018), https://www.economist.com/christmas-specials /2018/12/18/establishing-identity-is-a-vital-risky-and-changing-business (accessed 28 December 2018).

Chapter 5

1. James C. Scott, *Seeing Like a State: How Certain Schemes to Improve the Human Condition Have Failed* (New Haven: Yale University Press, 1998), 87.

2. Ibid. 11.

3. Max Weber, *Economy and Society: An Outline of Interpretative Sociology*, ed. Guenther Roth and Claus Wittich (Berkeley: University of California Press, 1978), 9.

4. Scott, op. cit., 316.

5. Ibid. 320.

6. Barbara Aneil, *John Locke and America: The Defense of English Colonialism* (Oxford: Clarendon Press, 1996), 45ff.

7. Thomas Hobbes, *Leviathan* (London: G. Routledge & Sons, 1894), 12.

8. Stephen Metcalf, 'Neoliberalism: The Idea That Swallowed the World', *The Guardian*, 18 August 2017, https://www.theguardian.com/news/2017/aug/18/ neoliberalism-the-idea-that-changed-the-world (accessed 21 August 2017).

9. See Daniel Stedman Jones, *Masters of the University: Hayek, Friedman, and the Birth of Neoliberal Politics* (Princeton: Princeton University Press, 2012).

10. F. A. Hayek, *The Road to Serfdom* (London: Routledge, 1944), 3.

180

11. Ibid. 157.

12. F. A. Hayek, 'The Use of Knowledge in Society', *The American Economic Review* 35 (September 1945): 522.

13. Hayek, *The Road to Serfdom*, 38.

14. Ibid. 42.

15. Immanuel Kant, *Groundwork for the Metaphysic of Morals*, trans. Allen W. Wood (New Haven: Yale University Press, 2002), 14–15.

16. Randall Lahann and Emilie Mitescu Reagan, 'Teach for America and the Politics of Progressive Neoliberalism', *Teacher Education Quarterly* 38(Winter 2011): 13. One may, of course, raise the serious question about how 'progressive' such progressive neoliberalism really is. If Joseph Schumpeter famously characterised capitalism as a process of 'creative destruction', can it then be said, as Michael Grimshaw has observed in an informal exchange with this author, that progressive neoliberalism constitutes the creative destruction of what we normally mean by 'capitalism' as a whole?

17. Ibid. 14.

18. Julie Wilson, *Neoliberalism* (New York: Routledge, 2018).

19. 'Perhaps', Foucault confessed, 'I've insisted too much on the technology of domination and power. I am more and more interested in the interaction between oneself and others, and in the technologies of individual domination, in the mode of action that an individual exercises upon himself by means of the technologies of the self.' Michel Foucault, 'Technologies of the Self', in *Essential Works of Foucault*, vol. 1, 225.

20. Michel Foucault, *Security, Territory, Population: Lectures at the Collège de France, 1977–1978* (New York: Picador/Palgrave Macmillan, 2009), 125.

21. Ibid. 148.

22. Hannah Arendt, *The Promise of Politics* (New York: Schocken Books, 2005), 93.

23. Foucault, *Security, Territory, Population*, 149.

24. Ibid. 179.

25. See Dotan Leshem, *The Origins of Neoliberalism: Modeling the Economy from Jesus to Foucault* (New York: Columbia University Press, 2016).

26. See Hannah Arendt, *The Human Condition* (Chicago: University of Chicago Press, 1958).

27. Carl Schmitt, *Political Theology: Four Chapters on the Concept of Sovereignty*, trans. George Schwab (Chicago: University of Chicago Press, 1985), 36.

28. Giorgio Agamben, *The Kingdom and the Glory: For a Theological Genealogy of Economy and Government* (Stanford: Stanford University Press, 2011), 3.

29. Aristotle, *Complete Works of Aristotle*. Delphi Ancient Classics Book 11. Kindle Edition, loc. 48152.
30. Ibid. loc. 48158.
31. Leshem, op. cit., 155.
32. Ibid. 159.
33. Ibid. 155.
34. Arendt, op. cit., 41.
35. Leshem, op. cit., 28.

Chapter 6

1. As scholars of Greek religion are wont to point out, there was no formal, institutionalised 'priesthood' in ancient Athens. But the priestly focus on upholding 'piety', which consisted of participating in prescribed communal rites and adhering to the traditional representations of the deities for whom these practices were performed, was very much in evidence. The *polis* could not function if these representations were brought into question. That is why the charge against Socrates of 'impiety' had such force and led to his death sentence. For a careful analysis of the context of the 'religious' context of Socrates's trial and sentence, see Robin Waterfield, *Why Socrates Died: Dispelling the Myths* (Toronto: McClelland and Stewart, 2010), 173ff. A somewhat different take can be found in Shadia B. Drury, *The Bleak Political Implications of Socratic Religion* (Basingstoke: Palgrave Macmillan, 2017).
2. Michel Foucault, *Security, Territory, Population: Lectures at the Collège de France, 1977–1978* (New York: Picador/Palgrave Macmillan, 2009), 117.
3. Ibid. 118.
4. Ibid. 123.
5. Ibid. 126.
6. Ibid. 127.
7. Ibid. 237.
8. Michel Foucault, *The Birth of Biopolitics: Lectures at the Collège de France, 1978–1979*, trans. Graham Burchell (New York: Picador, 2008), 85.
9. Slobodian writes: 'The core of twentieth-century neoliberal theorizing involves what they called the meta-economic or extra-economic conditions for safeguarding capitalism at the scale of the entire world. I show that the neoliberal project focused on designing institutions – not to liberate markets but to encase them, to inoculate capitalism against the threat of democracy, to create a framework to contain often-irrational human behavior, and to reorder the

world after empire as a space of competing states.' Quinn Slobodian, *Globalists: The End of Empire and the Birth of Neoliberalism* (Cambridge, MA: Harvard University Press, 2018). Kindle Edition, loc. 93–7.

10. Foucault, *The Birth of Biopolitics*, 102.

11. Ibid. 283.

12. Consider Foucault's discussion of market fundamentalism in the early sections of *The Birth of Biopolitics*.

13. Foucault, *The Birth of Biopolitics*, 323.

14. Adam Smith, *The Theory of the Moral Sentiments* (Glasgow: R. Chapman, 1809), 357.

15. Adam Smith, *An Inquiry into the Nature and Causes of the Wealth of Nations* (Edinburgh: Thomas Nelson and Peter Brown, 1827), 183.

16. Kant speculates about how world order is gradually forged not through conscientious human efforts but through seemingly chaotic strife and conflict, which is history's own kind of 'invisible hand', and which he terms the 'unsocial sociability' of the human race as a whole. See his 'Idea for a Universal History with a Cosmopolitan Purpose', in *Kant: Political Writings*, trans. H. B. Nisbet (Cambridge: Cambridge University Press, 1991), 41–53.

17. Smith, *Wealth of Nations*, 57.

18. Francis Fukuyama, *The End of History and the Last Man* (New York: The Free Press, 1992), xii.

19. Ibid. xvi.

20. Ibid. 152.

21. Nancy Fraser, *Justus Interruptus: Critical Reflections on the 'Postsocialist' Condition* (New York: Routledge, 1997), 2.

22. Ibid. 3.

23. Nancy Fraser, *Fortunes of Feminism: From State-Managed Capitalism to Neoliberal Crisis* (London: Verso, 2013), 224.

24. Ibid. 224–5.

25. The distinction between 'negative' and 'positive' freedom was first made by Isaiah Berlin. See his 'Two Concepts of Liberty', in Isaiah Berlin, *Liberty* (Oxford: Oxford University Press, 2002), 166–217.

26. Axel Honneth, *Freedom's Right: The Social Foundations of Democratic Life*, trans. Joseph Ganahl (New York: Columbia University Press, 2014), 29.

27. Ibid. 46.

28. Georg Hegel, *Phenomenology of the Spirit* (New Orleans: Pettis-Lovell, 2013). Kindle Edition, loc. 2759–62. 'Es sind zu dieser Reflexion die beiden Momente der Furcht und des Dienstes überhaupt, sowie des Bildens notwendig, und

zugleich beide auf eine allgemeine Weise. Ohne die Zucht des Dienstes und Gehorsams bleibt die Furcht beim Formellen stehen, und verbreitet sich nicht über die bewußte Wirklichkeit des Daseins.' Loc. 13160–2.

29. See Franz Fanon, *Black Skin, White Masks*, trans. Charles Lam Markmann (London: Pluto Press, 1986), 113–14.

30. Georg Lukács, *History and Class Consciousness: Studies in Marxist Dialectics*, trans. Rodney Livingstone (Cambridge, MA: The MIT Press, 1971), 86. Consider Lukács's subsequent comment that 'just as the capitalist system continuously produces and reproduces itself economically on higher and higher levels, the structure of reification progressively sinks more deeply, more fatefully and more definitively into the consciousness of man' (Ibid. 93). For a series of in-depth studies of these issues in Lukács, see Istvan Meszaros (ed.), *Aspects of History and Class Consciousness* (New York: Routledge, 2016).

31. Lukács, op. cit., 78.

32. Lisa Duggan, *The Twilight of Equality: Neoliberalism, Cultural Politics, and the Attack on Democracy* (Boston: Beacon Press, 2003).

33. Ange-Marie Hancock, *Intersectionality: An Intellectual History* (New York: Oxford University Press, 2016).

34. Duggan, op. cit., 83.

35. Olivier Roy, *Holy Ignorance: When Religion and Culture Part Ways* (New York: Oxford University Press, 2014).

36. See Jaap Koojman, *Fabricating the Absolute Fake: America in Contemporary Pop Culture* (Amsterdam: Amsterdam University Press, 2008).

37. It is not coincidental that the coke song appears at the end of the Netflix series *Mad Men* when advertising genius *extraordinare* Don Draper ostensibly retires from his career and joins a California New Age commune on the Californian coast in the region known as Big Sur. The association of the scene with the historical beginnings of the 'bohemian bourgeoisie', the cannon fodder for the rise of the global empire of progressive neoliberalism, is unmistakable.

38. Jeff Chang, 'What Coke Taught the World', *Slate*, 18 May 2015, http://www.slate.com/articles/arts/culturebox/2015/05/coca_cola_s_it_s_the_real_thing_ad_how_the_mccann_erickson_ad_changed_american.html (accessed 21 March 2018).

39. Ami Sedghi (4 November 2012), 'UK's Million-selling Singles: The Full List', *The Guardian*, https://www.theguardian.com/news/datablog/2012/nov/04/uk-million-selling-singles-full-list (accessed 22 March 2018).

40. Koojman, op. cit., 32.

41. Ibid. 33. The irony was also noted by music critic Greil Marcus. 'As pop music, "We Are the World" says less about Ethiopia than it does about Pepsi – and the true result will likely be less that certain Ethiopian individuals will live, or anyway live a little bit longer than they otherwise would have, than that Pepsi will get the catchphrase of its advertising sung for free by Ray Charles, Stevie Wonder, Bruce Springstein, and the rest.' See Greil Marcus, *Bob Dylan by Greil Marcus: Writings 1968–2010* (New York: Public Affairs), 108–9.

42. See John Naisbitt, *Megatrends: Ten Directions Transforming Our Lives* (New York: Warner Books, 1984). Interestingly, one can find almost exactly the same vision thirty-five years later in a report to its clients by the German strategic marketing firm Z-Punkt. The report, published in 2008 and also entitled 'Megatrends', celebrates in its introduction the prophetic insights of Naisbitt, which supposedly have virtually all come true. See 'Megatrends', Köln, Z-Punkt GMBH, The Foresight Company, 2008.

43. See John and Doris Naisbitt, *China's Megatrends: The 8 Pillars of a New Society* (New York: HarperCollins, 2010).

44. Christian Stöcker, 'Interview with John and Doris Naisbitt', *Spiegel Online*, 5 February 2010, http://www.spiegel.de/international/world/interview-with-john-and-doris-naisbitt-china-is-a-country-without-an-ideology-a-675615.html (accessed 22 March 2018).

Chapter 7

1. Michel Foucault, *The Birth of Biopolitics: Lectures at the Collège de France, 1978–1979*, trans. Graham Burchell (New York: Picador, 2008), 243.
2. Ibid. 244.
3. Nancy Fraser, 'From Progressive Neoliberalism to Trump – and Beyond', *American Affairs* 1(Winter 2017): 53.
4. See Gary Wills, *Reagan's America: Innocents at Home* (New York: Open Road Media, 2017).
5. See J. F. Jekel and D. F. Allen, 'Trends in Drug Abuse in the 1980s', *Yale Journal of Biology and Medicine* 60(January–February 1987): 45–52.
6. See Doug Rossinow, *The Reagan Era: A History of the 1980s* (New York: Columbia University Press, 2015), 2.
7. Harvey Cox, *The Secular City* (New York: The Macmillan Company, 1965), 1.
8. See Max Weber, *The Vocation Lectures*, trans. Rodney Livingstone (Indianapolis: Hackett Publishing, 2004), 13.
9. Cox, op. cit., 4.

10. Ibid. 3.

11. The development of this whole movement is masterfully traced by Gary J. Dorrien in *The Making of American Liberal Theology: Idealism, Realism, and Modernity, 1900–1950* (Louisville, KY: Westminster John Knox Press).

12. Ingolf U. Dalferth, *Radical Theology: An Essay on Faith and Theology in the Twenty-First Century* (Minneapolis: Fortress Press, 2016), 165.

13. Jeffrey Robbins, *In Search of a Non-Dogmatic Theology* (Aurora, CO: The Davies Group, 2004), xiii.

14. Diana Coole and Samantha Frost, 'Introducing the New Materialisms', in Diana Coole and Samantha Frost (eds), *The New Materialisms: Ontology, Agency, and Politics* (Durham, NC: Duke University Press, 2010), 7.

15. Clayton Crockett and Jeffrey Robbins, *The New Materialism* (New York: Palgrave Macmillan, 2012), xvi.

16. Ibid. 28.

17. Ibid. 39.

18. Ibid. 145.

19. See Costas Douzinas, *Human Rights and Empire: The Political Philosophy of Cosmopolitanism* (New York: Routledge, 2007), 142ff.

20. Ibid. 156.

21. Foucault, op. cit., chapter 7.

22. See Marilyn Ferguson, *The Aquarian Conspiracy: Personal and Social Transformation in Our Time* (New York: Penguin, 2009).

23. This argument was made implicitly by Frederic Jameson in *Postmodernism, Or The Cultural Logic of Late Capitalism* (Durham, NC: Duke University Press, 1991), 391. See also Adam Possamai, 'Alternative Spiritualities and the Cultural Logic of Late Capitalism', *Culture and Religion* 4 (2003): 31–45; P. Heelas, 'Prosperity and the New Age Movement: The Efficacy of Spiritual Economics', in B. Wilson and J. Cresswell (eds), *New Religious Movements: Challenge and Response* (London: Routledge, 1999), 51–78; P. Roberts, 'Power and Empowerment: New Age Managers and the Dialects of Modernity/Postmodernity', *Syzygy: Journal of Alternative Religion and Culture* 3(3–4): 271–88; Michael York, *The Emerging Network. A Sociology of the New Age and Neo-Pagan Movements* (Lanham, MD: Rowman & Littlefield Publishers, 1995).

24. John Naisbitt, *Megatrends: Ten Directions Transforming Our Lives* (New York: Warner Books, 1984), 259.

25. See Joshua Ramey, *The Hermetic Deleuze: Philosophy and Spiritual Ordeal* (Durham, NC: Duke University Press, 2012).

26. See Harald Wydra, 'The Politics of Transcendence', *Cultural Politics* 7 (2011): 265–87. See also Vittorio Lanternari, *The Religions of the Oppressed: A Study of Messianic Cults* (New York: Alfred A. Knopf, 1963).

27. Romans 13:1, NIV.

28. Paul insists in Romans 13:5 (NIV) that 'therefore, it is necessary to submit to the authorities, not only because of possible punishment but also as a matter of conscience (συνείδησῃ)'. The principle of divine conscience is introduced into Christian theology by Saint Jerome (370–420 CE) and is elaborated by Thomas Aquinas in the thirteenth century. See Donald P. Verene, *Moral Philosophy and the Modern World* (Eugene, OR: Wipf & Stock, 2013), 89.

29. Michel Foucault, *The Government of Self and Others: Lectures at the Collège de France 1982–1983* (New York: Picador, 2011). Kindle Edition, loc. 902–3.

30. Ibid. loc. 3014–15.

31. Immanuel Kant, 'Aufklärung ist der Ausgang des Menschen ausseiner selbst verschuldeten Unmündigkeit', in *Beantwortung der Frage: Was ist Aufklärung?* (Berlin: Dearbooks Verlag, 2016), 7.

32. Wendy Brown, *Undoing the Demos: Neoliberalism's Stealth Revolution* (New York: Zone Books, 2015), 133.

33. Foucault, op. cit., loc. 686.

34. Ibid. loc. 706–9.

35. Ida Danewild, 'White Innocence in the Black Mediterranean: Hospitality and the Erasure of History', *Third World Quarterly* 10 (2017): 10.

36. Alex Sager, *Toward a Cosmopolitan Ethics of Mobility: The Migrant's Eye View of the World* (Berlin: Springer, 2018), 80. A rich and more detailed historical backgrounding of this argument is developed in Sager, 'Immigration, Rights, and Equality', doctoral dissertation, University of Calgary, 2008.

37. *Charter of the United Nations and the International Court of Justice*, San Francisco, 1945.

38. *South Dakota* v. *Wayfair, Inc. et al.* Certiorari to the Supreme Court of South Dakota. No. 17-494. 17 April–21 June 2018.

39. Ravi Chandra, MD, 'Is Facebook Destroying Society and Your Mental Health?', *Psychology Today*, 29 January 2018, https://www.psychologytoday.com/us/blog/the-pacific-heart/201801/is-facebook-destroying-society-and-your-mental-health (accessed 21 June 2018).

Chapter 8

1. Amy Chua, *Political Tribes: Group Instinct and the Fate of Nations* (New York: Penguin Press, 2018), 9.

2. Karl Marx and Friedrich Engels, *The Communist Manifesto: A Modern Edition* (New Haven: Yale University Press, 2012), 40.

3. Quinn Slobodian, *Globalists: The End of Empire and the Birth of Neoliberalism* (Cambridge, MA: Harvard University Press, 2018). Kindle Edition, loc. 94–7.

4. Wendy Brown, *Undoing the Demos: Neoliberalism's Stealth Revolution* (New York: Zone Books, 2015), 27.

5. Alain Badiou, *Saint Paul: The Foundation of Universalism*, trans. Ray Brassier (Stanford: Stanford University Press, 2003), 21.

6. Colossians 3:11, NIV.

7. Plato, *The Republic*, trans. Alan Bloom (New York: Basic Books, 1968), 47–51.

8. Ibid. 50.

9. Emmanuel Levinas, *Otherwise than Being, or Beyond Essence*, trans. Alphonso Lingis (Leiden: Martinus Nijhoff, 1978), 13.

10. Emmanuel Levinas, *Totality and Infinity: An Essay on Exteriority*, trans. Alphonso Lingis (Leiden: Martinus Nijhoff, 1979), 21.

11. Ibid. 23.

12. Ibid.

13. Ibid.

14. See Jacques Derrida, *Specters of Marx: The State of the Debt, the Work of Mourning, and the New Internationale*, trans. Peggy Kamuf (New York: Routledge, 1994).

15. See Jacques Derrida, 'Faith and Knowledge: The Two Sources of "Religion" at the Limits of Reason Alone', in Gil Andijar (ed.), *Acts of Religion* (New York: Routledge, 2002). Derrida, writing in the immediate aftermath of the collapse of the Soviet Union, himself invokes the Roman imperial metaphor by characterising the process of emergent, communicative capitalism as 'globo-latinizaton'.

Index

EU representative:
Easy Access System Europe
Mustamäe tee 50, 10621 Tallinn, Estonia
Gpsr.requests@easproject.com